A NIGHT AT TH

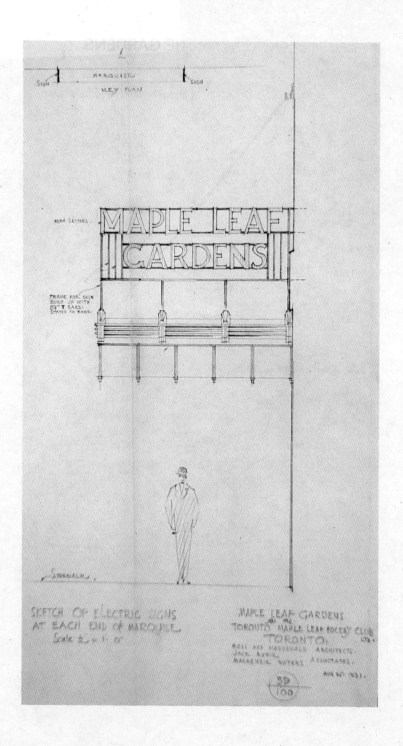

SKETCH OF ELECTRIC SIGNS
AT EACH END OF MARQUISE
Scale 2" = 1' 0"

MAPLE LEAF GARDENS
TORONTO MAPLE LEAF HOCKEY CLUB LTD.
TORONTO.
ROSS AND MACDONALD ARCHITECTS
JACK RYRIE
MACKENZIE WATERS ASSOCIATES

A Night at the Gardens

Class, Gender, and Respectability in 1930s Toronto

RUSSELL FIELD

UNIVERSITY OF TORONTO PRESS
Toronto Buffalo London

ISBN 978-1-4875-4702-8 (cloth)   ISBN 978-1-4875-4716-5 (EPUB)
ISBN 978-1-4875-4708-0 (paper)   ISBN 978-1-4875-4714-1 (PDF)

Library and Archives Canada Cataloguing in Publication

Title: A night at the Gardens : class, gender, and respectability in
1930s Toronto / Russell Field.
Names: Field, Russell, author.
Description: Includes bibliographical references and index.
Identifiers: Canadiana (print) 20230131557 | Canadiana (ebook) 20230131646 |
ISBN 9781487547028 (cloth) | ISBN 9781487547080 (paper) |
ISBN 9781487547165 (EPUB) | ISBN 9781487547141 (PDF)
Subjects: LCSH: Maple Leaf Gardens Ltd. – History – 20th century. |
LCSH: Arenas – Ontario – Toronto – History – 20th century. |
LCSH: Hockey fans – Ontario – Toronto – History – 20th century. |
LCSH: Hockey – Social aspects – Ontario – Toronto – History – 20th century. |
LCSH: Middle class – Ontario – Toronto – History – 20th century. |
LCSH: Toronto (Ont.) – Buildings, structures, etc. – History – 20th century.
Classification: LCC GV418.M37 F54 2023 | DDC 796.96209713/541 – dc23

Cover design: Heng Wee Tan

Cover illustration: a playoff game between the Maple Leafs and Boston, 1938 (City of
Toronto Archives, Globe and Mail fonds, Fonds 1266, Item 50393); frontispiece: elevation
sketch for the entrance marquee at Maple Leaf Gardens, 1931 (Ross & Macdonald Archive,
Collection Centre Canadien d'Architecture / Canadian Centre for Architecture, Montreal)

We wish to acknowledge the land on which the University of Toronto Press operates. This
land is the traditional territory of the Wendat, the Anishnaabeg, the Haudenosaunee, the
Métis, and the Mississaugas of the Credit First Nation.

This book has been published with the help of a grant from the Federation for the
Humanities and Social Sciences, through the Awards to Scholarly Publications Program,
using funds provided by the Social Sciences and Humanities Research Council of Canada.

University of Toronto Press acknowledges the financial support of the Government of
Canada, the Canada Council for the Arts, and the Ontario Arts Council, an agency of the
Government of Ontario, for its publishing activities.

Canada Council **Conseil des Arts**
for the Arts **du Canada**

In memory of Joyce Field

Contents

Illustrations

Figures

Tables

Acknowledgments

While only a single name appears on the cover, the effort that went into producing this book was a collaborative one. It is the work of friends and family, colleagues and strangers, archivists and librarians. And I want to acknowledge and give thanks for their many and varied contributions.

The most appropriate place to start is to thank the people who shared with me their experiences as spectators at Maple Leaf Gardens in the 1930s. Twenty-one people set aside time in their days and, in many instances, opened their homes to me. We met in Toronto, Kingston, Waterloo, Calgary, and Vancouver. My hope is that they will feel that I have done justice to their memories and accurately interpreted their experiences as hockey spectators. In some cases, I met these charismatic and enthusiastic former spectators through the efforts of administrators at assisted-living facilities, and I am grateful for their help.

A number of employees of Maple Leaf Sports and Entertainment, the corporation whose holdings include the Toronto Maple Leafs hockey club (and once included Maple Leaf Gardens) were very helpful, including Paul Beirne, who connected me with long-time Leafs' ticket subscribers. Absolutely invaluable assistance was also provided by Donna Henderson and her staff at the then–Air Canada Centre ticket office. It was Donna who alerted me to the existence of the Maple Leaf Gardens subscriber ledgers that comprise such a significant portion of the evidence upon which chapter 3 is based.

Like many historians, I relied heavily on archival collections. And, given the scarcity of accounts of spectator experiences, I combed through as many different archives as I could access. In all cases, the archivists at these facilities were generous with their time and knowledge. I am especially grateful to the reading room staff at the Archives of Ontario, the City of Toronto Archives, the National Archives in Ottawa, and the Centre for Canadian Architecture in Montreal, in particular Howard

Shubert. The staff of the resource centre at the Hockey Hall of Fame were also helpful, as were the data and geographic information systems librarians at the University of Toronto's Robarts Library.

This book began some time ago as a research project, whose finished form differs greatly from the current volume. That work was supervised by Bruce Kidd, now a cherished friend, mentor, and collaborator, and was also supported by Peter Donnelly, Margaret MacNeill, and Ian Radforth. I am equally grateful to Colin Howell, for his work as an external examiner, and to the anonymous reviewers whose feedback shaped the current volume.

Many other friends and colleagues offered support, often more valuable than they imagined, as this book trudged towards completion. It is not an exaggeration to say that this book would not exist without the supportive prodding of Nancy Bouchier, whom I value as a mentor and friend. From the graduate student cohort at "40 Sussex" to my disciplinary home in the North American Society for Sport History, I am grateful to have been sustained by such supportive communities. In particular, Malcolm MacLean and Carly Adams are excellent conspirators within the discipline and better friends beyond it. At the University of Manitoba, supportive colleagues and comrades have included Colleen Plumton, Sarah Teetzel, jay johnson, Dan Henhawk, Jon Singer, and Doug Brown. Elsewhere in the academy, that support network has included Simon Darnell, LeAnne Petherick, Moss Norman, and Andrew Loman, the latter always a willing companion (and better friend) when New York beckoned for research on Madison Square Garden (and off-Broadway productions and museum exhibits).

I am also in the considerable debt of Len Husband at University of Toronto Press. His patience coupled with his support and enthusiasm for this book were sustaining and are deeply appreciated. Thanks also to Janice Evans, Stephanie Mazza, Emily Reiner, and the production and marketing teams at UTP for all they did to ensure this book saw the light of day; to Nate Wessel for the map that appears in chapter 2; and to Celia Braves for the index appended to the end of this volume. I am pleased that this book is as well illustrated as it is (another debt owed to Len). My thanks for assistance in sourcing images and securing permissions to the staff at a number of archives, museums, and public libraries (all of which are credited within the text). In particular, I want to thank the reading room staff at the City of Toronto Archives, and at the Baillie Special Collections Centre in the Toronto Reference Library, as well as Lindsey Winstone at the Archives of Ontario, Céline Pereira at the Canadian Centre for Architecture in Montreal, and Alexander Jackson at the National Football Museum in Manchester.

While this book covers the 1930s, it was only late in that decade that hockey photographers moved beyond fixed positions high above the ice, where they focused only on the action of the players below, to locations closer to the ice, where they captured hockey's broader milieu. As a result, some of the photographs that appear in this book were taken after the 1930s, although care has been taken in all but a few cases to not extend the timeframe of these illustrations beyond the 1940s. Maple Leaf Gardens remained largely unchanged through the Depression and the Second World War. It was only in the 1950s with the installation of escalators (1955) and a Wurlitzer organ (1956), as well as the coronation of a new monarch (1952), which necessitated the hanging of a different portrait, that the arena underwent significant renovations for the first time. It should also be noted that the images that appear in this book are meant to be illustrative of the themes that appear in the analysis; they are not a feature of the analysis itself. An interrogation of sport photography and the ways in which representations shaped understandings of modern sport is a worthwhile endeavour; this, however, is not that project.

My final thanks are reserved for family. Carolyn Snider came into my life while I was in the middle of the initial project that became this book. Although she faced her own hurdles at the same time, Carolyn has filled our time together with warmth and joy. Sharing a wanderlust, we escaped the rigours of grad school and residency by travelling around the world and naively dreaming of the day when there will be less work to escape from and more time to travel (and, it turns out, fewer pandemics). A move to (and from) Winnipeg brought more adventures, this time with Alice – the enduring joy of my life and an excellent travel companion in her own right. Carolyn's parents, Mel and Elaine, and all of the extended Snider clan have, from the moment I first met them, warmly welcomed me into their family – although some no doubt wondered, "What is it exactly that Russell does?" I am grateful for the ways in which they opened both their homes and their family to me.

My own family is much smaller, although no less supportive. My parents, Lloyd and Joyce, instilled in me a love of education and study. (Where I got my love of sport from is more of a mystery.) Nevertheless, from the moment that I announced my interest in returning to school to pursue graduate work, my parents supported me through good times and bad. My mother did not live to see the publication of this book. She did, however, take me to my first game at Maple Leaf Gardens, in 1975 or '76. The petulance I displayed then at learning it was a Toronto Toros game (argh) and not a Maple Leafs game is topped only by the iconoclastic joy I feel now that it was a Toronto Toros (!) game. It is in her memory that I dedicate this book.

A NIGHT AT THE GARDENS

Chapter One

Historicizing the Hockey Spectator

In early 1937, the five-year-old Maple Leaf Gardens was already an important institution in Toronto. While the arena played host to a wide variety of sporting, entertainment, and political events, it was known primarily as the home of the city's professional ice hockey franchise.[1] On the evening of Saturday, 27 February 1937, 13,380 spectators filed into "the Gardens" – as it was popularly known – to watch a midseason game between the hometown Maple Leafs and the Montreal Maroons.[2] The two clubs were in a heated battle for second place in the National Hockey League's (NHL) Canadian division.

On the following Monday, 1 March, the sports pages of Toronto's daily newspapers reported on the home team's 3–2 victory, with the "highlight of a rousing struggle" being a ten-player, third-period brawl. Each of these reports also made mention of a spirited first-period encounter between Maroons defenceman Lionel Conacher and a local spectator. Conacher, a talented multi-sport athlete who would be named Canada's male athlete of the half century in 1950, was by 1937 already venerated by the central Canadian press as the "Big Train," and events involving him regularly merited comment. During this particular game against the Maple Leafs, he found his stick being held by a man sitting rinkside in one of the Gardens' more expensive rail seats. Annoyed by the spectator's interference and, as sports editor Tommy Munns noted in the *Globe and Mail*, "exasperated," Conacher "wrenched the stick free and brought the hickory down on the head of the interfering one." The audience enjoyed the spectacle. Even though "Conacher was given a ten-minute penalty ... the crowd cheered him when he returned to action."[3]

With accounts of Maple Leafs games appearing in all four of Toronto's daily newspapers during the 1930s, descriptions of interactions between players and spectators were not uncommon. Pucks would fly into the crowd, and without the Plexiglas partitions of modern arenas, rinkside

spectators would encounter players who were battling along the boards.
What made Munns's report unusual was that the spectator who became
entangled with Conacher's stick took exception to his resulting injuries
being characterized as the product of "a fairly gentle tap." He made
this point clear to the *Globe and Mail*'s editors. The spectator was John
McGinnis, general manager of the Toronto office of Buffalo Beardmore
Gold Mines Limited. His indignant response was printed the following
day in the paper's sports pages:

> Dear Sir: After reading your column in The Globe and Mail this morning,
> I am certainly very much surprised at your version of the attack Conacher
> made on a spectator, as I am the one who got the "gentle tap."
>
> Being so far away, it may have looked like a gentle tap to you, but I had
> two stitches put in it, and it really requires three.
>
> In all due fairness to sport, I'd like to clear this matter up, so that in
> future you might make an effort to get a few details before you write your
> story.
>
> There was a mixup in front of me, and the players were trying to get the
> puck. A woman sitting beside me was hit with one of the three sticks, and I
> put up my arm to protect my face. While my arm was up, Conacher thrust
> his stick in under my armpit. When I lowered my arm he tugged and pulled
> to free his stick. When he pulled it out he turned around and deliberately
> hit me on the head ...
>
> It is evident from your comments this morning that you are in favor of
> this sort of thing. All I can say is that as an example to the juniors every
> effort should be made to enforce a proper sporting spirit, instead of rank
> cowardice.
>
> If this is a new style in hockey, why not start a hickory club, and then the
> spectators could come armed with bottles and other weapons, and when
> they felt so inclined (without provocation) they could take a few pot-shots
> at the players.
>
> The President of one of the large drug houses of Toronto was sitting
> near-by, along with at least fifteen others who were close enough to actually
> see what happened. They requested me to have Conacher arrested for as-
> sault, but I declined, as I hope I am a better sportsman than he is ...
>
> I suppose that had the woman next to me been in my place and the stick
> had been caught in the same way it would have been just the same. Or had
> the stick been caught in the seat I was sitting in, I suppose that, according to
> you, Conacher would have had the right to take it out on the seat.
>
> My suggestion to you is to first find out what you are talking about before
> you go so far as to print your opinions.
>
> Yours very truly, John McGinnis[4]

A letter such as this is a valuable introduction to a history of indoor, commercial sport facilities constructed during the interwar years, such as Maple Leaf Gardens, and an examination of the lived experiences of the spectators who inhabited them. McGinnis reveals something of the experience that sports spectators encountered when they entered these new facilities. He highlights that both men and women attended commercial hockey games in 1930s Toronto and that the Gardens' more expensive seats, where McGinnis himself was sitting, were home to some of Toronto's better-off citizens, including the "President of one of the large drug houses." One intention of this book is to offer a more thorough consideration of the identity of hockey spectators in the interwar years.

But McGinnis's protest against the treatment he received in his seat and on the pages of Monday's newspaper also reveals the public discourses that surrounded the practice of spectating. In a city such as Toronto where cultural traditions, including sporting ones, were closely linked to the British origins of the vast majority of its citizens, the values of late nineteenth and early twentieth-century amateurism persisted. McGinnis fancied himself a "better sportsman" and he believed that not only should a "proper sporting spirit" be valorized, if necessary it needed to be enforced. Indeed, respectable behaviour was to be expected of all spectators and players, including Conacher, whose behaviour, McGinnis asserts, was sufficient to warrant arrest in the minds of some spectators. A second theme explored in this book is how spectators were expected to act and behave – how to spectate – in the new sport spaces of the interwar years.

Finally, the reaction of the audience at Maple Leaf Gardens to the McGinnis-Conacher altercation – cheering the latter's return from the penalty box – suggests that many in the crowd enjoyed physical play that could at times impact spectators. McGinnis hints at the role that the media played in promoting physicality as one of the attractions of hockey as a consumer spectacle. But regardless of McGinnis's opinion of these efforts, his sarcastic observation that spectators needed to arrive at the arena "armed with bottles and other weapons" reveals that spectators were far from passive observers and regularly interacted with the spectacle that they were paying to "observe." A final line of enquiry in this book explores the nature of the spectating experience and what it meant to the men and women who filled the stands at commercial hockey arenas.

The primary aim of this book is to examine the consumption of commercial entertainments in Toronto during the interwar years, through an examination of the experiences of hockey spectators at Toronto's Maple Leaf Gardens after the building opened in 1931. The traditional narrative surrounding such venues was that they were built in such a

way as to make visiting them a more appealing proposition than similar experiences at older venues. NHL owners and managers, including
Toronto's Conn Smythe, hoped to attract a "new" clientele, one willing
to spend its disposable income on tickets to hockey games. Maple Leaf
Gardens, according to one popular history, was to be "a place that would
lift hockey forever out of the realm of cigar-chomping hustlers and
back-alley knockabouts."[5] Reflecting upon the apparent success of their
endeavour, Smythe's right-hand man, Frank Selke, recalled that after
Maple Leaf Gardens opened, "Hockey crowds now had real class."[6] This
book interrogates such claims, while foregrounding the experiences of
the spectators who purchased tickets and attended games at the new
arena. The final section of this chapter outlines how this argument un-
folds in the remaining chapters.

   Prior to that, this chapter sketches out the broader landscape of sport
spectating and places this practice within the consumption of commercial entertainments during the interwar years. A consideration of both
the scholarly literature and popular histories reveals the ways in which
spectators have largely remained absent in the history of commercial
hockey, despite their centrality to the profitability of the very enterprise.
This was true of Toronto, which emerged as the centre of professional
hockey in English Canada in these decades. The intentions behind the
design and construction of Maple Leaf Gardens as well as the experiences of the men and women who attended games at this new arena also
need to be understood in the context of the facility that preceded it. As a
result, the profile of Toronto in the 1920s that follows in the penultimate
section of this chapter highlights hockey's professional home in the city
from 1912 to 1931: Arena Gardens.

Considering the Historical Sport Spectator

The experiences of hockey spectators in 1930s Toronto are best understood within the wider historical experience of spectating. Sport spectators have received their fullest examination by scholars of British football
(soccer) and, to a lesser extent, American baseball.[7] Jeffrey Hill notes
of the former that there is "some conjecture in the remarks that historians have made" but that it "seems likely that working men and their
sons made up the vast majority of them [spectators], with a sprinkling
of (probably unmarried) younger women and middle-class men."[8] Such
accounts have proceeded from a relatively straightforward premise that
characterized interwar football spectators as "decent, ordinary folk"
and presumed a fairly homogeneous crowd, one that was white, male,
and predominantly working class (see Fig. 1.1).[9] While there is likely a

WILES

3 0

ALBION V. CARDIFF...

Fig. 1.1. Early British soccer crowds like this one at a 1920s match at Brighton and Hove Albion have been characterized as predominantly male and working class. (Courtesy of the National Football Museum)

significant degree of truth in these suppositions, they are not grounded in an in-depth empirical analysis of spectators.

In contrast, studies of late twentieth-century spectators enumerate the ways in which members of the middle class and wealthier elites are more common in contemporary stadiums.[10] Examining the shifting socio-economic standing of spectators is relevant when considering the historical composition of the crowd. Allen Guttmann, whose *Sports Spectators* is the most comprehensive historical study of spectatorship, connects social standing, the regulation of spectator violence, and the design of early modern sport venues, as entrepreneurs sought "to construct stadiums and arenas to which access was strictly controlled and within which social classes tended to be separated by different ticket prices."[11] Guttmann's observations about stadium design point to the presence of spectators representative of a variety of economic and social circumstances. While in the 1880s "a significant proportion of a good many football crowds was made up of the better-off or middle classes," at the end of the century their membership was increasingly drawn from the ranks of England's working men, so much so that by 1915, "the majority of the spectators who went to watch professional football matches were working class in origin, occupation and life style."[12] Tony Mason, however, notes that spectators were not "a monolithic group," highlighting diversity within the working classes as well as the possibility of geographic differences and changes over time.[13] In arguing for the need to more thoroughly consider the composition of pre–Second World War crowds, Martin Johnes makes this point clear: "The existence of stands charging a 3s [three-shilling] entrance fee suggests that affluent people must have attended in reasonable numbers, even if they were always a small minority ... [S]occer was clearly not the preserve of the working class alone."[14]

The gender makeup of the crowd was similarly heterogeneous. Women have historically been sports spectators; their presence reflected their own interests and contoured the experience of male spectators, requiring that their involvement be incorporated into any analysis. Working-class women through the early twentieth century were frequent spectators, though among the minority. Upper- and upper-middle-class women were less likely to patronize the terraces at football grounds or the stands of indoor arenas and were instead more commonly found accompanying men at country clubs, where the aristocratic atmosphere made their presence far "safer" in keeping with contemporary social mores. Guttmann notes that in the representations of the day – be they the popular press or lithographs – the prevailing sentiment was that women as spectators were adjuncts to men, who were the more knowledgeable, real fans. Women were companions, not interested observers.[15]

This does not mean that women were not consumers of entertainment, and by the 1920s new amusements had the potential to impact gender relations. Lewis Erenberg notes that, "unlike the entertainments of the Victorian era, various forms of popular culture in the twentieth century sought to bring men and women together."[16] Moreover, as Mark Jancovich, Lucy Faire, and Sarah Stubbings argue in a cultural geography of film consumption, "a whole series of new spaces and public activities emerged which were not only acceptable for women, but actively courted them: exhibitions, amusement parks, galleries, libraries, restaurants, tea rooms, department stores and, of course, picture houses."[17] At the same time, traditional assumptions about the role that women played within the spaces of sports spectating had evolved.

Nevertheless, prevailing attitudes retained strong residual elements of late-Victorian beliefs about women's "public" role as a purifying element. This was especially true of baseball entrepreneurs across North America, who had witnessed the commercial expansion of the sport in the latter half of the nineteenth century accompanied by more frequent public comment on the rowdy behaviour, drunkenness, and presence of gamblers among an increasingly working-class crowd. While female respectability could be maintained by keeping women away from such

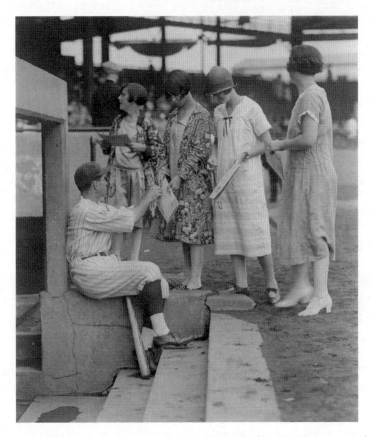

Fig. 1.2. Washington Senators player-manager Bucky Harris signs autographs on Ladies Day, 8 September 1925. (Library of Congress)

environments, baseball club owners began to target women as potential spectators, specifically invoking notions of feminine respectability. The *New York Chronicle* argued in 1867 that "the presence of an assemblage of ladies purifies the moral atmosphere" and suppresses "the outburst of intemperate language which the excitement of the contest so frequently induces."[18] Many clubs offered women free admission to their grounds and covered grandstand seating for particular games (often identified as "Ladies Days"), away from the working-class male patrons standing along the foul lines and beyond the outfield boundary, to attract what Colin Howell calls the ideal "'lady' spectator" (see Fig. 1.2).[19] This woman, Howell goes on to observe, embodied "an ideological construct that served at once to constrain class rowdiness and promote a conformist definition of respectable behaviour that transcended class lines."[20]

These notions had undergone a subtle shift by the interwar years, and to reinforce the idea that sports spectating – in this case soccer spectating – was not the male bastion that it has been assumed to be, it is worth quoting at length from Johnes as he discusses Wales in the decades prior to the Second World War:

> Soccer may have been a predominantly male activity but women were getting more involved, especially in the years before marriage, just as they were in many traditionally male facets of life. Indeed, had the practical constraints that dogged the lives of many women been removed, it is reasonable to suggest that they would have been there in even greater numbers. This recognition of the role of soccer in the lives of at least some women is an indication of the need to question conventional assumptions and narratives about gender roles. Working-class women's lives were not simply the stuff of motherhood, home and burden, and their involvement in soccer marked the game's incorporation into mainstream popular culture.[21]

While the gender composition of the crowd has drawn the attention of sport scholars, less consideration has been given to spectators' ethno-cultural identities. One exception is the narrative history of professional baseball in the United States, which is dominated by the view that, in the late nineteenth and early twentieth centuries in large urban centres in the northeast, supporting the local team was a vehicle of immigrant acculturation, in particular for newcomers from eastern and southern Europe. In his study of sport and the Jewish experience in the early twentieth century, Peter Levine asserts that "aspiring immigrants eagerly embraced obvious and accessible avenues that permitted immediate identification as Americans."[22] Steven Riess, on the other hand, argues that "new immigrants from eastern and southern Europe generally did not become baseball fans." Rather, it was their children who were ardent fans, so that baseball fandom and spectatorship in the early twentieth century was an instrument of acculturation primarily for second-generation Americans.[23]

This comparatively limited scholarship on sports spectators makes it clear that assumptions about the composition of spectators need to be grounded in further historical research. Even moving beyond identity categories, as Jeffrey Hill observes, spectators "have proved a difficult entity for historians to grapple with," in part because, as Jack Williams notes, scholars have had to rely on little more than "impressionistic evidence."[24] This book offers a more detailed consideration of the spectator experience by focusing on three themes, each of which is considered briefly below.

The first of these themes highlights the ways in which the new sports spaces of the 1920s and early 1930s were designed with spectators in mind. No doubt instrumental priorities influenced building architecture and operation. As late nineteenth and early twentieth-century sport entrepreneurs sought to maximize the profits of their enterprises, they attempted to maintain respectable behaviour both on and off the field, in part by charging a variety of entrance fees for the different sections within their facilities.[25] The architecture of the earliest commercial football facilities in England, for example, offered differential entry to the seating in the grandstand on one side of the ground and the standing spaces on the sloped embankment (the "bank") or terrace on the other. As the sport increasingly appealed to working-class men beginning in the mid-1880s, "stadia were certainly designed with the 'popular' element uppermost in mind."[26] Across the pitch, according to Mason, "the 'stand' [was] a bourgeois island in a sea of working class faces."[27] Women were also more likely to be found in the grandstand, among middle-class spectators, perhaps accompanying them. Similar distinctions were made in American baseball stadiums at the turn of the twentieth century, where the covered grandstand was more frequently home to middle-class spectators, both male and female, while the bleachers featured "rowdy, lower-class fans," who, Riess notes, "comprised the majority of spectators in the low-priced sections."[28] These different spaces engendered a variety of spectator experiences, so that historians need to ask how these spaces were designed? With whom in mind? And to accommodate what nature of spectator practices and behaviours?

Secondly, while historians recognize the importance of spectators to the financial and cultural success of the commercial sport ventures of the interwar years, a question remains: How do we identify, even in general terms, who filled the stadiums, ballparks, and grounds across Europe and North America? Little demographic data and few published recollections or diaries exist from which to paint a picture of the "typical" sporting audience. Historians have had to rely on "contemporary comment" in newspaper accounts, written by journalists "whose main interest lay in describing or analysing something else, usually an actual ... match."[29] Mason uses newspaper accounts that listed the victims of a terrace collapse at Glasgow's Ibrox Park in 1902. The disaster resulted in 550 casualties whose names and addresses were reported by the press; 249 also had their occupation listed. This allows Mason to comment on the socio-occupational nature of the spectators who attended the England-Scotland friendly that afternoon – a match whose importance and increased ticket prices may have attracted an atypical audience of skilled craftspeople, rather than unskilled labourers.[30] Similarly, Dean A. Sullivan uses ticket sales data from Cincinnati Reds professional baseball games between 1886 and 1888 to paint a portrait of the class composition of the crowd. He notes that despite the rhetoric of baseball's cross-class appeal, management in Cincinnati often blamed unruly behaviour in the stands on working-class customers, who it was presumed were prominent in Sunday afternoon audiences (having that time free from work). In turn, club management "attempted to discourage blue-collar fans from attending by instituting seating, pricing and scheduling policies designed to isolate and exclude them," which "resulted in largely homogeneous white-collar crowds."[31]

Historians have also accessed non-textual sources to add nuance to their characterizations of spectators. Nicholas Fishwick uses photographs to observe that women, though a minority, did attend football matches in England during the interwar years, while Johnes notes that images of the embankment "show a sea of the flat caps that characterized working-class male dress," but that also "disguised differences of age and region."[32] Riess also uses photographs to characterize professional baseball spectators in the US as "a largely male, middle-class audience," based on the clothing worn by the men pictured in the crowd. Like Johnes, Riess notes that this may be deceiving as spectators dressed in "dark jackets and ties topped with either a derby or straw hat" could well have been "manual workers outfitted in their best church-going suit" who were adhering to social norms of public appearance.[33] Photographs offer a limited glimpse into the nature of spectatorship as they provide only a snapshot of certain spectators at certain events – often those closest to the playing surface – usually captured in a frame where the game action held the photographer's attention. Newsreels have similar limitations. A relatively new medium in the early twentieth century, moving images of sporting events were often filmed from fixed positions with the camera focused on the sporting action and revealing little of the crowd in attendance.

Despite the absence of a representative portrayal of spectators from historical images of sport spaces, Riess goes on to note that by the 1920s baseball was attracting "fans from all social classes" and had become America's most popular spectator sport, as part of a proliferation in commercial entertainments, from sport to cinema.[34] Benjamin Rader argues that the "fundamental characteristic" of sport in this era, at least in the American case, was the "ascendancy of the spectator." He notes the essential role of the person in the stands, who "ultimately determined the broad contours of American sport" as entrepreneurs took advantage of the burgeoning sport media and also changed the very rules of their contests to make them more exciting.[35] Rader labels the interwar years the "Age of the Spectator." Although this moniker suggests the popularity of sport as an entertainment in the 1920s and 1930s, Rader does not enumerate the men, women, and children who purchased tickets and populated the stands at baseball, basketball, and football games, watched tennis and golf matches, and attended track meets. Spectators were important, but little is known about their identity in the "Age of the Spectator."

While a greater understanding of the demographic composition of spectators is important to our understanding of the growth of commercial sport, as Fishwick observes, "the composition of the crowds tells us more about the cast than the play."[36] Spectators were engaged actors in the theatre of commercial sport and the third consideration of this book is the nature and meaning of sports spectating as a lived experience and cultural practice. Bruce Kuklick, in his history of Philadelphia's Shibe Park baseball stadium, recalls the "Huckster," a famed vendor who walked through the stands selling his wares. His trademark booming voice added texture to the experience of watching Philadelphia Athletics baseball in a way that box scores do not reveal.[37] Similarly, fans who gathered on the roofs of buildings on Twentieth Street to watch games over the right-field wall found their own meanings in their spectating practices, narratives that are largely absent from the historical record of commercial sport.

The behaviour of spectators, specifically acts deemed unruly, dominates many analyses at the expense of studying the experience of being a spectator, and is a result no doubt of the influence of soccer hooliganism on the study of spectatorship. Nevertheless, Fishwick rejects the idea that soccer crowds were "unruly mobs" and argues that emphasizing these kinds of behaviours obscures the experiences of the vast majority of fans. To make this error is to miss the historical experience of spectating, as he asserts that "The nature of the communities to which most spectators belonged, of the composition of crowds, meant that most spectators shared norms of behaviour according to which enthusiasm was not incompatible with restraint. It is a serious distortion, therefore, to study football spectators from the point of view of their occasional misbehaviour: it is simply not an adequate reflection of the relationship between the spectators, the game and society."[38] While Fishwick observes that many fans engaged in cheering, taunting (barracking), and (infrequent, he argues) acts of violence, spectatorship allowed for other sensations. It had a symbolic value, and in the industrial cities of England's northeast especially, being a supporter of the local team enhanced membership in the wider community.

At an elemental level, Fishwick asserts that the pleasure offered by spectating must enter into any historical account of the experience. "No event could give such intense excitement and colour to so many working class people, combining passionate commitment in varying degrees with a sense of fun," he argues, "as did a big football match."[39]

Johnes notes that for spectators at football matches – whether standing on the bank (and later the terraces) or sitting in the grandstand – the experience of spectating varied widely. It could include coping with the crush of an often overcrowded stadium. Furthermore, admission to a ground's embankment was the cheapest available ticket and came without the overhead cover found in the more expensive grandstand seats. In inclement weather spectators would have to endure rain and mud. At some grounds, the banks were heaps of garbage covered in dirt, which could mean an olfactory battle with the "evil smell" from the underlying refuse.[40] The experience of being a football spectator also usually involved alcohol, as a spectator who had imbibed, being among others who had, or both.

As suggested above, the experience was also influenced by a spectator's location – where they sat or stood – within the ground, stadium, or arena. Locating oneself, both literally and figuratively, was part of the construction of spectator identities. These, however, were not rigid and immutable, and Johnes argues, not always the overriding concern of spectators. Of a 1920 soccer match between Cardiff City and Swansea Town, he notes that "there was a rush from the queue for the grandstand to the popular bank after news spread that there were no seats left. Seeing this eagerly anticipated derby was more important than remaining separated from the 'bob bankers,'" a nickname for the predominantly working-class crowd who paid a "bob," or a shilling, for a ticket to stand on the embankment.[41] The experience at extraordinary games (e.g., FA Cup matches that were part of football's oldest and most prestigious single-elimination tournament) was often quite different from midseason league matches. High-profile contests might attract different people who "were turning out more for a social affair and an excursion than a game of soccer. This was especially true of females of all classes whose numbers increased significantly at big matches."[42] Yet, the more typical football spectator experience was played out in the majority of matches that were league fixtures without the hype of a Cup match or derby.

Examining the meaningfulness of the practice of spectating in the lives of spectators, whether at hockey arenas or in the context of British football grounds, is a useful starting point for foregrounding the spectator experience in the history of sport. As Johnes observes "for many supporters, soccer's attraction ran deeper than a fun day out, and the sport was an integral and routine part of their lives."[43] It is not surprising then that he asserts that Welsh soccer spectators were "as much a part of the game as the players on the pitch."[44] Yet the experience of the spectator did not occur within a vacuum, but happened amid a growing array of entertainment possibilities in the 1920s and 1930s.[45]

Many analyses agree that the "size of football crowds thus seems to have been broadly determined by the ability of working-class people to pay for fairly cheap entertainments, and implicitly by the lack of alternatives to football available to them."[46] However, Johnes's assessment of female spectators, while somewhat paternalistic, makes a direct comparison to the movie house as a viable alternative to soccer spectatorship: "Compared with the comforts of the increasingly popular cinema, soccer, with its standing in uncomfortable conditions for long periods, probably held little appeal for many working-class women anyway."[47] Despite his claim of a "lack of alternatives," Fishwick's look at football in Sheffield in the interwar years catalogues the many possibilities open to a predominantly working-class audience:

> League matches between the wars cost 1s to see, no mean sum for 90 min-
> utes' entertainment. There were cheaper luxuries available to the working
> class that competed with football in times of hardship. There were, for ex-
> ample, at least 49 picture palaces in Sheffield in 1932, charging only 6d [six
> pence] for a matinée in drier, warmer and more comfortable conditions
> than generally prevailed at Hillsborough or Bramall Lane. Nationally the
> number of cinemas rose during the 1930s from 3,300 in 1929 to 4,967 in
> 1938. There was also competition from the local greyhound track, which
> charged 6d in Sheffield, and perennially from cigarettes (1s a packet in the
> 1930s) and beer (8d a pint).[48]

The popularity of sport as a commercial amusement at the time meant that, as Hill notes, many English football clubs "set their ground re-cords for attendances" during the interwar years.[49] In the same decades in North America, sport entrepreneurs financed the expansion of the fledgling NHL in the mid-1920s out of its central Canadian base into American metropolises such as New York and Chicago.[50] They built large indoor ice venues that were designed primarily to attract spectators – as opposed to participants interested in public skating – and "provided the spectator with a much more comfortable viewing experience, making spectator sports appealing to affluent new audiences."[51] The evolution of professional hockey in the early decades of the twentieth century is central to a history of hockey spectatorship, especially as these changes included attempts to enter new markets and attract paying customers.

Hockey's New Spectating Spaces

The meaningfulness of spectatorship as a demonstration of fandom was as significant for hockey in Canada as it was for soccer in Britain or baseball in the US, although the spectator is largely absent in both popular and scholarly considerations of Canada's national winter sport. Moreover, paying customers were just as important to entrepreneurs in the nascent days of commercial hockey in the 1910s and 1920s as they were to purveyors of other amusements, sporting or otherwise. In her study of arts institutions in Canada, Maria Tippett cites a commentator on the musical scene in Montreal who, in 1907, observed that "there was 'seldom any excitement manifested over concert tickets' while it was 'not unusual to see a line of men two blocks in length waiting patiently for the opening of the box office where tickets for a hockey match are on sale.'"[52] Such a level of commitment among spectators would, twenty-eight years later, lead to press reports of Stanley Cup celebrants in Montreal in 1935 where "a mob of fans occasionally surged and heaved against the [dressing room] door."[53] Arena construction projects were one element in conscious attempts on the part of NHL owners to invest commercial hockey with a culture of respectability, enhancing the position of hockey spectatorship within the pantheon of cultural entertainments as a way of capitalizing on fan passions, such as those of Montreal's hockeygoers, and increasing revenues.

According to Richard Gruneau and David Whitson, NHL owners attempted to civilize the experience of watching hockey and not the game itself (i.e., the on-ice product), playing up "the idea that hockey had indeed 'put on a high hat'" (a reference to a December 1927 *Maclean's* article).[54] The gentrification of spectating took place even though some stakeholders worried about the effect of the on-ice product on attendance. Major Frederic McLaughlin, owner of the Chicago Black Hawks, wrote NHL president Frank Calder in 1927, worried that rough play and violence "will both have a serious sporting and financial effect on the future of professional hockey."[55] To be sure, team owners and hockey officials debated changes to the rules of on-ice play in the 1910s and 1920s. Following on earlier innovations made by Frank and Lester Patrick when they ran the Pacific Coast Hockey Association, the NHL experimented with more liberal forward passing and offside rules, as well as limiting the ways in which goaltenders could operate.[56] Such changes were designed to increase offence on the assumption that higher-scoring games would be more enjoyable for casual fans, attract new paying customers to the sport, and ultimately increase profits. Nevertheless, there is little doubt that hockey entrepreneurs were concerned with improving the image of their product off the ice, and to good effect, as Gruneau and Whitson observe: "Such self-conscious attempts at gentrification may not have convinced many highbrows of the cultural value of hockey, but there seems little doubt that as hockey moved into new sports palaces in Toronto, Montreal, Chicago, and Detroit in the 1920s and 1930s it gained new levels of popularity and a larger share of urban middle-class audiences – which also began to include more women spectators."[57]

These assertions suggest profits were to be gained by appealing to "urban middle-class audiences." Yet, beyond the financial benefits, it remains to ask what form these "civilizing" attempts took.[58] Were they successful? And did this "high hat" image of hockey spectating reflect the diversity of spectator experiences? The claim that crowds at interwar commercial hockey games included "more" women also merits greater interrogation. Women were playing organized versions of hockey by the 1890s, but from the earliest games, they were also spectating.[59] Michael McKinley cites newspaper accounts of a number of nineteenth-century games that make explicit reference to the presence of female spectators. On the occasion of what is considered the first game to follow modern rules, 3 March 1875, the *Kingston Whig-Standard* noted: "A disgraceful sight took place at Montreal at the Victoria Skating Rink after a game of hockey. Shins and heads were battered, benches smashed, and the lady spectators fled in confusion." [60] It is unclear whether more women were attending games half a century later, but debates persisted over behaviours that would be considered respectable, as opposed to "disgraceful," in the presence of a "lady."

Elsewhere Gruneau and Whitson argue that efforts to make commercial hockey more reputable were similar to other middle-class attempts to reform popular culture. The growing popularity of professional hockey in the 1920s coalesced around the NHL, whose hegemony was fuelled partly by its distribution through the new medium of radio and by the capital generated by successful expansion into US markets such as Boston, Chicago, Detroit, and New York (in spite of failed ventures in Philadelphia, Pittsburgh, and St. Louis).[61] As a result, the building of an arena such as Maple Leaf Gardens has been framed within a na-tionalist discourse – saving hockey in Canada in the face of American influence – consistent with attempts in the 1920s to promote national public broadcasting and foster Canadian art, music, drama, and litera-ture.[62] This discourse has also had implications for assumptions made about hockey spectators, assumptions which often take the form of ob-servations about the power of hockey as a unifying force in Canadian society: "There was no other cultural form, no other popular practice, that brought the 'two solitudes' [anglophone and francophone Canada] into regular engagement with each other in quite the same way. More-over, although millions of immigrants from other European countries had brought their own popular recreations with them when they moved to Canada, it wasn't long before their children and grandchildren were watching and playing hockey."[63]

What basis do generalizations about acculturation have in lived expe-rience? The cultural similarity that this argument bears to the rhetoric of immigrant children playing stickball in Brooklyn's streets and sneaking into Dodgers baseball games at Ebbets Field is unmistakable. But does this narrative reflect lived experience? Do we know that the same boys and girls were cheering on the Rangers and trying to get into Madison Square Garden for hockey games in the winter? Or whether Toronto's early twentieth-century eastern European Jewish population or post–Second World War Italian and Portuguese immigrant communities sought out Maple Leaf Gardens as a place to "practice" being Canadian?

Generalizations about the consumption of hockey as a unifying na-tional force persist, in part, because it is on the role of spectating in the lives of spectators in the interwar years that the socio-historical understanding of North American hockey spectators falls most short. The published history of hockey is dominated by popular works by writers such as Brian McFarlane, Stan Fischler, and others.[64] There is an established and growing scholarly literature on hockey, led by the work of Gruneau and Whitson and Bruce Kidd, which now includes notable monographs by Stephen Hardy and Andrew C. Holman, J. An-drew Ross, and John Chi-Kit Wong, among others, as well as important anthologies and collections.[65] The focus of much of this literature is the historical origins of the NHL and hockey's cultural significance in Canada and its presumed (and contested) connection with notions of national identity.[66]

This scholarship details how the period of franchise expansion and arena construction in the NHL that occurred between 1924 and 1931 was central to the league's hegemonic project, raising the barrier to en-try into what Kidd argues had become a "cartel."[67] Making this transition, which included building expensive new arenas, required investment from among North America's capitalist elite. It is perhaps not surprising that, after 1926, "professional hockey was no longer the domain of mid-dle-class entrepreneurs. Ownership of a franchise now rested with men of substantial wealth."[68] Yet, as much as these men (and they were all men) were involved in financing the construction of the new arenas in Montreal, New York, Boston, Chicago, Detroit, and Toronto, the rhetoric surrounding the buildings' construction often centred on the need to create environments to attract people of just such standing so that they would be comfortable spending both their money and their evenings in these new surroundings.

Tickets to games in these new venues were only one alternative within the panoply of public amusements. But what united hockey entrepreneurs with other amusement capitalists were their aspirations. Vaudeville, theatre, and movie house owners all sought to infuse their entertainments with an aura of respectability. As a result, the architectural details of these sport spaces also alluded to elements of the new consumer culture. "Several of the new arenas," Howard Shubert notes, "featured the kind of marquees with flashing lights more typically associated with theatres and cinemas." This was no accident, as Shubert goes on to observe: "Two of the arenas, at New York and Detroit, were even designed by noted 'theatre' architects – Thomas W. Lamb and Charles Howard Crane, respectively."[69] Crane was in such demand in Detroit that "he designed over fifty theatres in the city, including all the major houses in two successive theatre districts."[70] In 1927, he opened his first NHL arena, Detroit's Olympia. Crane's subsequent projects included the Allen (later Tivoli) Theatre in Toronto, but it was Lamb who made a name for himself as the most prolific North American theatre and movie house architect of the early twentieth century.[71] In New York, his designs included the Capitol and the Strand, while in Toronto he was the primary architect on Loew's Yonge Street and its companion, the Winter Garden, as well as the Pantages, and the Regent. "In 1920," Constance Olsheski notes, "of the five vaudeville houses in Toronto, three had been designed by him."[72] Five years later, Lamb designed the seminal indoor sports arena of the period, Madison Square Garden in New York.

While the new arenas of the NHL drew upon the talents of theatre architects and were designed in such a way as to promote (and profit from) respectable attendance, they each also housed their own unique spectator cultures. Frank Selke, an assistant manager with the Maple Leafs who eventually left Toronto to manage the Montreal Canadiens, claimed that Montreal's new Forum, which opened in 1924, was "the first of its kind to depart from the old-fashioned, skating-rink type of building to a construction that would give thousands of people a clear view of the playing area."[73] Frank "King" Clancy, who played for both the Maple Leafs and Ottawa Senators, recalled crowds at the Forum as "rough and ready": "Many a night in Montreal I got next to the fence there [separating the playing surface from spectators at either end of the rink], somebody push you into the fence, you be getting up and somebody hit you, punch you in the mouth, that is, a spectator."[74] Even after his playing career was over, when Clancy worked as a referee for the NHL, he remembered that Montreal spectators "threw everything that they could lay their hands on out on the ice at me." Radio broadcaster Foster Hewitt also recalled that working in the Montreal Forum could be a dangerous proposition. His broadcast position was located within the stands, "smack in the centre of over-enthusiastic fans who were famed for their noisy hilarities." One particular evening "something whizzed past my left ear ... a whiskey bottle (empty, of course)." Attempts by security officials at the Forum to eject the offending patron resulted in "a real Donny-brook," during which Hewitt continued his broadcast, despite "a likelihood that a body might shortly be draped over my shoulders."[75]

Behaviour such as this was often associated with a group of spectators seated in what was sarcastically dubbed the "Millionaire's Section," which Selke described as "some fifteen hundred fans willing to pay fifty cents for the privilege of standing."[76] The association between a section in the arena such as this, with its low admission cost, pedestrian appointments, and rowdy behaviour, suggests a working-class and predominantly male crowd. In Montreal, this requires additionally a recognition of the ways in which anglophone-francophone identity politics accompanied spectators into the Forum. Popular representations, such as the 2005 French-Canadian motion picture biography of Maurice "Rocket" Richard, *The Rocket*, portray the Forum's standing-room audience in the 1940s and 1950s as predominantly working-class, francophone men, squeezed into a small section at the end of the rink and separated from the rest of the crowd by a chicken-wire fence.[77]

At a seating capacity of nine thousand, the Forum was slightly larger than Toronto's existing Arena Gardens (built in 1912), and only hinted at the spectator revolution that was to come. Despite Shubert's assertion that "the next generation of hockey arenas [was] constructed between 1920 and 1931," a more convincing and precise case can be made that it was in 1925, with the opening of the new Madison Square Garden in New York, that a new era of spectator facilities was inaugurated.[78] Madison Square Garden was essentially the first, and Maple Leaf Gardens the last in a series of new buildings constructed in this period and intended, at least in part, to host professional hockey and house spectators. Madison Square Garden opened in 1925 with nearly twice the seating capacity (seventeen thousand) of the one-year-old Montreal Forum. This building was, in many ways, representative of the infusion of US capital into the NHL, which prior to 1924 had been a central Canadian commercial enterprise. More than this, the opening of Madison Square Garden ushered in a new era of hockey spectatorship, which, in addition to its unprecedented seating capacity, signalled a new emphasis on sports spectator as distinct from sport participants (see Fig. 1.3).

Fig. 1.3. The new Madison Square Garden, pictured here set up for boxing (c. 1925–26), offered the largest indoor spectating experience in North America. (Collection of the New York Historical Society)

Built by boxing promoter Tex Rickard, Madison Square Garden was the third building of that name in New York's history and the first not located on the eponymous square, where Broadway meets Fifth Avenue, but instead on Eighth Avenue between 49th and 50th Streets in Manhattan. This location on the western boundary of New York's amusement corridor – Times Square – highlighted the affinity that the arena shared with the entertainment district. Madison Square Garden played host to major indoor sporting events, including professional hockey, and the city's first NHL team, the New York Americans, started play with the opening of the new arena in December 1925. The gala opening was presented as a benefit for the Neurological Institute and hosted by the Canadian Club of New York, which after the game hosted a dinner-dance at the Biltmore Hotel. The Prince of Wales donated a trophy to be awarded to the winner of the game. Box seats were sold in advance and the society pages in the days before the game enumerated just who would be sitting in each box.

Exhibitions of both fancy and speed skating were included between periods in part to entertain a New York sporting public somewhat unfamiliar with hockey, as well as to mark hockey spectating as a more respectable practice, and thus attract a more middle-class crowd than boxing events, which already had an established clientele from Rickard's days operating the previous incarnation of Madison Square Garden.

Such festivities were not the norm. The building's design created a physical separation between spectators with seats in the more expensive main portion of Madison Square Garden, who entered through the lobby on Eighth Avenue, and balcony patrons, who were shepherded towards more pedestrian entrances and staircases along the north and south sides of the building. A unique spectating culture developed in the balcony, where seats were sold general admission – first come, first served – with sight lines for hockey spectators that were far from ideal. Madison Square Garden was built primarily as a boxing and circus venue, so the seats were installed, and the balcony and mezzanine tiers positioned, in such a way as to focus the spectators' gaze on the centre of the floor below. Hockey spectators, whose visible field of interest was both wider and deeper, were able to see the entire ice surface from only the first two rows of the balcony. As a result, spectators would line up early and, once the arena doors opened, run up the stairs to try and get a treasured seat in the balcony's first two rows.

The involvement of the NHL in New York's new arena also symbolized the shift of the NHL towards major northeastern and midwestern US cities where entrepreneurs had invested in large indoor facilities that included artificial ice plants. Within five years, Boston, Chicago, Detroit, and St. Louis all had new arenas, the first three of which would remain NHL venues through the 1970s. Boston Garden opened in 1928 and closed in 1995, Chicago Stadium was home to an NHL franchise from 1929 to 1995, and the Detroit Olympia was in use from 1927 to 1979 (see Fig. 1.4). The Pittsburgh Pirates, who joined the NHL in the 1925–26 season, the same year that the New York Americans opened Madison Square Garden, played in Duquesne Gardens, which opened in 1890. The Pirates moved to Philadelphia in 1930 and lasted one season as the Quakers, playing out of the Philadelphia Arena, which opened in 1920. The Ottawa Senators, an original NHL franchise, spent their final decade playing in the ten thousand-seat Ottawa Auditorium, which opened in 1923. The Senators became the St. Louis Eagles, who played their only NHL season, 1934–35, in the relatively new St. Louis Arena, which was built in 1929.

The Boston Bruins were the NHL's first American franchise, joining the league for the 1924–25 season, a year before the New York Americans

Fig. 1.4. The NHL saw a boom in arena construction in the late 1920s, including Chicago Stadium (top), opened in 1929, and the Detroit Olympia (bottom) opened in 1927. (top: Courtesy of the Newberry Library, Chicago; bottom: Library of Congress)

inaugurated Madison Square Garden. Owned by grocery store magnate
Charles Adams, the Bruins played their first four seasons in the Boston
Arena, built in 1910. Unlike Rickard and Madison Square Garden, the
Boston Arena had a lengthy history of hosting hockey games. The spectating experience in Boston was shaped by hockey's association in the
city with the amateur game: "a rich base of schools and colleges, which
became incubators for players and fans alike."[79] Although Hardy notes
the ways in which spectators at amateur games could be no less rowdy
than those at professional ones, Adams was as concerned as his contemporaries about presenting NHL hockey within a respectable environment. For example, the Boston Arena enforced a differential smoking
policy: "Smoking in any place in the auditorium is positively forbidden.
Smoking is permitted, however, in the main foyer."[80] This typically male
public pastime was permitted, but not around the ice surface; smoke-
filled arenas were more commonly associated with less respectable boxing crowds and, after the first incarnation of the Boston Arena burned
down in 1918, with the threat of fire.[81] Much like Smythe would with
Maple Leaf Gardens, Adams sold professional hockey in Boston through
"a strategy to build the fan base by convincing female listeners [of radio
broadcasts] that Bruins games were the 'in' thing."[82]

As professional hockey in the form of the Bruins became a commercial
success, Adams moved his club to a new arena, the Boston Garden, which
was built by Rickard – and originally called the Boston Madison Square
Garden – as part of a short-lived plan to build of series of Madison Square
Gardens across the United States (see Fig. 1.5).[83] Throughout the 1930s,
Boston spectators were portrayed as the rowdiest in the league, at least by
the Toronto press and Maple Leafs' personnel, which reflected tensions
between the two clubs. These opinions became entrenched after a 12
December 1933 game at the Boston Garden where a violent hit by the
Bruins' Eddie Shore left the Maple Leafs' Ace Bailey in the hospital with
what would turn out to be career-ending injuries (see Fig. 1.6). Charles
Higginbottom of the Amateur Athletic Union of Canada, a bastion of
respectability in sport, told the *Star* that the Bruins had "the most rabid
crowd on the circuit. He felt that their extreme enthusiasm may have had
a great deal to do with the starting of the trouble."[84] Characterizations
such as these persisted throughout the 1930s. More than four years after
the Bailey-Shore incident, a *Globe and Mail* writer reported:

> I'd heard about the paper-throwing for which the top galleryites of the Bos-
> ton Garden are famous, but didn't expect it so soon. The fans here are like
> baseball pitchers. They warm up before game time. Torn paper was flutter-
> ing from the uppermost gallery twenty-five minutes before the teams were
> scheduled to resume action.

Fig. 1.5. Boston Garden, which opened in 1928, was owner Charles Adams's attempt to profit from commercial hockey and was home to Smythe's and the Maple Leafs' rival in the 1930s, the Bruins. (Courtesy of the Boston Public Library, Leslie Jones Collection)

> There was a chorus of boos, loud and prolonged, and more showers of torn paper from the gallery when the Leafs, first to come on the ice, made their appearance. Then what cheering when the Bruins followed them – the kind of ovation one would expect to be given an athlete on the winning of a world championship.[85]

Reports such as these that detailed the manner in which spectators were an active component of the spectacle – in ways that were often seen as disreputable, which is likely why they were commented upon or remembered – were obviously not unique to Boston. Contemporary newspaper accounts highlight that spectators were actively involved in minor league professional games as well.[86] Officials were sent to investigate a game at the Detroit Olympia, nine days before the Bailey-Shore incident, after a "game was held up for several minutes when fights between players occurred, and numerous spectators swarmed onto the ice."[87]

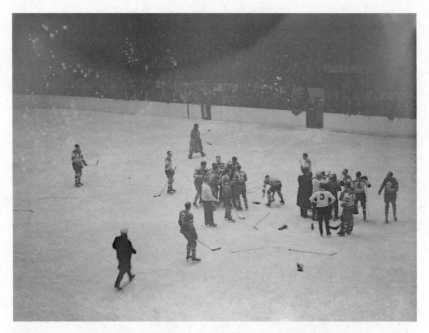

Fig. 1.6. Scene on the ice after the Shore-Bailey incident, Boston Garden,
12 December 1933. (Courtesy of the Boston Public Library, Leslie Jones
Collection)

As spectating cultures developed in all of the NHL's cities in the 1920s
and 1930s, hockey's leading capitalist entrepreneurs faced similar concerns as they sought to fill their new arenas: reconciling the desire to
present a respectable and, they presumed, profitable spectacle with the
ways in which spectators chose to shape their own experience. In Toronto, the pursuit of the riches of respectable sporting entertainment
was taken up by Smythe. A veteran of both a working-class upbringing
and First World War military service, the Maple Leafs' managing partner
doggedly pursued success on his way to becoming a larger-than-life figure in the hockey capital of English Canada.

Toronto before Maple Leaf Gardens

Smythe's fame was inextricably linked to the hockey team he managed
and the arena he built to house it, which quickly became a civic landmark in Toronto. All of this was achieved in a city that had a population

that was essentially one-tenth the size of New York's (and smaller than many other NHL cities), where ethnic tensions reflected divisions between Orange Order Protestants and Irish Roman Catholics.[88] The city, however, did experience growth during the interwar years, from a population of 489,681 in 1918 to 606,370 in 1929.[89] The percentage of people not of British origin grew from less than 5 per cent to 19 per cent over the course of the 1920s, with Jews and Italians comprising the largest immigrant communities. Despite this, Toronto remained overwhelmingly British, which led local historian Jesse Middleton to assert that "no other city of comparable size ... is as homogenous."[90]

In the 1920s, Toronto's financial industries had begun to overtake the historically dominant position held by the originally Scottish-Canadian banks of Montreal. Taking advantage of the resource boom in the Canadian economy, Toronto became the metropolitan centre to the resource hinterlands. This boom resulted largely from the extraction of resources – predominantly in the pulp and paper and mining industries – that were in turn exported to the US to fuel manufacturing south of the border. While control of the firms in these industries was increasingly held by US interests, their financiers and headquarters were more often than not to be found in Toronto.[91] Such concentration of wealth changed the urban landscape of Toronto in dramatic ways. Although skyscrapers were far rarer than in cities like New York and Chicago, "seven went up between 1922 and 1927 and, in 1928 alone, seven more were added."[92] The most prominent changes to Toronto's streetscape were the Bank of Commerce building (completed in 1931) and the Royal York Hotel (opened in 1929), which at thirty-four storeys and over one thousand rooms, respectively, were promoted as the tallest building and largest hotel in the British Empire. The economic downturn that began in 1929, however, ended this construction boom and, as James Lemon observes: "The physical fabric of Toronto changed less in the 1930s than in any other decade of the twentieth century. The Royal York Hotel, Eaton's College Street, Maple Leaf Gardens and the Customs Building on Front Street were all finished by 1932 ... these projects marked the end of downtown development for many years."[93]

Characterizations of the 1920s as a period of booming economic times are far more representative of the last half of the decade, as "it was not until the autumn of 1924 that Canada's economic health was largely regained" following the post-war downturn.[94] For most Torontonians the 1920s were a period of only moderate prosperity, as from 1921 to 1929 average annual earnings only rose from $1,261 to $1,306.[95] During the Depression, Toronto's wage-earners were the hardest hit and construction in the city almost stopped. As an October 1930 article in *Canadian*

Magazine noted: "The idea of a vacation, of travel, or of having a radio or of indulging in even the slightest luxury is not even considered."[96] By 1929, women comprised 17 per cent of the labour force, yet the average working woman earned only $559 annually in 1931 in a career that would last eight years, while her male counterpart brought home $942 – still well below the incomes of the 1920s – but would work on average for thirty-nine years.[97]

Although the Toronto business community's "dominant financial ties were with New York," Lemon observes that there was concern among moral reformers and the press about "American influence" on Canadian cultural institutions, including the shows staged at the city's vaudeville theatres and playhouses.[98] However, the influence of American commercial interests was most visible in the products of popular mass culture. There was a "northbound tidal wave of American mass culture: radio programs, professional spectator sports, magazines."[99] American magazines dominated the market – US publications had the four largest circulations – and radio programs from nearby US stations held sway over Toronto's airwaves.

Debates over issues such as these, as well as increasingly prominent sports coverage, were a staple of Toronto's daily newspapers in the interwar years. There were a quartet of dailies, ranging from the respectable to the sensational: the *Globe* and *Mail and Empire* published in the morning while evening editions were offered by the *Star* and *Telegram*. The *Globe* was Toronto's most established paper and historically a Liberal party organ, while the *Mail and Empire* was the Conservative party paper. (The two merged in 1936 to form the *Globe and Mail*.) The *Telegram* also took conservative, pro-Empire stances, usually in sensationalist fashion, while the *Star* offered a more liberal populism and enjoyed the largest circulation in the city. These latter two papers "framed much of the debate of the 1920s, certainly outdoing their more respectable morning rivals."[100] There were also more salacious news and rumour sources, as "between the wars, Toronto became the tabloid capital of Canada."[101] One of these was a scandal-seeking tabloid called *Hush*, which, while it occasionally covered sport and did comment upon the city's new hockey arena, dedicated itself to "the furtherance of public morality and decency."[102]

Beyond US capital interests enabling NHL expansion – and challenging Smythe's ability to compete – the impact of American popular culture was also seen on the stages of the city's theatre and vaudeville houses. Lemon notes that "American influences insidiously worked their way into the entertainment of Torontonians," specifically "musicals and revues at the Royal Alexandra and movies, particularly the talkies which arrived in 1927, were considered immoral by many."[103] As early as 1923, historian Jesse Middleton was moved to note that "In outward semblance Toronto is an American city ... The shop windows are all dressed in the alluring New York manner."[104]

Department stores were well established in Toronto by the interwar years. Two companies in particular, built upon national mail-order operations facilitated by factories in Toronto, vied for both local customers and respectability by building flagship stores in the city. The T. Eaton Company (or Eaton's, as it was popularly known) was founded in 1869 and erected a store in Toronto at the intersection of Yonge and Queen Streets in 1883. Directly opposite Eaton's, on the south side of Queen Street, was its primary competitor, Simpson's. The flagship store of the Robert Simpson Company was built in 1896 and expanded in 1929. Significantly for the story of Maple Leaf Gardens, Eaton's, instead of mirroring its competitor's expansion on Queen Street, built a new flagship store further north on Yonge Street, at the intersection with College Street, in 1930.

Yonge Street, which remains Toronto's major north-south artery, was also home to a number of the city's highest-profile theatres and movie houses, with Massey Hall, the city's major concert venue, one short block east of the thoroughfare. Massey Hall opened in 1894 with a seating capacity of 3,500, which made it Toronto's largest indoor venue.[105] But it was in the vaudeville market, in the years before and after the First World War, that competition was most intense. In a marketplace that already boasted the Grand Opera House (built in 1874 on Adelaide Street, just west of Yonge Street), Shea's operated two large theatres in Toronto: the Victoria (built in 1910 and seating two thousand, on Victoria Street, just east of Yonge Street) and the Hippodrome (built in 1914 and seating 3,200, on Bay Street). A second US interest, Marcus Loew's Theatres Limited, opened Loew's Yonge Street in 1913 (seating 2,194) and its upstairs companion, the Winter Garden (seating 1,422) a year later. In 1920, N.L. Nathanson opened the 3,626-seat Pantages Theatre, also on Yonge Street, which with a price tag of between $600,000 and $1 million was Toronto's costliest theatre.[106] All of these theatres were built in and around what was becoming known as the "theatre block" in Toronto, with the "legitimate" Royal Alexandra on King Street being the furthest removed from this concentration (see Fig. 1.7).[107]

It was within this entertainment economy that Smythe positioned his new arena. He made a direct connection between respectability and the regard in which theatre-going was held at the time. The spectator experience Smythe offered before building Maple Leaf Gardens failed to, in his words, "compete with the comfort of the theatres and other places where people can spend their money."[108] Indeed, as one popular

Fig. 1.7. Prominent Toronto entertainment venues, contemporary with Maple Leaf Gardens, included Shea's Hippodrome (above), pictured here in 1955, and Loew's Yonge Street theatre (left), looking north (c. 1935–37). (above: Courtesy of Toronto Public Library; left: City of Toronto Archives, Fonds 1488, Series 1230, Item 1097)

account has observed, Smythe "pitched the grand new edifice as a kind of sporting Carnegie Hall."[109]

Connections already existed at the managerial level between Toronto's amusement venues and commercial sport. When Loew's Theatres, financed by the Shubert brothers, New York's pre-eminent theatre impresarios, was incorporated in February 1913, Lawrence Solman was listed as a member of the board of directors. At the time he was a partner in and manager of the Royal Alexandra Theatre. The Shubert brothers employed him as the manager of their Canadian operations. In Toronto during the 1920s, Solman also operated the Toronto Island Ferries and Sunnyside Amusement Park, owned the city's professional baseball team and its stadium on Toronto Island, and was involved in Mutual Street Arena.[110] Loew's northern competitor on Toronto's Yonge Street theatre block, N.L. Nathanson's Pantages, was financed in part by J.P. Bickell.[111] The president of McIntyre Porcupine Mines, Bickell was also a primary investor in professional hockey in Toronto.[112] It was by convincing Bickell to remain invested in the St. Patricks hockey club in 1927 that Smythe was able to purchase the franchise. Bickell, in turn, would become president of Maple Leaf Gardens, while Nathanson was also invested in the local hockey team.[113]

The St. Patricks were neither Conn Smythe's initial foray into hockey management nor his first business venture (see Fig. 1.8). He had played hockey at the University of Toronto prior to the First World War before turning his hand to managing and coaching teams, also primarily at the University of Toronto. A squad he assembled – the Varsity Grads – represented Canada at the 1928 Olympics, although Smythe did not accompany the team to St. Moritz. By that point his NHL journey was already underway. While managing the Varsity team, Smythe continued to operate the sand and gravel business he had started and develop his stable of racehorses. A believer in hard work – to say nothing of his very public loyalty to the British Empire – Smythe's stature as a self-made man grew as potentially apocryphal stories of his gambling success were linked to the acquisition of Toronto's NHL club and the subsequent purchase of defenceman King Clancy from the Ottawa Senators. As much as he was the public face of the Maple Leafs and Maple Leaf Gardens, he was, for quite some time, only a minority stakeholder in both ventures. Nevertheless, as one biographer noted, Smythe's exploits in hockey would result in him becoming "one of the best-known figures in the country, see his arena become a national sports shrine, and turn Saturday night into a near-religious experience as Canadians from one coast to the other gathered around the radio to listen to Foster Hewitt describe the latest exploits of Canada's favourite team."[114]

Smythe's entry into professional hockey – which was still in the 1920s a poor cousin to the amateur game in many parts of Canada – came not

Fig. 1.8. Conn Smythe with Maple Leafs coach Dick Irvin, visiting Boston Garden, c. 1938–39. (Courtesy of the Boston Public Library, Leslie Jones Collection)

in Toronto, but in New York. In March 1926, he had accepted the position of manager with New York's second NHL team, the Rangers, eight months before the club's first game. He was charged with assembling a competitive squad, which he did before suffering a falling out with Col. John Hammond, the man who ran the hockey operation at Madison Square Garden and who replaced Smythe with Lester Patrick. But while in New York, Smythe had seen the financial benefits that could be reaped from hockey teams owning their own large, modern arenas. He understood the transformational (and financial) potential of modern spectator-oriented arenas. Upon returning to Toronto, Smythe assembled a group of backers that enabled him to purchase the St. Patricks – so named in an effort "to lure Toronto's large Irish community" – and promptly renamed the club the "Maple Leafs."[115]

The team played in Arena Gardens, also known because of its location as the Mutual Street Arena, or in the press as just the "Arena" (see Fig. 1.9).

Fig. 1.9. Located on Mutual Street, Arena Gardens was typical of arenas that catered as much to public use as to spectator events. (City of Toronto Archives, Fonds 1646)

Before the 1923–24 NHL season, Arena Gardens was the league's largest venue. Opened in December 1912, it was "highly esteemed because it was the first artificial ice rink in Ontario" with "room for 2,000 skaters and 7,000 spectators."[116] Similar to other arenas built in this era, when facilities were intended as much for participation as spectating, Arena Gardens' management let it be known in 1912 that "Friday nights will be devoted to public skating."[117] The arena was renovated in 1925, increasing its seating capacity to 7,105, perhaps in time for the inaugural meeting of the United Church of Canada, which took place there on 10 June 1925.[118]

Long-time spectator Tom Gaston recalled Arena Gardens as "an old brick building on Mutual Street, near Shuter, right downtown."[119] It was a pedestrian arena typical of the period during which it was constructed, with a similar exterior to a building such as the Amphitheatre in Winnipeg, though able to accommodate more spectators than many of its contemporaries.[120] An interior photograph of Arena Gardens, circa

Fig. 1.10. Home to the first artificial ice rink in Ontario when it opened in 1912, Arena Gardens held far fewer spectators than its US contemporaries by 1931. (City of Toronto Archives, Fonds 1646, Item 36)

1920–21, shows a single tier of wooden benches and two rows of box seats (see Fig. 1.10). Gaston, also recalled that "there was standing room in the tiers. Chicken wire kept the people in standing room from trying to move down into the seats."[121] Sportswriter Henry Roxborough wrote of Arena Gardens in 1950 that "When all reserved seats were sold, the rush sections jammed, the aisles and corridors packed, with more fans huddled on the window sills and a few lying flat on high steel girders, the massed attendance was 8500."[122] Those who could be squeezed in to watch a hockey game at Arena Gardens by the late 1920s and who weren't standing were more than likely sitting on "wooden benches, kind of like church pews," Gaston recalls.[123] Long-time Maple Leafs employee Tommy Naylor recalled that Arena Gardens "was more like a barn. The box seats were planks."[124]

Not that seat material was the only issue affecting spectator comfort in the stands on Mutual Street. "Nutsy Fagan," a pseudonym and alter ego for well-known Toronto athlete-turned-sportswriter Ted Reeve, writing in the 1930–31 *Arena Gardens Programme*, complained: "Is it right that

every time the [Montreal] Canadiens or [Boston] Bruins come to town
we should be packed in so closely that we have to clap our hands up and
down instead of sideways and that even in the box seats there is hardly
room to swing a chair?" Moreover, Fagan/Reeve, a former rugby football player who was well-schooled in that sport's turns of phrase, went
on: "Is it proper that during the intermissions you cannot reach the re-
freshment stand without gaining yards six times on plunges?"[125] Without
losing sight of the fact that Reeve was paid by the Maple Leafs hockey
club so that "Nutsy Fagan" could lobby programme purchasers at Arena
Gardens to support Smythe's pursuit of a new hockey arena in Toronto,
it is ironic that Reeve's metaphor for Arena Gardens' cramped stands
was the space "to swing a chair." One former spectator remembers that
the box seats had "kitchen chairs in them to sit on." As they tell the
story: "some of the people didn't like the way the game was going ... and
they'd pick up a chair and throw it out on the ice. Smash it. That's why
they had to take out all the chairs and put in some tacked down, nailed
down seats."

Such descriptions of the atmosphere at Arena Gardens were less true
in the early 1920s. Clancy, who visited as a member of the Ottawa Senators between 1921 and 1930, remembered the Arena Gardens crowd as
"a little different" from other audiences in the NHL, especially, as noted
above, Montreal: "It wasn't as tough playing in Toronto at that time, as
it was in Montreal." Clancy also recalls that in the 1920s "in the Mutual
Street Arena, we had lots of room for people over there; at that time, the
[professional] hockey wasn't what it was" in the 1930s. Smythe may have
been "the one who put professional hockey over in Toronto," as Clancy
goes on to assert, but when Arena Gardens opened in 1912 the financial
success of professional hockey in the city was by no means assured.[126] In
fact, press accounts of the first game played at the arena by the Toronto
franchise of the National Hockey Association, the precursor to the NHL,
estimated the crowd at four thousand, only slightly more than half of the
capacity of Arena Gardens.[127] Hockey was undoubtedly a popular spectator activity, but Clancy also recalled that even into the 1920s, "the senior
OHA [the amateur Ontario Hockey Association] was the big league here
[in Toronto]."[128] The amateur game was, at the beginning of the interwar
period, more popular in Toronto than professional hockey. One spectator remembered watching an Allen Cup playoff game between the senior
amateur Winnipeg Falcons and University of Toronto Varsity squad in
1920 at Arena Gardens: "I lined up on Dalhousie Street from 2 oclock
[sic] to eight and only got standing room, but it was worth the effort,
that was in 1920 when the Falcons went from Toronto after the games to
Antwerpt [sic], the first time the hockey was on the Olympic agenda."[129]

Cultural and economic circumstances were markedly different for commercial hockey in Toronto a decade later. The Maple Leafs' final year at Arena Gardens (1930–31) was called "one of the most successful seasons a local pro team has ever enjoyed" by one newspaper, as "no other pro team ever reaped the financial benefits this aggregation, coached by Connie Smythe did." The same writer "estimated that the club was forced to turn away many thousands of dollars at the gates this winter because of the lack of accommodation. The great majority of the home games were sell-outs."[130] Such assertions of the Maple Leafs' popularity prior to the opening of Maple Leaf Gardens are difficult to confirm since attendance figures for the team's four seasons at Arena Gardens have not survived. However, during these years gate receipts certainly grew under Smythe's management from almost $123,500 in 1927–28 to nearly $202,000 just three years later in the team's final season on Mutual Street.[131] This is suggestive of an increasing demand among spectators – assuming stable ticket prices and a somewhat fixed capacity – that is also confirmed by anecdotal evidence. Gaston recalled his first Maple Leafs game at Arena Gardens, tickets that were gifted to him at Christmas 1930, and remembered a full house: "even though money was scarce and the Leafs weren't a great team, the place was usually full and it was tough to get seats."[132]

This reality was not lost on Smythe who claimed that at Arena Gardens "about half the time we were packing in nine thousand counting standees, but still weren't grossing enough to pay our players what they could have been getting with the richer teams in the US."[133] He believed that there was untapped consumer demand for commercial hockey in Toronto. But the motivation to build Maple Leaf Gardens in 1931 was not just to create a larger arena, although this was a factor. Smythe was also looking to escape a rental agreement with the owners of Arena Gardens, to whom the club had to remit approximately 30 per cent of gate receipts.[134] As a tenant at Arena Gardens, Smythe's hockey club was contractually limited to home games every other Saturday night, the most desirable and profitable time slot, with remaining games scheduled for weeknights. Kidd has noted the boost to attendance that the playoffs gave the Maple Leafs and that, without onerous rental stipulations, these additional revenues flowed back to Smythe and the Maple Leafs. Another analysis has estimated the substantial impact that playoff games and the additional attendance enabled by the new, larger rink, had on the team's bottom line.[135]

The influx of American capital into the NHL, which Smythe had witnessed first-hand in New York in 1926 and on road trips with the Maple Leafs in subsequent years, had dramatically altered the financial landscape of commercial hockey. Maple Leaf Gardens – a building owned rather than rented – was Smythe's response to these changing circumstances. All the other teams in the league were playing in arenas newer than Arena Gardens, with the major facilities in Boston, Chicago, Detroit, New York, and Montreal offering substantially greater spectator capacity. To realize the economic benefits of a new arena, Smythe and the team's board of directors argued that a larger building needed to be accompanied by an effort to change the perceptions of sports spectating as a cultural practice.

A prospectus, prepared by Frank Selke and available to the public for ten cents, made the case for the new arena. Ted Reeve donned his other literary guises to support these efforts. "Moaner McGruffey" noted that a new arena that offered a more respectable spectating environment would, if not improve the behaviour of all spectators, allow him to "be able to get at least seven thousand seats away from the paper throwing boo-boo bird who has been next to me all winter" at Arena Gardens.[136] Smythe was determined, as a biographer noted, to "get rid of the dinginess, the drunkenness, and the rowdiness that tainted hockey's image."[137] To contribute to these efforts, another of Reeve's alter egos, "Miss Alice Snippersnapper," introduced the notion of feminine respectability – while reaffirming perceptions of female frailty – with which Smythe would attempt to imbue attendance at his new arena. She and the other "sopranos don't care how big the new Arena may be as long as a good portion of it is devoted to a rest room for excitement-frayed females."[138] Moreover, the physical environment at Arena Gardens was too crowded – "it is positively panicking, if you know what I mean, to find oneself powdering someone else's nose in the crush" – and too smoky – "all a damsel had to do for a satisfying inhale was to take a few deep breaths of the surrounding ozone and blow it out her ears."[139]

At Maple Leaf Gardens, the club's games would be the only Saturday evening attraction and the city's highest-profile destination most every week of the NHL season.[140] The new arena quickly became a primary focus of Toronto's social scene during the 1930s. The lived experience of this transformation is the focus of this book. Trying to understand how spectators experienced this new facility, especially as it differed from experiences at an earlier venue such as Arena Gardens, is the lens through which Maple Leaf Gardens' construction is placed within the socio-historic context of the North American entertainment economy of the interwar years.

Chapter Outline: Centring the Spectator

This book examines the historical significance of the construction of Maple Leaf Gardens in 1931, with specific attention given to the role of spectators – in particular their class and gender composition, and the expectations that accompanied these. The Gardens ended the arena construction boom in NHL cities. After its opening in 1931, the NHL would not welcome a new building until the league expanded in 1967. The Maple Leafs contended that the hockey club needed an arena of the capacity and grandeur necessary to attract crowds both sizeable enough and sufficiently well off to compete with what was being offered in New York and elsewhere. While motivated by considerations of profit, the building of Maple Leaf Gardens also fundamentally changed the nature of sports spectating in Toronto. And, given Maple Leaf Gardens' place in the anglophone, pan-Canadian imagination – thanks to national radio broadcasts – the influence of spectator expectations and behaviours extended far beyond Toronto.

. The central argument that follows is that the new stadium- and arena-building of the 1920s and 1930s fundamentally changed the spectator experience by altering the appointments of the spaces that surrounded the playing surface at the same time that the NHL was expanding to new markets and making rule changes designed to result in higher-scoring games that would attract more fans. The focus here is placed squarely on the experience of the paying customer, which integrated sport within the emerging consumer economy, including developments such as the growth of theatres and movie houses.

The meaning of the experience to spectators is important because of how sport entrepreneurs such as Smythe were positioning their attractions in the interwar years as a respectable alternative to, for example, a night at the theatre. In this context, then, this book is an examination of what it was like to be a spectator in the 1930s, specifically a spectator of professional hockey in Toronto. Such a topic raises a number of issues, including understanding why spectating was organized in the interwar years in the way that it was (i.e., in newly built arenas, substantially different and larger than their predecessors); how this new organization of spectating differed from earlier experiences as a spectator at commercial sporting events; and how hockey spectatorship was integrated into the broader consumption of urban entertainments. These issues are explored by answering three central questions: What nature of spectator was preferred or anticipated by Maple Leaf Gardens? Who attended games during the interwar years? And, what was the nature of their spectating experience and what did it mean to them?

The concept of "respectability" is central to addressing these questions. Class and gender norms were mobilized in an effort to build and operate an arena that expected and promoted respectable spectatorship, aims that were fully implicated within the desire for profit accumulation that had motivated the arena's construction in the first place.[141] Smythe attempted to gentrify the practice of spectating by invoking middle-class notions of respectability to realize greater profits from the increased seating capacity of his new arena. To reap the financial benefits of owning his own arena, he took advantage of these middle-class sensibilities by making the arena a desirable destination for the respectable consumption of entertainment. Cultural institutions of the late nineteenth and early twentieth centuries had endeavoured to produce respectable environments for the public consumption of entertainment. An "exhibitionary complex," Tony Bennett contends, frames the museum as a space where preferred notions of an ordered world could be displayed both within the artefact cases and among the spectators themselves, who would be educated in Victorian notions of respectable society, act these out, and model them for others, all in the same moment.[142] Bennett proposes that nineteenth-century museums be considered alongside other cultural institutions that also attracted the attention of middle-class reformers, such as libraries, public parks, and department stores. These reformers were interested in using public spaces to communicate and inculcate what were perceived to be respectable, Christian, middle-class values. Sport and physical activity fell well within the rubric of social reform, as movements such as muscular Christianity and institutions such as the YM/YWCA and Boy Scouts make clear. The physical spaces of sport were also put to the same reforming ends. Social reform movements reached their apogee in the late nineteenth century, yet these debates continued into the post–First World War era as theatres and movie houses, along with commercial sport spaces such as Maple Leaf Gardens, competed for consumers.

Having set the stage in this chapter by placing the development of commercial hockey alongside the emerging consumer entertainments of the 1920s and the spaces being created for these audiences, as well as considering the spectator experience at the generation of arenas that preceded the construction boom of the 1920s – in particular Arena Gardens in Toronto, which would have been the site where the city's hockey spectators "learned" to spectate – the focus shifts to the book's three themes: what nature of spectator the building was designed to anticipate, who actually attended hockey games there, and what spectator experiences were.

These are addressed in the subsequent chapters, each of which is based upon a unique evidentiary foundation. The first of these themes examines how NHL entrepreneurs – using Smythe in Toronto as the case study – designed and operated their new arenas to host a "preferred" spectator, one who responded to the different (from previous venues)

spectator experience offered by the new arena. How were design princi-
ples and operating practices intended to influence who spectators would
be and how they would act? Who was the desired audience? What were
the preferred spectator behaviours, and what role did the preferred spectator play in modelling respectability for other arena patrons? Chapter
2 examines these questions in the context of how Maple Leaf Gardens
anticipated particular spectators in its location, design, and operation.
Central to this analysis are the debates surrounding the physical location
of Maple Leaf Gardens that took place between the hockey club and
the T. Eaton Company department store, which controlled the parcel of
land that Smythe desired for his new building. The construction of the
respectable spectator is also examined by looking at the architectural
decisions that influenced the interior design of Maple Leaf Gardens and
the subsequent operations practices implemented by arena management. Chapter 2 concludes with a look back at 12 November 1931, the
opening night of Maple Leaf Gardens. The local press, not surprisingly,
paid considerable attention to the arena's inauguration. There is much
to be gleaned from these accounts. However, the pomp and circum-
stance of opening night might not have been the most representative of
occasions, or indeed have attracted the most typical of crowds.

If Smythe, his financial backers, and his architects anticipated a preferred spectator in their new arena, did the people who attended games
at Maple Leaf Gardens in the 1930s conform to these expectations?
Chapter 3 focuses on this question through an examination of the 1933–
34 Maple Leaf Gardens' subscriber ledger. This heretofore unexplored
source – a list compiled by arena staff of all of subscribers to Maple Leafs'
hockey tickets during the 1933–34 NHL season, complete with the name,
address, and seat location of account holders – offers a wealth of data on
the composition of hockey crowds at Maple Leaf Gardens that season.
The analysis in chapter 3 compares the contents of the ledger to the
1934 *Might's City of Toronto Directory* and the 1931 *Seventh Census of Canada*
to paint a fuller demographic portrait of the interwar hockey spectator.
The audience that filled the stands at the new arena – and whose ticket
purchases filled the hockey club's coffers – was overwhelmingly male.
Nevertheless, the composition of the crowd was more diverse than this
may suggest. Ticket subscribers were more likely to hold managerial jobs
than the average Torontonian. Moreover, ledger data hint at the ways in
which spectating was an opportunity for socializing and reveals the ways
in which women were active, engaged attendees.

After examining who spectators were and how they were expected
to comport themselves, it remains to enquire into the nature of their
spectating experiences. Relying on the memories of former spectators,

chapter 4 begins by recreating the experience of an evening spent spectating at Maple Leaf Gardens. Following the rhythm of a visit to the arena, it traces preparations for the game, how one arrived at the arena and whether this included visiting a local restaurant, how the arena was entered, and the sensory experience of the game. Chapter 4 also acknowledges that determining the identity of spectators is only a part of the story. Based upon interviews with twenty-one former spectators at and employees of Maple Leaf Gardens, this chapter examines how hockey spectators in Toronto in the 1930s understood the spectating experience, what it meant to them, and what they took away from it. Why, during the Depression, did they dip into their disposable incomes to purchase tickets to hockey games? What was it about the experience that spectators enjoyed? For some, it was a chance to view the new civic landmark. For many, it was an opportunity to watch in person their hockey heroes, whose exploits they read about in the papers or listened to on the radio. But for almost all, spectating was a social experience, a practice they shared with friends and family.

Chapter 5 concludes the examination of the spectator experience by acknowledging that hockey spectatorship was a meaningful cultural practice to those who watched and that the commercial nature of the game shaped the ways in which hockey was presented but not entirely the ways in which it was consumed. Coexistent with efforts to structure their experience, spectators were active agents in the making of commercial hockey within the boundaries of the entertainment as presented. On any given evening there were multiple spectator experiences occurring at Maple Leaf Gardens. Spectators engaged with the spectacle that was taking place on the ice in ways that shaped their experience. In considering the manner in which people both observed preferred behaviours and perhaps sought to subvert them, how did spectators at Maple Leaf Gardens acquire the culturally specific skills needed to be a spectator, conform to these expectations, and perhaps resist them in ways that made the spectating experience more meaningful? These questions are addressed through a consideration of the lived experience of Smythe's attempts to create a respectable spectating environment, exploring in turn the ways in which norms of respectability were promoted, relaxed, and resisted. Chapter 5 offers a theoretical consideration of the experiences of spectators – using the historical to inform the theoretical – as a means to suggest a larger framework for the inclusion of the spectator within historical accounts of twentieth-century commercial sport and the consumption of consumer entertainments more broadly.

In considering the people who attended hockey games at Maple Leaf Gardens, this book explores the composition of the sporting audience and broadens our understanding of the spectator experience. In the context of Maple Leaf Gardens in the 1930s, it is important to recognize the ways in which entrepreneurial expectations intersected with spectator practices. The analysis highlights the ways in which class distinctions and dominant gender norms were mobilized, capitalized upon, and at times subverted. Understanding who spectators were and what meanings their spectating experiences held for them inserts underappreciated actors into both the socio-cultural history of sport (and commercial entertainments more generally) and the economic history of sport during the interwar years when facilities such as Maple Leaf Gardens were built to generate the revenues necessary for commercial sport to thrive.

Chapter Two

Constructing the Preferred Spectator

Two opening-night paeans to the arena underscore the original vision of Maple Leaf Gardens. The first is from Conn Smythe, who proclaimed: "Regardless of how enticing an attraction may be, it is ever so much more pleasant to spend an evening in comfortable surroundings where the architectural design and interior decorations are in harmony with the tastes of the clientele of the arena."[1] The second, entitled "President's Address to Sports Followers of the Queen City," was written by J.P. Bickell, then president of Maple Leaf Gardens Ltd., and included in the official programme of the opening night at Maple Leaf Gardens, 12 November 1931: "The enthusiastic support of our patrons during the past few years encouraged and warranted us in providing enlarged, better-planned and more comfortable quarters. The citizens of Toronto and the country surrounding have always given generous support to clean, well-organized athletic activities, and we are confident in the hope that our management will continue to merit a patronage commensurate with our expanded effort."[2]

These two quotations, contemporary with the building's opening, get at the heart of the rhetoric surrounding the design and construction of Maple Leaf Gardens. They explicitly link the architecture and design of the building with the spectators it was presumed would occupy it as well as the notions of gentility and civility it was hoped would prevail. These links reveal fundamental assumptions surrounding hockey spectatorship in Toronto in the interwar years, which were reflected in how such spaces were designed. This chapter suggests the existence – even if never explicitly defined – of a "preferred" spectator. In such a context, what were expected spectator behaviours? How were arenas designed and operated to anticipate these?

The anticipation of a preferred hockey spectator invoked notions of respectability that were articulated around a particular intersection of

class and gender expectations. Respectability in the consumption of
hockey was tied not only to attracting a "civilized" crowd, but also to creating an environment suitable for and appealing to the presumed tastes
of a female audience. Prior to the building of Maple Leaf Gardens, and
in marshalling public support for the project, Smythe worried that "as a
place to go all dressed up, we don't compete with the comfort of theatres
and other places where people can spend their money. We need a place
where people can go in evening clothes, if they want to come there from
a party or dinner. We need at least twelve thousand seats, everything new
and clean, a place that people can be proud to take their wives or girl
friends to."[3]

In 1931, while raising funds for his new arena project, Smythe made
it clear that women were among the audiences that he hoped to target
upon the completion of Maple Leaf Gardens. A cartoon that appeared
in a prospectus Smythe prepared to help raise money for his new arena
from among members of the public contains interesting messages about
the female spectator (see Fig. 2.1). Within the cartoon, women discuss
how a more comfortable arena will make them more likely spectators,
and are pleased that the new Maple Leaf Gardens will offer a "ladies
lounge."[4] Throughout his life, including in his memoirs, Smythe reit-
erated, as noted above, that his goal in building Maple Leaf Gardens
was to create "a place that people can be proud to take their wives or
girl friends to."[5] These "people" were obviously men, reinforcing older
notions of women spectators as companions to "real" spectators, while
the idea that a place was only of sufficient comfort and social standing
when it appealed to the tastes of women harkened back to separate
spheres ideologies.[6] The fact that Smythe was considering his building
an evening "destination" placed it firmly within the constellation of restaurants, theatres, cinemas, opera houses, nickelodeons, cabarets, and
vaudeville houses that had come to compete for disposable income in
Toronto in the late 1920s. Among these choices, Maple Leaf Gardens
would be built and operated in such a way as to make it a respectable
destination for Smythe's preferred spectator.

Based upon documentary and visual evidence, including archival
collections such as the T. Eaton Company Fonds and Conn Smythe Papers at the Archives of Ontario, and the Ross & Macdonald Collection
at the Canadian Centre for Architecture, as well as contemporary press
accounts, this chapter examines the articulation and anticipation of preferred spectators at Maple Leaf Gardens. This occurred in three "spaces":
the *exterior* of the arena and its situation within 1930s Toronto; the architectural design of the *interior*; and, finally, the ways – both formal and
informal – in which Maple Leaf Gardens was *operated*. Opening night in

Fig. 2.1. "Tired of Being Stay-at-Homes, the Ladies Are Buying Shares in the New Arena": one of the cartoons that appeared in a prospectus aimed at raising public funds for the new arena project. (Maple Leaf Gardens prospectus, 1931)

November 1931 was the first evening on which Smythe's and the club's efforts were realized, and this chapter concludes with a consideration of that event. But first, to uncover the preferred spectator, we begin with an examination of Maple Leaf Gardens' exterior "space" and the building's situation within the downtown Toronto consumer economy of the 1930s.

Exterior: "A Splendid Architectural Treatment"

Any examination of the location of Maple Leaf Gardens, as well as the ways in which the arena was envisioned, needs to begin one block to the west with another major commercial Toronto landmark built in the 1930s, Eaton's College Street store. Similar to Madison Square Garden's proximity to Times Square in Manhattan, but on a much smaller scale, Maple Leaf Gardens was located near Toronto's "theatre block." Further north on Yonge Street and closer to what was to become the site of the new hockey arena, at the intersection with College Street, the streetscape would come to be dominated by the T. Eaton Company's flagship department store.

Department stores and hockey arenas can be considered within the constellation of cultural and consumer institutions that sought to influence tastes by invoking notions of respectability. Both Eaton's College Street store and Maple Leaf Gardens shared this project in interwar Toronto. On a more practical level, the land on which Maple Leaf Gardens was built was controlled by Eaton's and had to be purchased with the retailer's approval by the hockey club. An examination of Eaton's reaction to and influence over the hockey arena being built in its backyard is a lens through which to view the exterior space of Maple Leaf Gardens. As Cynthia Wright observes in her study of Eaton's College Street store in Toronto, "The spatial organization of the department store can be understood at a number of levels. One approach is to examine the relationship between the department store and the city."[7]

Eaton's opened its new College Street store, which targeted a higher-end trade than the existing Queen Street location, at the southwest corner of Yonge and College Streets, in October 1930 (see Fig. 2.2). The vision for the store included "an explicit link ... made between the modernity of the College Street building and the transformation or 'modernization' of shopping itself."[8] This reform project, directed as it was at the female "carriage trade," included "the architecture of the College Street premises [which] was planned with a view to 'the transformation of the store's image.'"[9] Moreover, while the store "was conceived primarily as a corporate landmark," notes William Dendy, "its elegances and fine materials reflected the company's concern that it be seen to be enhancing the

Fig. 2.2. Eaton's College Street store, built in 1930 to cater to a more upscale clientele, one that often arrived by automobile. (Archives of Ontario, T. Eaton Company Fonds, Item F 229-308-0-517.7)

appearance of the city."[10] A new hockey arena was envisioned one block east, at the northwest corner of Carlton and Church Streets. For Smythe's project to go ahead on this site, he and his partners needed to convince Eaton's executives that the building would alter their perceptions of the clientele that hockey arenas attracted and would not compromise Eaton's own efforts to create and attract a respectable bourgeois consumer.

From the outset, Eaton's executives were concerned both about locating a hockey arena within the neighbourhood of the College Street store generally and, more specifically, with selling the prime lot at the northwest corner of Church and Carlton Streets in which Smythe and the Maple Leafs were most interested. Eaton's attempted to negotiate – ultimately unsuccessfully – to get the team to accept an "inside" lot, first to the north on either the smaller Wood or Alexander Streets, with some frontage on Church Street, and later west on Carlton Street, with no frontage on Church Street (see Fig. 2.3).

Fig. 2.3. Street map of Maple Leaf Gardens' neighbourhood. (Prepared by
Nate Wessel)

The nature of Eaton's objections to the location of the hockey arena
and the use of the corner lot is instructive. Frank Selke, Smythe's right-
hand man in running the Maple Leafs, remembered that Eaton's executive J.J. Vaughan "hit the roof" upon learning of the hockey club's desire
to acquire frontage on Church or Carlton Streets, preferably both. Selke
believed that "Eaton's did not want a hockey arena so close to their spacious College Street store. The people who attended sports events were
hardly the type to whom Eaton's catered."[11] An internal Eaton's memo,
prepared by executive secretary James Elliott, dated 3 January 1931,
but recalling earlier board discussions about the project, summarized
the retailer's concerns: "I looked up some notes made ... at the time

Fig. 2.4. The intersection of Carlton and Church Streets, looking northwest. The construction of Maple Leaf Gardens changed the commercial makeup of the surrounding neighbourhood. (*Construction*, December 1931)

the matter was up at the Directors' Meeting, which are – that the Arena would be dead most of the day – keep it off Church St. – keep it off Carlton St. – would kill or at least interfere with property in developing a retail district but it might be alright if the Arena were inside the block leaving the frontage for retail purposes."[12]

By contrast, Smythe "felt that the Eaton name attached to his project would help dispel pro hockey's slightly unsavoury image."[13] To try and negotiate the purchase of the desired corner lot, the Maple Leafs argued that their operation would bring not only potential customers, but the right calibre of customer to the College Street vicinity. Moreover, they assured Eaton's that the architectural design of the exterior of the arena would make it the valuable addition to the commercial neighbourhood that the retailer desired (see Fig. 2.4). As J.A. Gibson, the agent acting for Eaton's in this matter, relayed back to his client:

> The intention is to have a building of handsome appearance with first class modern store fronts to produce the maximum amount of rental and give the best possible appearance.
>
> It would appear to us that such a project would bring a great many additional people to this section thus having a beneficial effect on property in this district.[14]

Eight months later, with negotiations for the corner lot stalled by the Eaton's board's objection to having this property used for a hockey arena and their insistence that the Maple Leafs take an inside lot, Gibson again detailed the arguments in favour of just such a sale to Eaton's executives. These arguments had been articulated to him by E.W. Bickle, an executive with the hockey club.[15] Bickle tried to address Eaton's concerns over pedestrian traffic during business hours by arguing that not only would crowds visit the new arena at night, but "also in the day time when school and inter-club games are played and when practices are attended by many onlookers." The facility would be the largest in the city, and therefore would draw crowds to a variety of events throughout the calendar. The nature of these events was explicitly linked to the building's design, which "can be made attractive in appearance and it will be to the interests of those erecting the building to make it attractive." Finally, Bickle argued that the arena would offer Eaton's potential advertising and publicity opportunities, and he offered to call the as yet unnamed building "Eatonia Gardens."[16] Selke attributed considerably more bravado to Bickle's stance, noting that the hockey executive told Eaton's, "You should consider yourselves lucky that the best people in Toronto would build such a fine building so close to your store! We'll bring thousands of customers who wouldn't otherwise know Eaton's have a store on College Street!"[17]

The primary architects on the arena project also sought to reassure Eaton's. Ross & Macdonald, a leading Montreal firm, had designed such landmark Toronto buildings as the Royal York Hotel, the renovated Union Station, and most importantly in this context, Eaton's College Street store.[18] The firm was well positioned to comment on the respectability of the new hockey arena. In response to a telephone call from Gibson, "requesting our opinion as to the desirability of constructing the proposed new Arena Building on the north-west corner of Church and Carlton Streets," Ross & Macdonald asserted that "the location is admirably suited for the project in mind," and that Eaton's and the Maple Leafs would also do well to consider the concurrent development of a commercial shopping district in the surrounding area:

> The site in our judgement lends itself to the development of modern stores or specialty shops, both on the Carlton and Church Street frontages of the building. These modern shops would form a base to the Arena building and offer the opportunity of a splendid architectural treatment for the entire structure.
>
> We are of the opinion that the development of attractively designed stores in conjunction with the Arena Building would develop an interesting

shopping centre in a short time, greatly assisted by the numbers of people drawn to the attractions to be offered by the Arena Company both in their programme for daytime and evening events.[19]

Gibson was clear in his recommendation that Eaton's should reconsider its opposition to selling the corner lot. Despite his support for the position taken by the Maple Leafs and Ross & Macdonald, Gibson argued against any optimism about creating a commercial district, noting that it was unlikely that "Church St. will ever be a real business street," as it was "extremely difficult to interest purchasers in land located east of Yonge Street."[20] Gibson was prophetic, as attempts to create a shopping district at Carlton and Church Streets were unsuccessful. By the post-war era, the major east-west commercial corridor was found north of this area along Bloor Street. Indeed, as early as 1920, Loew's signalled the northward shift of Toronto's public amusements by adding the three thousand-seat Uptown theatre on Yonge Street, south of Bloor Street. In the 1930s, the 1.25 km (0.8 mile) stretch of Carlton Street east from Yonge Street to Parliament Street hosted its share of what the Eaton's board might have considered to be unsavoury elements. Efforts at making the neighbourhood surrounding the new arena more respectable began during the building's construction as a crackdown on "the Legions of the Scarlet Sisterhood" sought to reduce prostitution in the vicinity of the Church and Carlton intersection.[21] Despite this, there were still rumours of "speaks" and "booze-dives" on Carlton Street in the winter of 1935.[22]

Eaton's misgivings about the location of the arena and scepticism concerning the hockey club's counterarguments about the building's potential impact on the neighbourhood led the retailer to do its homework before entering into any agreement. As Elliott indicated to C.N. Mills of the College Street store, "This is a matter which affects the College Street Store and the development of the surrounding district, particularly to the East."[23] Concerned as they were about the ability of a hockey arena to generate the human traffic that might translate into a successful commercial district, Eaton's went to the length of determining the automobile traffic that occurred on the evening of a Maple Leafs game at their current home, Arena Gardens on Mutual Street. A.E. Stuart of Eaton's architectural office reported back to Elliott that "the number of motor cars parked in the area bounded by, and including George St., Gerrard St., and Queen St., and up to but not including Yonge St., was 2,698."[24] This was no make-work project for Stuart, to which the handwritten note at the bottom of his memo attests: "[Senior Eaton's executives] Mr McGee and Mr Vaughan aware of this."

The automobile was becoming increasingly important to both transportation and commerce in Toronto, with the number of cars in the city increasing from ten thousand in 1916 to over eighty thousand by 1928.[25] Moreover, in conjunction with the opening of Eaton's new store in 1930, the city rerouted Carlton Street so that it met College Street at Yonge Street, creating a continuous east-west thoroughfare. Automobile traffic was central to the commercial streetscape that Eaton's envisioned for the College Street store. As Wright notes of the new consumption patterns of the interwar years, "access to these shops from outside the store was designed to accommodate the woman in an automobile," and Eaton's wanted to ensure that a nearby hockey arena would support and enhance these efforts. Smythe, as noted at the beginning of this chapter, was similarly – though with different motives – catering to feminine tastes.[26]

To determine both the nature of retail operations that hockey arenas had attracted in other cities and the subsequent impact upon the commercial neighbourhood, Eaton's engaged representatives in both New York and Montreal. W.G. Mills of Eaton's advertising office, while in New York, "looked over the district in and around Madison Square Garden" and provided a sketch of the arena (built in 1925) and surrounding area, including the shops contained within the building's Eighth Avenue frontage (see Fig. 2.5, top).[27] J.E. Dodds, of Eaton's Montreal store, provided a similar drawing along with his assessment of the impact of the Montreal Forum (built in 1924) on the St. Catherine Street neighbourhood west of downtown Montreal (see Fig. 2.5, bottom). His concerns reflect both middle-class assumptions about the hockey arena and its presumed fan base, while at the same time acknowledging the commercial impact on the surrounding businesses:

> Frankly speaking, we don't think the stores are particularly attractive but, notwithstanding, they do not appear to have had a detrimental effect on the district.
>
> Since the erection of the Forum – prior to 1925 – St. Catherine Street that far west has improved greatly. There are new buildings and the section seems to have become an automobile district. On streets between St. Catherine and Sherbrooke in recent years a number of very good apartment houses have been erected. We understand they are very well tenanted. We are advised that rents in the vicinity are very much higher than – and in some instances double that of – five years ago.
>
> With the opening of the Bus Service from Verdun up Atwater Avenue to St. Catherine Street, considerable traffic has been drawn to this corner. On the corner opposite to the Forum running west on St. Catherine Street is

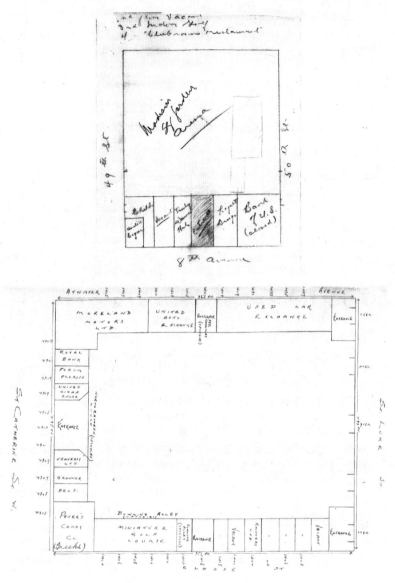

Fig. 2.5. Sketches of the commercial establishments surrounding arenas
contemporary to the proposed Maple Leaf Gardens: shops that shared the
Eighth Avenue frontage with Madison Square Garden's main entrance (top);
and sketch of the neighbourhood surrounding the Montreal Forum (bottom).
Both prepared by Eaton's staff in January 1931. (top: Archives of Ontario,
T. Eaton Company Fonds, F 229–82, File M-103; bottom: Archives of Ontario,
T. Eaton Company Fonds, F 229–82, File M-103)

vacant land which is now being built up as an automobile row. Two blocks east of the Forum on St. Catherine Street a moving picture house has been erected.

In view of the activities the above section of the City is steadily appreciating.[28]

Eaton's initial reticence about selling the prime parcel of land at the Church-Carlton intersection to the Maple Leafs is revealing. Attempts by Eaton's to get the hockey club to accept an "inside" lot might well have been a negotiating tactic in the hopes of driving up the price for the land that the team truly wanted. However, this seems unlikely. The economic depression and falling real estate prices had already made the Eaton's board unsure of what they could recoup for this land, and their agent suggested that they were getting fair market value from the Maple Leafs. Indeed, he argued that "the erection of the Arena building will increase the value of the land purchased by them and it will also increase the value of the remaining Carlton Street frontage held by International Realty Company Limited," the corporation that legally owned the land and whose shares were owned by the estate of Sir John Eaton (late son of the department store's founder and the company's president from 1907 to 1922) and managed by the Eaton's board.[29]

It appears that Eaton's was concerned more about the use to which the land would be put rather than the sales price they would receive. Their board members wanted the land to be used in a way that complemented their intention to make the College Street store an "arbiter of distinctness and correctness."[30] The department store was not afraid of commercial competition, having tried unsuccessfully to induce their most prominent competitor in the Toronto market, Simpson's (which was located directly across the street from Eaton's main Toronto store on Queen Street), to join in the move north to College Street.[31] The concern was not competing shops, but the right kind of shops, as Elliott worried "that there would not be any stores of any importance on any property the Arena people may purchase but rather a lot of small shops."[32]

Even after an agreement had been reached to sell the northwest corner lot to the Maple Leafs, Eaton's approval was so important that the lead architect on the Gardens shared the working drawings and specifications for the new arena with the department store so that "the T. Eaton Company should have the privilege of reviewing the plans and specifications so that we might endeavour to make any modifications that they might suggest."[33] However, the modifications that interested Eaton's on a philosophical and financial level, the idea of reaping the

Fig. 2.6. In addition to Eaton's College Street store and the Toronto Hydro building, Maple Leaf Gardens, pictured on 14 March 1939, dominated the skyline of the surrounding neighbourhood. (City of Toronto Archives, Globe and Mail fonds, Fonds 1266, Item 57300)

profits of respectable middle-class consumption, interested the Maple Leafs as well. These concerns were reflected in the exterior of the new arena, which would come to dominate the Toronto landscape (see Fig. 2.6), as well as in its interior design.

Interior: From Box Seats to Benches

While Eaton's vice-president, Harry McGee – who was chosen to represent Eaton's on Maple Leaf Gardens' executive committee ten months before the building's opening – was reviewing Ross & Macdonald's designs for Toronto's new arena he would have learned of the architects' vision for what was to become the city's largest indoor gathering place.[34] Early architectural drawings of the building indicate that the arena had been thought of in part as an amusement palace, including as they did a bowling alley and billiards room on the first floor of the Wood Street (north) side of the building.[35] In one photograph from the 1930s,

Toronto mayor Sam McBride bowls the ceremonial first ball to get a tournament underway at the Maple Leaf Gardens' alley.[36] Amusements such as these, however, were likely inconsistent with Eaton's perception of the respectable nature of its carriage trade, and the Gardens was emblematic of a shift in arena design and operation from participation to spectating. Eventually pastimes such as bowling and billiards gave way to consumer spectacles, with the emphasis firmly placed on facilitating the movement of people through the building to their seats within the arena.

While Maple Leaf Gardens' design, on the exterior and interior, marked it as a building different both in kind and degree from anything that had previously dotted Toronto's sporting landscape, it was still a building that catered to masculine tastes. Wright has argued that the interior of Eaton's College Street store was designed as a "feminine" space, where "the very spatial organization of the store's interior was 'feminized'" (see Fig. 2.7).[37] There were men's departments, but these were invariably found on the ground floor, assuming that men who felt the necessity to shop would prefer to conduct their business as quickly as possible and would be unlikely to be interested in browsing through the store's upper floors in the way that it was presumed women would want to do. By this measure, Toronto's new hockey arena was a predominantly masculine space, despite Smythe's claims of appealing to feminine notions of respectability. Indeed, architecture historian Sherry McKay asserts that physical activity spaces, both private and public, historically have been designed to anticipate the male body.[38] "Sports landscapes can, therefore," Patricia Vertinsky also argues, "be appropriately read as masculine landscapes."[39]

The arena was also very much an architectural artefact of the interwar years. It was built in a period when architectural styles that displayed the "flamboyance and ostentation of the early twentieth century were replaced by post–First World War sobriety." Buildings that one history of architecture calls "modern classicism" were "purposely frugal in character" and represented "a serviceable style for public buildings of all kinds."[40] Some architectural historians have chosen to celebrate Maple Leaf Gardens' design for using "the language of a[n Art] Deco skyscraper deftly translated to a colossal box with set-back angular façade and Art Moderne decorative touches."[41] Still others have praised the "sleek, horizontally oriented style [that] symbolized progress and the promise of a better future."[42] However, critics have tempered these assessments by noting that the arena was "a distinctive building both staidly traditional and cautiously *moderne*" whose design was "characterized by 'coarseness of materials,' 'utter functionalism' in its interior arrangements and 'superficiality' of exterior ornament."[43]

Fig. 2.7. The interior of Eaton's College Street store, a space intended to cater to stereotypically feminine tastes. (Archives of Ontario, T. Eaton Company Fonds, Item F 229-308-0-520-2)

Architectural drawings indicate that entrances were planned on three sides of the building, two on Wood Street (at the building's northeast and northwest corners), two on Church Street (northeast and southeast corners), and the main entrance, three sets of double doors at the centre of the building's south face on Carlton Street.[44] The latter led into the main lobby, which did not take up a considerable amount of the building's footprint. It housed box offices on either side of the main entrance, past which were turnstiles at the southeast and southwest corners of the building.

Despite a 1931 account that praised the "spacious lobby," former spectators recall that not only the lobby but the entire interior of the building was more functional than grand (see Fig. 2.8).[45] One popular historian notes that "its finest attribute was its outer appearance. Inside it was plain and unglamorous."[46] Another commentator asserted, at the time of the arena's closing while the building was being celebrated for its place in public memory, that its origins in the Depression ensured that

Fig. 2.8. The lobby of Maple Leaf Gardens was a functional and utilitarian space rather than a grand entrance to the new building. (*Construction*, December 1931)

"the building was never quite the architectural accomplishment Smythe had originally intended it would be." (Neither was Eaton's College Street venture, it should be noted, with a planned thirty-eight-storey tower never built on top of the department store.) In fact, Maple Leaf Gardens suffered from "a utilitarian plainness" as "windows had been reduced in number and size, and cinder blocks had been used to line lobbies and entranceways which, in another decade, might well have been faced with polished marble or tile."[47]

From the lobby, patrons made their way into the arena itself whose "initial impressions ... are those of size, scale and colour."[48] The focus of the building's planners on the central arena space – an emphasis on the most masculine of spaces – is indicated by the architectural drawing, "Interior Study," which includes a hockey player drawn on a fictive arena floor with a consideration of sight lines from a variety of seat locations (see Fig. 2.9).[49] Additional drawings – such as "Details of Boxing Ring" and "Boxing Ring Elec. Fixture" – are evidence that other sporting events were also considered during the planning of Maple Leaf Gardens.[50]

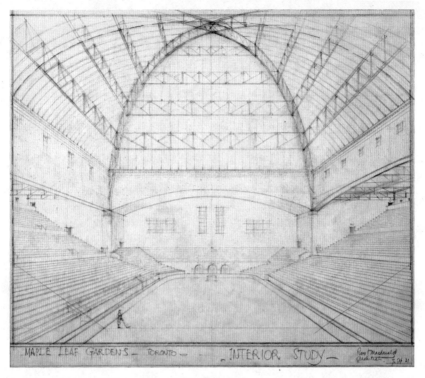

Fig. 2.9. Unlike Madison Square Garden, for example, Maple Leaf Gardens was designed with sight lines for the hockey spectator in mind, as this "Interior Study" from 1931 highlights. (Ross & Macdonald fonds, Collection Centre Canadien d'Architecture / Canadian Centre for Architecture, Montreal)

While there was social space within the building where people could linger and, in the 1930s, smoke, the primary focus of the arena's interior design was to move people through the building to their seats. On the occasion of Maple Leaf Gardens' opening, Lou Marsh of the *Star* remarked on the "gray and blue lines on the wall" that led spectators to the sections whose seats were the same colours. "Just like Times Square subway, isn't it?"[51]

Spectators with rail or box seats entered the arena through a series of ground-floor passageways, otherwise staircases along the east and west corridors as well as in each of the building's four corners delivered people to the level of the arena on which their seats were located. Passageways led into the arena, where spectators would descend another flight of stairs to reach their assigned seats. Maple Leaf Gardens was clearly a space marked out for able-bodied people.[52] (Escalators were not installed in the building until October 1955.) Indeed, while reviewing the plans for the new arena, Eaton's executive J.J. Vaughan recommended reducing the number of stairways in favour of ramps, though this was likely more for aesthetic than inclusive reasons.[53]

There are other markers that indicate this space was intended, primarily, for men. On the most mundane but necessary level, the arena was designed with considerably more washrooms for men than women. As Table 2.1 indicates, 87.3 per cent of the available washroom spaces were found in the men's toilets, and this ratio was consistent on every level of the building. Male patrons in the arena's most expensive seats were well treated when heeding nature's call, using porcelain toilets rather than the stainless-steel troughs found on the upper floors, which acquired almost mythological status in the memories of many former spectators.[54] There were, however, attempts to cater to women's comfort. Every women's toilet, though offering limited "seating," included (as was the custom) an anteroom. Moreover, if, as Wright suggests, feminine spaces are marked in part by allowing for leisurely strolling (browsing, in the department store context), each level within Maple Leaf Gardens did include "lounge space." These were spaces where people could congregate between periods of the game to socialize and smoke, a practice which was prohibited by Smythe within the arena itself. And these spaces, at least on the building's opening night, were occupied by women. As the *Telegram's* women's sports columnist Phyllis Griffiths noted, "The wide promenades at the Maple Leaf Gardens gave the women a chance to enjoy a walk and a cigarette between periods, although many preferred to do their puffing in privacy in the rooms provided on each floor."[55]

Griffiths's observation of smokers highlights shifts that were occurring in the ways in which public space in Toronto was gendered. Female spectators who chose to enjoy "a walk and a cigarette" during intermissions at Maple Leaf Gardens reflected the changing perceptions of public smoking. Whereas at the turn of the twentieth century "respectable smoking was only possible for men," Jarrett Rudy notes that, "by the twenties and thirties, the idea that women might smoke was more acceptable yet still contentious."[56] Despite this, especially in a socially conservative city such as Toronto, Donald Davis and Barbara Lorenzkowski argue that until "the 1940s smoking was still considered a gendered habit."[57] This may account for those female hockey spectators who "preferred to do their puffing in privacy." While smoking "gave odour and visible shape to spaces socially constructed as male," as noted of Toronto's streetcar patrons, Rudy argues that deference and self control were equally important male smoking behaviours.[58] "Not smoking while with a woman in public," he

Table 2.1. Washrooms at Maple Leaf Gardens

Seating section	Seats	Total seats	Men's urinals	Men's stalls	Men's total	Women's stalls
Boxes	784	–	–	–	–	–
Rails	237	1,021	9	2	11 (73.3%)	4 (26.7%)
First tier	3,784	–	–	–	–	–
Ends	1,554	5,338	88	8	96 (88.9%)	12 (11.1%)
Second tier	–	3,076	48	8	52 (89.7%)	6 (10.3%)
Third tier	–	3,031	40	4	44 (84.6%)	8 (15.4%)
Total	–	12,466	185	22	207 (87.3%)	30 (12.7%)

Source: "Maple Leaf Gardens – Arena," RG 7–137, rolls, L133–1140, Factory Inspection Branch blueprints and drawings, Archives of Ontario, Toronto, Ontario.

contends, "was nothing less than a performance of masculine respecta-bility."[59] The operating practices of Maple Leaf Gardens – discussed in greater detail below – which prohibited smoking in the arena's main seating areas, required this performance of respectability of all the build-ing's male customers. Nevertheless, the ban on smoking in the arena did not prohibit the Maple Leafs from reaping the financial benefits of this cultural practice. By the late 1930s, the score clock at Maple Leaf Gar-dens promoted Sweet Caporal Cigarettes and the arena programme was paid for, in part, by prominent advertisements from Sweet Caporal (back cover), and British Consols Cigarettes (scorecard insert).[60]

Maple Leaf Gardens' design not only marked out gendered space, it also mapped out the social hierarchies of Toronto's entertain-ment consumers. While one contemporary observer noted of the arena's seats that "contrasting colour marks each of the sections, *all* of which are equipped with folding seats of the opera type," in ac-tual fact, the nature of the seating changed dramatically the further one moved up from the floor of the arena.[61] The box and rail seats were opera seating with red leather padded chairs, each with their own arms (see Fig. 2.10).[62] Box seats were also 19" or 20" wide, while individual seats in the rest of the arena were predominantly 18"-wide wooden seats, with hinged bases that raised as patrons stood up to let others pass by on the way to their seats.[63] The uppermost (grey) section only offered spectators long wooden benches (see Fig. 2.11), with neither cushioning nor separated seats. (The nature of Maple Leaf Gardens seating is discussed in greater detail in chapter 3.)

There were not just material distinctions between the arena's individ-ual sections. The building's design precluded spectators from moving between the tiers of seats. Box and rail seat customers entered on the ground level, while ticket holders in each of the upper three tiers or

Fig. 2.10. A view of the box and rail seats in one corner of Maple Leaf Gardens.
The home team lost 5–1, which may explain some of the empty rail seats
(Maple Leafs versus New York Rangers, 9 February 1937). (City of Toronto
Archives, Globe and Mail fonds, Fonds 1266, Item 43154)

in the end seats had to ascend staircases. These took them to the top
of their section, where they descended to their seats. The location of
standing room areas at the back of each tier, with a substantial rise to the
front row of the above section, meant that there was no easy way to move
between sections.

The interior of Maple Leaf Gardens was considerably grander than its
forerunner, Arena Gardens, and the *Telegram* contended that the new
arena boasted "the last word in setting and appointment."[64] Despite the
assessment that a space designed primarily to move patrons towards their
seats was masculine space, the new arena's "appointments" did invoke
notions of feminine respectability in pursuit of the preferred spectator.
Selke asserted that, upon the opening of the arena, "women, who previously hated to dress for the stodgy old arenas of yesteryear, were glad to
wear their best to see the Maple Leafs in their new arena." In turn, "as the
apparel of the lady fans stepped up in quality, that of the men followed
suit. Hockey crowds now had real class."[65] This increasingly respectable

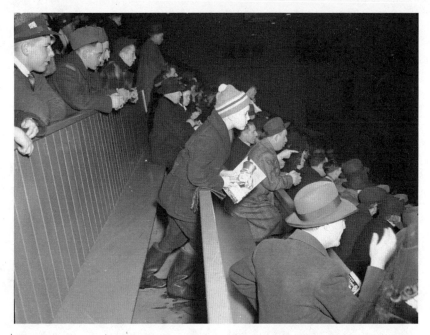

Fig. 2.11. The long benches that distinguished the third-tier grey seats at Maple Leaf Gardens. (City of Toronto Archives, Fonds 1257, Series 1057, Item 7509)

audience was attracted in part by the design of Maple Leaf Gardens, but also by the nature of the experience that they were promised. The "apparel," what it was hoped if not expected that spectators would wear while attending hockey games at the new arena, suggested that Maple Leaf Gardens would be operated differently than earlier venues. This space was to be home to the respectable middle-class spectator, whose spectating experience and behaviours were ultimately influenced by how the arena was operated, both formally and informally.

Operations: "Enforce a Proper Sporting Spirit"

The preferred spectator was produced not only by the design of Maple Leaf Gardens, but also through the ways in which the arena was operated. While no detailed operating plans survive, if they ever existed, there are ways in which this theme can be explored. Media accounts not only reported on fans and spectators, but also offered commentary on what was appropriate and what, in the minds of columnists, went beyond the bounds. An examination of these and other contemporary accounts reveals that Maple Leaf Gardens was operated during the 1930s in such a way as to produce a spectator who inhabited an ideal intersection of class, gender, and (to a less overt extent) racial expectations. At this nexus existed the preferred spectator, one who was both respectable and respectful. They were valuable not only in maintaining respectability but in modelling the correct behaviours for others.

Respectability and behavioural expectations were intertwined with spectators' attendance at hockey games. Praise was bestowed on spectators who supported the home side through rapt attention and "respectable" cheering. The *Globe* noted in 1936 that "support from the crowd ... [was] given ... in a manner that showed what Toronto fans ... think of their team in the final analysis."[66] In advance of praise, however, came education. Local readers learned of spectators elsewhere, acquiring guidance on how to behave by way of comparison. Ed Allan, sports editor of the *Mail and Empire*, asserted that he had "never heard a more rabid or partisan crowd than the Boston fans, but many would not be allowed into Maple Leaf Gardens owing to their language." Indeed, "Boston used to boast of having the most fair crowd that ever attended any sport ... but that was before the coming of the alleged bootleggers, and then the tenor of the crowd is said to have changed completely."[67] To rise above such behaviours, which were clearly inflected by civic and club rivalries, J.P. Bickell outlined the manner in which Toronto's spectators could best demonstrate their support for the Maple Leafs: "To the patrons may I suggest that they match the players' skill and energy with their cheers, so that when the game starts, dull care departs, and entertainment such as no other game provides, will be our lot."[68]

The well-behaved crowd who supplied Bickell's "cheers" attended hockey games within an environment where the expectations of behaviour, if not posted at the entrances, were at least understood to be significantly different from the experiences of earlier commercial sports crowds. One way that the expectation of public behaviour associated with middle-class respectability could be maintained was by charging appropriate entrance fees. In the first season at Maple Leaf Gardens, 1931–32, ticket prices ranged from $1.00 to $3.00, with the colour of tickets corresponding to the colour of the seat sections within the arena.[69] Prices were raised the following year, to a maximum of $3.30, before being decreased part way through the season. For the rest of the 1930s, the top ticket price was $2.50. On one hand, the cost of tickets made it challenging to attend hockey games during the Depression, especially in the seats closest to the action. High prices for the best seats ensured that the latter would be filled with preferred customers. But Smythe and the Maple Leafs were still in the business of selling tickets, at a variety of price points. So, on the other hand, multiple ticket prices worked to establish expectations yet not preclude working people from attending, usually in the upper reaches of the arena. (More on who attended Maple Leafs games in chapter 3.)

Ticket selling practices served to further distinguish spectator groups from one another. Patrons looking to buy seats for an evening's game or to pick up their subscribed tickets used the two box offices located inside Maple Leaf Gardens' main lobby off Carlton Street. General admission tickets to the standing-room-only sections, however, were primarily sold "at the north entrance on Church and Wood Sts." with the line-up of admission seekers obscured from the main entrance on the south side of the building.[70]

Smythe, in both the design and operation of Maple Leafs Gardens, wanted to create an environment that rivalled the finest nights out in Toronto, where people could attend hockey games in their evening wear. Smythe's contribution to this goal, after Maple Leaf Gardens opened, was to ensure that the arena was kept immaculately well maintained – as well as to ensure that the public perception of his staff's attention to cleanliness represented a break with earlier arena management practices. Selke recalled that "the over-all cleanliness and swank of the new building ushered in a new era for long-suffering hockey patrons."[71] Regardless of whether Toronto's hockey spectators had indeed been "suffering" before 1931, former Maple Leaf Gardens employees recall the considerable number of hours they worked to clean the arena before and after games.

This asserted new spectating environment, whether it accurately reflected who actually attended games at the Gardens and how they dressed and behaved, became wrapped up with expectations of how the entire crowd should act and behave. Such performances of public respectability were sustained through a dress code that was enforced even if it was not posted at the entrance, although it is instructive to consider to whom such expectations did and did not apply. The requirement to "dress" for hockey games in Toronto is most often attributed to Smythe – and his enterprise may have been responsible for creating a more respectable venue within which this could occur – but this behaviour was ultimately tied to larger social forces.[72] As Paul O'Leary notes: "The way an individual dressed in public was a crucial symbolic marker of his or her position in society."[73] For working-class men, Gareth Stedman Jones argues, respectability "meant the possession of a presentable Sunday suit, and the ability to be seen wearing it."[74] Similar societal expectations held true for women, whose "dress, cleanliness, and more general corporal reserve,"

Kate Boyer observes, "were important elements in the constitution of respectability, even across class lines."[75]

Expectations of public appearance may have differed among spectators who purchased tickets within differently priced sections at the Gardens, but many – if not most – spectators followed their own sense of propriety regarding dress. Nevertheless, one former spectator felt that Maple Leaf Gardens "had to be a place where the women were happy to wear their mink stoles and their furs and where the men would have Sammy Taft's hats on."[76] This certainty about the nature of the spectating environment was shared by other patrons, as "people occasionally did sit in the reds with, we'll say, a windbreaker on, but they didn't do it twice." The knowledge of how one dressed to attend a game at Maple Leaf Gardens was learned from those who occupied the space with you: "It would just be peer pressure rather than some officious attendant coming to them and saying, 'I'm sorry you're not allowed here dressed like that.'"

While male spectators who sat in the arena's less costly seats rarely recall dressing in more than a windbreaker and slacks to attend a game, two long-time Maple Leaf Gardens' staff recounted in 1981 that "Smythe could insist that male customers in the box seats wear ties, holding a threat of cancelled season tickets over their heads."[77] Indeed it was in Maple Leaf Gardens' more expensive box and rail seats, where patrons were as much on view to the spectators seated in the sections above them as the game itself, that the Maple Leafs went to the greatest lengths to ensure that ticket holders donned the garments of middle-class respectability. Harold Ballard, the eventual Maple Leafs owner who attended the first game at Maple Leaf Gardens in 1931, noted, "I can recall when ushers would walk around and make a note of a box in which the customers weren't properly dressed. The box owner received a warning letter that the next time, he or his guest wouldn't be allowed into the Gardens without proper attire. You really had to be careful when giving your tickets away. At any rate, you had to make sure that person was properly dressed, or you risked losing your tickets."[78]

Such disciplinary practices – whether overt or the result of "peer pressure" – were used to establish a respectable environment for hockey spectating. If Smythe's motivation was to create an atmosphere in which women would be comfortable, the popular record has credited him with success. However, it was not only Maple Leaf Gardens, but all the new arenas of the interwar years that "provided the spectator with a much more comfortable viewing experience, making spectator sports appealing to affluent new audiences, women, and children."[79]

At the time of the building's opening, *Star* columnist Lou Marsh remarked, tongue in cheek, on "the fiendish rumor that things are so high hat around the new Gardens that the peanut men only be allowed to sell salted almonds!"[80] One source of "fiendish rumours" in 1930s Toronto was the scandal-seeking tabloid *Hush*. One of its gossip columnists was quick to reassure its readers who might have had "the idea that tuxedos will be do rigor [*sic*] or whatever the fashion magazines call it," that, in their opinion, formal attire was not required at the opening of Maple Leaf Gardens. Rather, the Maple Leafs were more interested in a large crowd: "All they want is the gang to turn out in large numbers, roll neck sweaters, coon coats, or any old benny and root what promises to be the smartest team Toronto ever had."[81]

Nevertheless, during the new arena's first three seasons, *Hush* waged a campaign against what it felt were the unreasonably high admission prices being charged by the Maple Leafs. In the autumn of 1932, *Hush* began questioning why, during hard economic times and in the face of dwindling attendance, the management at Maple Leaf Gardens refused to reduce ticket prices. It noted sarcastically that "hockey [radio] broadcasts are more popular than ever, as witness the great open spaces in the $3.00 seats."[82] Moreover, "55 cents for S.R.O. tickets at the pro games [is] ... Nothing but a hold-up."[83] The tabloid remained suspicious that the motives behind this practice were purely financial, as this would surely backfire: "Everyone and Sunday seems to have a knock to throw at the Maple Leaf Gardens management ... [and] the prices being asked for pro hockey. No doubt the men at the helm have their own ideas on the subject, but if by this brainstorm they hope to make a little extra dough to pay a dividend, the lack of full houses may act as a boomerang."[84]

Ticket prices and attire created spaces associated with very specific class expectations. The distribution of men's and women's washrooms gendered the hockey arena masculine. Racial and ethnic identities, however, were not so clearly delineated. While less explicitly articulated than class and gender expectations, Maple Leaf Gardens was also a racialized space, one that was both colonized and colonizing.[85] At the time of the building's inauguration, 81 per cent of Toronto's population were of British ancestry and two-thirds of non-native Torontonians hailed from the United Kingdom.[86] In part because of Smythe's well-publicized support of Canada's place in the British Empire – evidenced by his service in the Canadian forces in both the First and Second World Wars, with the latter beginning at age forty-five – the new arena fit within the cultural landscape of Protestant, British Toronto in the 1930s.[87] From the opening of Maple Leaf Gardens, the imperial project went unchallenged. If, as Vertinsky suggests, the inclusions and exclusions which revealed the power relations inherent in physical spaces marked sporting sites as masculine places, these same processes also operated at Maple Leaf Gardens to exclude – or at least render less visible – non-British bodies. The 48th Highlanders regiment playing "God Save the King" and the Union Jack hung prominently at one end of the arena reminded spectators of Toronto's British majority and the nation's ties to the Empire. (The tradition of the 48th Highlanders playing at the Maple Leafs' first home game of each NHL season continues to this day.)

Nevertheless, the proportion of Toronto's residents of non-British origins during the 1920s grew from 5 per cent to 19 per cent of the city's population. Jews and Italians were the city's largest non-British immigrant groups, and were subjected to both overt and hidden forms of racism. That these acts of racism could be connected to sport in Toronto was brought home in August 1933 when anti-Semitic riots broke out at a baseball game at Christie Pits Park.[88] Physical separation in ethnic neighbourhoods and racist stereotypes combined to render non-British minorities invisible within public spaces such as Maple Leaf Gardens. Conventions like the playing of "God Save the King" were common at other public spaces, such as movie houses, so that audiences were to some degree inured to these practices. Nevertheless, the Gardens was a space that marginalized non-British Torontonians. Indeed, *Hush* questioned why "Maple Leaf Gardens' ... officials are discriminating against the employment of Jews in the face of the fact that a great portion of their support comes from this sport-loving race."[89]

The criticism by *Hush* of Maple Leaf Gardens' hiring practices highlights another important element in the arena's operation: the staff. Ushers, concessionaries, and others should not be ignored for the role they played in constructing the preferred spectator. The staff set the tone – from demeanour to dress – and enforced the behaviours that projected and preserved Smythe's respectable environment. The Maple Leafs' manager felt that arena staff were, in part, responsible for keeping spectators from interfering with players, coaches, and officials. Smythe was involved in an altercation with a spectator following a December 1933 game in Boston. Despite his well-known tempestuous personality, he placed the blame for this incident squarely at the feet of the management of Boston Garden, who should have seen to it that "the runway between the rink and the players' dressing room is heavily policed to prevent fans from starting a disturbance."[90] Smythe and the Toronto press, by contrast, were much more complimentary towards the security at Madison Square Garden after a December 1931 game, during which a spectator confronted Red Horner of the Maple Leafs, when the Garden's staff ensured that "the fan who started the attack on Horner was noticeable by his absence during the remainder of the game."[91]

Fig. 2.12. Maple Leaf Gardens' staff, including the usher pictured here on 26 March 1947, policed spectator behaviours and modelled respectability. (Archives of Ontario, Fonds 4485, Item 26)

But staff served an instrumental role that went beyond security (see Fig. 2.12). Susan Porter Benson argues that, in the operation of department stores, "managers sought to acclimate the clerks sufficiently to the more luxurious aspects of a bourgeois way of life so that they could more effectively sell them."[92] Arena staff, too, modelled respectability through their attire and deportment while also enforcing it. As spectators passed through the turnstiles in the lobby, they presented their tickets to uniformed ticket takers. Visitors to arena concession stands were greeted by staff in aprons and caps. Regardless of where they worked, Gardens' staff strove to project an image of public respectability. On the occasion of the building's inauguration, the *Telegram*'s women's sports columnist, Phyllis Griffiths, praised the "girl ushers" who "looked neat and natty in blue and white uniform caps and blue capes ornamented with a white maple leaf and lined with flaming red."[93]

The division of labour among staff reflected traditional gender roles. Male and female ushers worked in differently priced sections. Women provided the comfort and respectability that Smythe sought in the more expensive box and rail seats, while the ushers in the least expensive seats were all male – and, it was thought, better able to deal with the potentially rowdier elements who would find their way up into the less expensive seats. Given women's stereotypical domestic roles, they too were most often used to staff the arena's concession stands. By contrast, male vendors moved throughout the tiers of the arena, and former employees recall that there were no female ticket takers.

The operation of Maple Leaf Gardens was also intertwined with the values of respectable, middle-class, Depression-era Toronto more generally. At times these values were revealed by the ways in which the arena's operation was critiqued. With jobs increasingly scarce, employed women were among the early victims of the Depression, forced to give way both to men who needed jobs and to normalized assumptions about gender.[94] The day of Maple Leaf Gardens' opening, the *Star*'s women's sports columnist, Alexandrine Gibb, received a letter from a male reader who was concerned "about the employment of girls for the duties of ushers at the Maple Leaf Gardens" at the expense of unemployed men, who it was presumed were more in need of employment and would be more competent ushers. In response, Gibb argued that

> men should realize that the girls have to earn a living for themselves as well as the men. And also remember that it is far more difficult for girls to get help when out of work than it is for the men. You do not hear anything about the desperate need of the girls who are out of work, who are living in one room wondering where the money is coming for the next week's room rent.
>
> So let's be fair about it. Give the girls a chance to earn a living.[95]

This interchange recalls the debate between historians Alice Kessler-Harris and Margaret Hobbs on the role that gender ideologies played in societal expectations such as these.[96] Gibb's reply to her reader demonstrates the sense of justice that Kessler-Harris argues pervaded attitudes towards waged labour during the Depression, as the earnings of both men and women often went to support other family members. Hobbs, however, notes that while arguments about economic injustice were put forth by both women and men, they should not be interpreted as "sweeping gender to the sidelines."[97] Gibb's correspondent, while highlighting what he perceived to be an inequity in Maple Leaf Gardens' hiring practices, "betrayed other fears of a non-material nature: fears about the social relations between men and women, fears about gender identity itself."[98] Gender identities, Hobbs and others argue, are relational. The presence of usherettes, unfair in some eyes, reinforced gender norms. Maple Leaf Gardens' operators invoked notions of femininity to transform hockey spectating into a respectable middle-class pursuit, but they did so in a way that affirmed rather than threatened traditional gender roles.

On two occasions, *Hush* sought to scandalize the management of Maple Leaf Gardens by accusing them of employing an usher and a ticket seller who were already employed elsewhere, as it was also considered inappropriate during the Depression to hire men who were already holding down other jobs.[99] Within the walls of the Gardens, as well, there were social norms that spectators believed needed to be reinforced. Recall the response to the newspaper account of the 1937 incident when Lionel Conacher hit a Gardens' rinkside spectator over the head with his stick where an earnest John McGinnis, a local office manager and Conacher's victim, wrote the *Globe and Mail* to remind the sports editor that such incidents should be taken more seriously. "All I can say," Mr. McGinnis wrote, "is that as an example to the juniors every effort should be made to enforce a proper sporting spirit, instead of rank cowardice."[100]

This rejoinder highlights the ways in which local newspapers and the radio contributed to the construction of the preferred hockey spectator. As Sandra Weathers Smith observes in her study of New York theatre audiences in the late nineteenth and early twentieth centuries, newspapers were instrumental in acclimating spectators to the norms of theatre performances. Reviews established the differences between quality and poor theatre for their readers. But, more than this, press reports helped audiences to map out the ways in which they were expected to consume theatre. As Weathers Smith notes: "City newspapers helped transform readers as consumers of news into a public of spectators active in the consumption of theatre."[101]

Similar processes were at work within North America's new commercial sport venues of the 1920s and early 1930s. In encouraging spectators to behave and support the Maple Leafs in particularly respectable ways the media were complicit in the construction of the Gardens' preferred spectator. The press not only encouraged citizens to patronize Maple Leaf Gardens, but sportswriters also participated in marking out the boundaries of respectable spectatorship. Their descriptions of the Gardens and the events that took place there painted a portrait of the new arena for Torontonians and established what potential spectators could expect to see and experience upon entering the building.

The hockey team offered the media ample assistance in promoting events at Maple Leaf Gardens. Stories of Smythe's influence over the local media – going so far as to threaten to pull advertising from the *Star* if the newspaper did not begin running stories more favourable to the team – are part of his popular mythology.[102] In two January 1944 letters to Smythe, who was serving in the 30th Battery, Canadian Army Overseas at the time, Selke recalled the ways in which Smythe in the 1930s had manipulated the media to generate fan interest in upcoming games at Maple Leaf Gardens.[103] Smythe's influence over the tenor of sports coverage in Toronto was well enough known that *Hush* could be moved to sarcastically remark, "Columnists' jobs are always considered easy but, brother, you have another think coming. We are wondering what Eddie Allen at the Mail and Empire will have to write about when the hockey season is finally finished. So far six of his eight paragraphs have been the Maple Leaf Gardens, Connie Smythe and the Maple Leafs … 'Ed' covered it all, with the exception of the usher's conversation."[104]

The pervasiveness of well-known Canadian radio pioneer Foster Hewitt's weekly national hockey broadcasts from Maple Leaf Gardens also allowed the medium of radio to influence spectator attitudes and behaviours. On Saturday nights in Toronto in the 1930s it was difficult to avoid Hewitt's weekly hockey broadcasts, sponsored initially by General Motors and then, as of 1934, by Imperial Oil. One history of the period noted that some listeners claimed "that they found games more interesting on radio than at the [Montreal] Forum or Maple Leaf Gardens." Indeed, "surveys suggested that almost three million Canadians listened to a Saturday night game."[105] Hewitt, in turn, noted that a "1937 survey indicated that over six million fans heard one Toronto-Detroit hockey game" on radio.[106] This became, briefly, another injustice for *Hush*: "Last Saturday, [local radio stations] CFCA, CKCL and CFRB, were all on a hook-up from the Maple Leaf Gardens, when one station carrying that feature would have been ample."[107]

Hewitt's broadcast position became a point of reference for people new to Maple Leaf Gardens. The "gondola," as it was famously known, was located in the arena's highest reaches, ostensibly to give Hewitt a view of the entire ice surface, although the broadcaster himself acknowledged that "the intention [was] to work close to ice level, but that would have involved blocking the view of many spectators and also occupying space that could provide much-desired revenue."[108] Nevertheless, his location in the rafters and its catwalk approach became iconic features of Maple Leaf Gardens. At the arena's first game, Lou Marsh of the *Star* wondered: "What's that big square thing up in the centre … Is that where Foster Hewitt broadcasts? … How'll he be able to tell the players from up there?"[109]

Gathering around the radio on Saturday nights and listening to hockey games was a feature of the social lives of many Canadians and Newfoundlanders in the interwar years. Peggy Moxton recounted that, while her parents were attending games at Maple Leaf Gardens, "We kids were at home listening to Foster Hewitt call the game on the radio and drinking Wilson's orange or ginger ale."[110] Similarly, Tom Gaston remembered the ways in which listening to broadcasts from Maple Leaf Gardens fit into the patterns of his family's life in 1930s Toronto: "We'd listened to Foster Hewitt on the radio every Saturday night for as long as I can remember ... I'd make fudge and my Mom would pop some corn, and the whole family would gather around our old Atwater-Kent radio. The broadcasts came on at the end of the first period, and we'd sit glued to the action."[111]

On the day following the first game at the Gardens in 1931, "Everyone from the patients at Christie Street Hospital to the kids in Cabbagetown talked about the broadcast."[112] More than seven years later, the Edmonton Grads women's basketball team attended a hockey game in person in Toronto. "None of the members [of the Grads] had ever eyed a National League pro game," wrote *Globe and Mail* women's sport columnist Bobbie Rosenfeld, "although [they were] well acquainted with the players through the voice of Foster Hewitt, whose broadcasts they never miss."[113] Even accounting for the popularity of Hewitt's national radio broadcasts, the famed announcer was unprepared for the effect his play-by-play accounts would have on spectating *within* the arena. "I was rather startled by the increasing number of spectators who took their radios with them right into the Maple Leaf Gardens," he recalls. "One night ushers counted no fewer than eighty-nine persons carrying their receiving sets."[114]

The radio played an important role, for those people accustomed to listening to rather than watching Maple Leafs games, in helping to orient them to the new arena. Hewitt's play-by-play would often mimic the reaction of spectators to the game unfolding on the ice below. His voice carried the excited atmosphere of being there in person across the airwaves and popularized his signature catchphrase upon a goal being scored, "he shoots, he scores." For many Canadians during the Depression, Hewitt's broadcasts extended the boundaries of Maple Leaf Gardens to include them. As one woman recounted to historian Barry Broadfoot: "Alone I was, my husband cutting wood in the bush and me with three kiddies on that farm miles from nowhere. It [radio] was the world talking to me. I had never seen a hockey game but I think I became quite something of an expert listening to Foster Hewitt doing the Saturday night games."[115]

Not only did the radio expand the boundaries of Maple Leaf Gardens, it extended the impact of Smythe's respectability project. People across Canada were brought into the Gardens but potential spectators were also educated in what to expect and how to act. Moreover, Hewitt's voice and the sounds of the crowd served to entice potential spectators into the arena. The radio established spectator expectations. "Even though we couldn't see what he was talking about," remembered Jack Warner, "we seemed to know what it all looked like: the game, the building, the players."[116]

Maple Leaf Gardens' Opening Night

After a remarkably brief construction period – groundbreaking took place on 1 June 1931, while some trades were coerced into working hours in exchange for pay in shares in the arena corporation (which only happened to prove to be quite lucrative) – the culmination of the efforts anticipating the preferred spectator occurred with Maple Leaf Gardens' inaugural game on 12 November 1931 (see Fig. 2.13). The press encouraged Torontonians to "come early" for the occasion and "get a real chance to see the new Gardens."[117] Those who did witnessed evidence of "the evolution of the conservative, easy-going Toronto of the now despised mid-Victorian era into the progressive, bustling, cosmopolitan city of today," which was highlighted by "the transformation of the junction of Yonge and Carlton Streets."[118] The integrated commercial nature of the district was reinforced by the goods in Maple Leaf Gardens' display windows on opening night. Both patrons and passers-by could examine the latest "Hockey Boots" from the Robert Simpson Co., Eaton's primary competitor, while "Ryrie's [Jewellers] are putting in a window display of Cups." Upon learning of these displays, Eaton's too got in on the act, "supplying Sweater Coats for the players."[119] Maple Leaf Gardens' position within this changing neighbourhood made the building itself as much of an attraction as the events that were to be staged within it.

The *Star*'s Marsh was among the spectators that evening walking along Carlton and Church Streets and disembarking from streetcars that were headed to Maple Leaf Gardens. Walking towards the new arena, past the "jam of cars," he was struck by the "stream of people ... They can't all be going to the game!"[120] Marsh's colleague at the *Star*, W.A. Hewitt, praised the arena staff's handling of the city's largest indoor audience: "No confusion, no crowding or rushing, everything done in the most orderly and systematic manner." Once inside, Hewitt, who was not coincidentally in charge of amateur hockey at the new arena, as well as the

Fig. 2.13. On-ice ceremonies on the occasion of the first game at Maple Leaf Gardens, Maple Leafs versus Chicago, 12 November 1931. (City of Toronto Archives, Globe and Mail fonds, Fonds 1266, Item 25804)

father of the Maple Leafs' radio announcer, Foster, lauded the space that the Maple Leafs had built as "a marvellous sight for all those fortunate enough to be present – 15,000 fans comfortably located in this amazing auditorium."[121] A Montreal *Gazette* reporter praised "the shining new sports palace with its colored tiers of seats rising spectacularly to a giddy height, its lofty ceiling webbed with tiny catwalks, its gaily-clad usherettes and its brilliant lighting."[122] Other contemporary accounts also focused on the "lofty ceiling," constructed in such a way that "no columns have been permitted to interrupt a clear view – from every seat in the house – of the great arena."[123] The unobstructed sight lines enabled patrons to take in the vast arena space in which "a ten storey office building could be erected."[124]

Marsh, too, was impressed: "Isn't it wonderful? ... Look at the size of it ... Looks like a cathedral." Using intentionally populist prose, he was quick to note that the experience of the "cathedral" would not be the same for all as "the blue seats are not as nice ... I'd rather be down there in those red leather chairs." Marsh, likely tongue in cheek, asked "Where are the [gallery] gods … Behind me? … They certainly get a great view."[125] Ted Reeve of the *Telegram* was more clearly sarcastic when he noted that "they can following [*sic*] the game fine up there and on clear nights can even see the lights of Rochester [across Lake Ontario in New York]."[126] Commenting on the behaviours of spectators on opening night, Marsh went on to wonder of the third-tier patrons: "What keeps them so quiet? … They're surely not afraid of the new building are they … Just wait you'll hear from them … They won't be afraid long."[127]

Despite these distinctions, spectators who attended the first game at Maple Leaf Gardens share relatively consistent memories, of well-dressed patrons, celebratory pomp, and somewhat lengthy ceremonies (see Fig. 2.14). Ballard, the future Maple Leafs owner, attended that game with the woman who would become his wife: "We sat in Box 22, elegantly dressed in evening attire."[128] Despite Ballard's assertion that "you really had to dress up to sit in the box seats," other spectators recall the Maple Leaf Gardens' opening as a night where "everybody was dressed up in 'soup and fish.'"[129] For Gaston this meant "a lot of men were in tuxedos and top hats. The ladies wore gowns or their best dresses." He, along with his father and brother, "sat in the east side greys, four or five rows from the top" and "wore shirts and ties plus our fedoras."[130]

Spectators also recall the ceremonies from that opening night. First came the music, supplied by the pipe-and-drum bands of the 48th Highlanders and the Royal Grenadiers. One account noted that the musicians "played 'Happy Days Are Here Again' when the Leafs came out on the blazing white sheet of ice for their practice" and, Gaston recalled, "they played 'Road to the Isles' on opening night in 1931, then they played 'God Save the King.'"[131] Then came the speeches, including those of Ontario premier G.S. Henry, Toronto mayor William Stewart, and Maple Leafs president J.P. Bickell, which for Reeve, constituted "enough speeches to open a parliament, let alone a hockey rink" (see Fig. 2.15). He went on to note that the ceremonies "marked the longest stretch that some of the Chi-Hawks [Chicago Blackhawks, the Maple Leafs' opposition that night] have been on the ice in three years."[132] Marsh's voice-of-the-people narrator questioned: "Do we have to listen to speakers?"[133]

An impatient crowd – "the somewhat lengthy opening ceremonies did not appeal to the dyed-in-the-wool fans" – began voicing its displeasure at the delayed start to the game.[134] One fan bellowed his civic demand for "wider highways" during the premier's remarks.[135] The ensuing booing and barracking was cause for rebuke in the popular press in the days after the arena's inauguration. The *Telegram* noted that "one fears, that

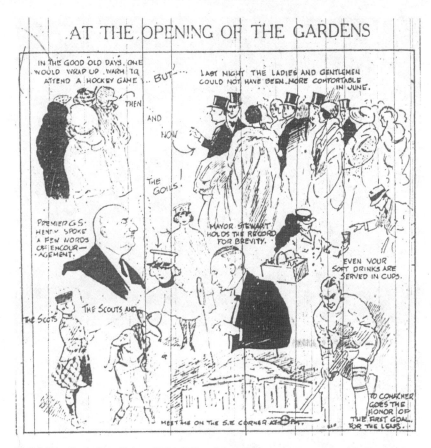

Fig. 2.14. Opening night of Maple Leaf Gardens, as captured in the *Toronto Telegram*, highlighting elements of the spectacle, including the attire of the crowd in the new arena. (*Toronto Telegram*, 13 November 1931)

the crowd was a little bit rude" and that "it is certainly deplorable that prominent men like the Premier and the mayor should be subjected to the howls of the impatient rabble."[136] Allan of the *Mail and Empire* remarked that Bickell and the other dignitaries were "entitled to a better reception." He went on to chastise an audience that was tiring of speeches, "but that's no excuse for the poor reception they gave some of the speakers."[137] Meanwhile, the *Mail and Empire*'s editorial page blamed the incident on "younger elements in the crowd," who needed to learn how to act in a "sportsmanlike" fashion.[138]

Fig. 2.15. Dignitaries who spoke at the opening of Maple Leaf Gardens (12 November 1931) drew the ire of impatient spectators. (City of Toronto Archives, Globe and Mail fonds, Fonds 1266, Item 25805)

Coming as they did from the more culturally conservative members of Toronto's sporting press – for example, Allan of the *Mail and Empire* and J.P. Fitzgerald of the *Telegram* – such rebukes were evidence of the media's complicity in Smythe's efforts to cloak Maple Leaf Gardens from the outset in middle-class respectability. However, as the spectators on opening night demonstrated, formal attire was not enough to ensure deference, especially as hockey spectating was likely not a new practice for many of the men and women in attendance. As Fitzgerald wrote on the morning of that first game: "The class of hockey in this new home will not be any faster or better than in the old Arena, but it will give more people an opportunity to see this, the speediest game on earth, in comfort."[139] The game had not changed with the opening of Maple Leaf Gardens, but the accommodations most certainly had – as had the expectations surrounding how spectators would comport themselves.

Conclusion

While Gibb of the *Star* noted that Maple Leaf Gardens' inaugural evening was "a wonderful spectacle ... the biggest show of the year," the effect that Smythe's respectability project might have on the practice and experience of spectating was not yet clear on that first night.[140] Fitzgerald lauded Toronto's hockey spectators for selling out the Maple Leafs' first game in their new home, but reminded local fans that they would have to "go further and pack in for every game up to or near capacity."[141] Indeed following the arena's inauguration, Marsh wondered "How'll they ever fill all those seats?" while Maple Leafs defenceman Frank "King" Clancy "used to say to the fellas, 'Where are they gonna get the people to fill this thing?'"[142]

Five months earlier, *Hush* had hoped that at the opening of the new arena the Maple Leafs would "cast out all this speech making and other blah blah usually forced on the public at these events."[143] Indeed, the tabloid encouraged the Maple Leafs to celebrate the average spectator and "get Joe Mush to throw the first programme." The socialist newspaper, *Labour Leader*, questioned why at the opening of Maple Leaf Gardens "16,000 people pay from one buck up – principally up – to see a 'restling bout" before also noting that, although the "hockey season opened in Toronto with those in attendance in full evening dress," if the arena was to be a success "the 'boys in overalls' will receive a royal welcome."[144] Invocations such as these of more "typical" fans, ones given to tossing programmes onto the ice, suggest that interrogating attempts to construct a preferred spectator requires looking beyond the opening night at Maple Leaf Gardens to consider the experience of hockey spectators at other games. That is the topic of chapter 4, but first chapter 3 considers who comprised the hockey audience in 1930s Toronto and whether the "boys in overalls" were in attendance.

Note

A version of this chapter appeared previously in Russell Field, "Constructing the Preferred Spectator: Arena Design and Operation and the Consumption of Hockey in 1930s Toronto," *The International Journal of the History of Sport* 25, no. 6 (May 2008): 649–77.

Chapter Three

Filling the Stands

As Maple Leaf Gardens prepared to open on 12 November 1931, Conn Smythe and the Maple Leafs set out to fill the new arena for the team's twenty-four home games in the 1931–32 season and beyond. These efforts took place during an economic crisis that limited the ability of many Torontonians to use their income on luxuries such as hockey tickets, even as hockey broadcasts became a prominent feature of the emerging radio culture of the 1930s. Yet the Maple Leafs attracted enough spectators to hockey games, as well as the variety of other events that Maple Leaf Gardens hosted, to make the arena a financial and cultural success. But while Smythe's new venture became a civic landmark, it remains unclear just who purchased tickets, attended games at Maple Leaf Gardens, and supplied the revenue that ensured the arena's financial viability.[1]

Writing about English football supporter clubs, Rogan Taylor observes that "it is easier to discover the conditions of the drains in Oldham in the late nineteenth century than to find out who went to football matches then."[2] Attracting paying customers was essential to the bottom-line success of commercial sporting ventures across North America and Europe in the 1920s and 1930s. Yet, few historical examinations of modern sport interrogate the nature of this consumption by exploring, in precise fashion, the composition of these audiences. This chapter features a detailed analysis of over 1,500 ticket subscribers for hockey matches at Maple Leaf Gardens during the 1933–34 NHL season and offers a unique look at the men and women whose consumption of spectating as a leisure activity contributed to the growth of North American commercial sport in the interwar years.

Census and city directory details are used in combination with ticket subscriber data to paint a demographic portrait of the men, women, and businesses whose interest in the spectator experience and the action on the ice fuelled the financial success of Smythe's venture. Indeed, despite the fact that "grinding poverty reduced the ability of many Torontonians to take any pleasure in the city's social life," in the 1930s, "the employed middle class enjoyed greater prosperity as prices fell and remained low."[3] It was within such a context and through the analysis of ticket subscriber data which follows that this chapter argues that the "employed middle class" contributed to Maple Leaf Gardens' gate receipts by subscribing to seats throughout the arena. Moreover, the subscriber ledger highlights the ways in which visiting Maple Leaf Gardens was not just a purchasing decision for spectators, but also offered an opportunity to socialize and share in the spectating experience. These ticket holders helped Smythe and the Maple Leafs realize the financial benefits they had sought from the respectability project that was their new arena.

The Maple Leaf Gardens Ticket Ledgers

There are three ledger books in a filing cabinet in the ticket office of the Maple Leafs' current arena, one for each of the hockey club's first three seasons at Maple Leaf Gardens: 1931–32, 1932–33, and 1933–34. These ledgers, presumably created by the arena ticket staff, list the names of all ticket subscribers, the seat(s) they purchased, how much they paid, and a contact (often home) address. A ticket subscriber was not necessarily the same as a *season's* ticket subscriber. The purchaser could buy an entire season's worth of tickets (called here "full" accounts), but a far more popular option – nearly 92 per cent of all accounts in 1933–34 – was to pay for the final two games of the season in advance and reserve the remainder of the year's tickets (called here "partial" ticket accounts), which were held at the ticket office until a certain period of time before the start of each game before being released for sale to the public.

Table 3.1 lists the number of ticket subscribers during Maple Leaf Gardens' first nine years of operation, as recorded by the arena, and the number of seats these subscriptions represented. At a building that opened with a capacity of 12,465 for hockey (not including standing room), these figures suggest the growing popularity of subscription purchases during the slow economic recovery of the 1930s, but more importantly they demonstrate the importance of subscriptions to Maple Leaf Gardens' bottom line.[4] Smythe himself boasted that, in the arena's inaugural year, "just about everybody who was anybody had season tickets" and, by 1940, "almost half the seats were sold before the season opened."[5] Without losing sight of the fact that thousands of people passed through Maple Leafs Gardens' turnstiles each year using single-game tickets, unable to or uninterested in purchasing ticket subscriptions, a

Table 3.1. Reported ticket subscribers, Maple Leaf Gardens

As of	Subscribers	Seats
21 December 1931	1,196	2,843
21 December 1932	1,721	3,777
22 December 1933	1,452	3,150
22 December 1934	1,616	3,442
21 December 1935	1,727	3,751
21 December 1936	2,022	4,449
17 November 1937	2,336	5,138
5 November 1938	2,661	5,912
4 November 1939	2,495	5,535

Source: "Maple Leaf Gardens Limited, Professional Hockey Subscribers," F 223-3-1-60: NHL – Summary of Box Office Receipts, Conn Smythe Fonds, Archives of Ontario, Toronto, Ontario.

detailed examination of subscribers reveals who hockey spectators were in Toronto during the 1930s.

This chapter focuses primarily on the 1933–34 ledger for a number of reasons: it includes nearly three hundred more names than the first season's ledger and considerably fewer complimentary accounts than the second season, although there may have been such accounts in 1933–34 that went unrecorded. It is the only one of the three ledgers that is typewritten (the first two seasons' ledgers are handwritten), reducing transcription errors as one possible source of misinterpretation. The Maple Leafs also reduced ticket prices slightly for the 1933–34 season, perhaps making spectating more affordable and leading to a more diverse audience being welcomed into the arena. And finally, since the ledgers began with the opening of Maple Leaf Gardens, an especially prominent building in the public landscape of 1930s Toronto, using the set of ticket subscribers furthest removed from the arena's opening mitigates to some degree against people subscribing to tickets because of the arena's novelty and offers the possibility of a more "typical" audience profile.

The 1933–34 ticket ledger, which lists all ticket subscribers for NHL games at Maple Leaf Gardens that season, is a valuable source of information on spectators at commercial hockey matches in Toronto in the interwar years. It contains 1,513 unique subscribers who accounted for 3,297 seats, which represented at minimum more than one-quarter of total attendance, presuming a sell-out crowd (see Table 3.2). But, during the 1933–34 NHL season, the Maple Leafs drew 228,181 spectators to their twenty-four home games. So, subscriber tickets, if all claimed by their owners, would have represented nearly 35 per cent of the average home crowd of 9,508. In addition, the ledger included at least 17 per cent of all the available seats in each of the five differently priced sections within the arena. Thus, the ledger represents a substantial cross section of a potential audience at Maple Leaf Gardens. In addition, subscriptions represented a significant portion of revenue for the arena. The accounts listed in the 1933–34 ledger represented $24,726.40 in "guaranteed" revenue, which includes the total amount collected from "full" accounts as well as the two-game prepayments for "partial" accounts. If partial accounts were prorated for the Maple Leafs' entire twenty-four-game 1933–34 home schedule – assuming each subscribed seat was sold for each game – and added to the receipts from full accounts, the "potential" revenue represented in the ledgers was $106,293.60. These were not insignificant sums. Team records indicate that gross gate receipts for Maple Leafs home games during the 1933–34 season were $253,584.66. As a result, "guaranteed" revenues from the sale of ticket subscriptions accounted for 9.75 per cent of revenues for the season, or 2.34 games' worth of revenue, based upon the average 1933–34 per-game receipts of $10,566.03. The accounts listed in the ledger could have accounted for nearly 42 per cent of season revenues if all "potential" revenues were realized.[6]

When cross-referenced with the city directory and census, the information in the ledger offers rich data on the composition of Toronto's hockey spectators in the interwar years. The 1934 *Might's City of Toronto Directory* included a name and address for each person listed, occupation and place of employment for many of the listings, and a register of each street address in Toronto. Entries in the 1933–34 ledger were cross-referenced against directory listings as well as Toronto-specific population and wage-earner data compiled in the 1931 *Seventh Census of Canada* to create a socio-occupational profile of ticket subscribers at Maple Leaf Gardens in the mid-1930s.[7]

It is important to note that being listed in the subscriber ledger did not guarantee that a person was actually a spectator. Any subscriber could have purchased seats for a purpose other than actually sitting in Maple Leaf Gardens to watch hockey. The ledger could include ticket speculators or purchasers whose tickets were used by other people. Nevertheless, the ledger could include the names of men and women who *did* attend hockey games at Maple Leaf Gardens. It also cannot be assumed that people with the financial means to purchase hockey ticket subscriptions in the middle of the Depression were representative of all spectators within the arena. As a result, the ticket subscription ledger only allows for a profile to be constructed of *potential* spectators.

Table 3.2. Ticket subscribers, Maple Leaf Gardens, 1933–34

	$0.75 seats		$1.25 seats		$1.40 seats		$1.75 seats		$2.20 seats		$2.50 seats		Total
	partial	full	partial	full	partial	full	partial	full	partial	full	partial	full	
Male subscribers													
Number of accounts	406	8	208	10	321	17	201	35	17	3	72	35	1,333
Number of tickets	748	18	408	22	678	37	466	89	39	8	176	136	2,825
Average tickets per account	1.84	2.25	1.96	2.20	2.11	2.18	2.32	2.54	2.29	2.67	2.44	3.89	2.12
"Guaranteed" revenue ($)	1,124.00	242.90	1,020.00	532.50	1,862.00	1,083.60	1,556.50	3,304.00	171.60	422.40	750.00	7,785.00	19,854.50
"Potential" revenue ($)	13,488.00	242.90	12,240.00	532.50	22,344.00	1,083.60	18,678.00	3,304.00	2,059.20	422.40	9,000.00	7,785.00	91,179.60
Female subscribers													
Number of accounts	62	2	21	3	29	2	14	2	1	2	5	2	145
Number of tickets	114	4	42	8	54	4	24	6	1	6	8	6	277
Tickets per account	1.84	2.00	2.00	2.67	1.86	2.00	1.71	3.00	1.00	3.00	1.60	3.00	1.91
"Guaranteed" revenue ($)	171.00	71.80	105.00	95.00	151.20	134.40	84.00	252.00	4.40	316.80	40.00	360.00	1,785.60
"Potential" revenue ($)	2,052.00	71.80	1,260.00	95.00	1,814.40	134.40	1,008.00	252.00	52.80	316.80	480.00	360.00	7,897.20
Corporate subscribers													
Number of accounts	0	0	0	0	3	0	13	7	0	1	1	2	35
Number of tickets	0	—	64	0	10	0	63	29	0	1	4	24	195
Tickets per account	—	—	8.00	—	3.33	—	4.85	4.14	—	1.00	4.00	12.00	5.57

													Total
"Guaranteed" revenue ($)	0.00	0.00	160.00	0.00	28.00	0.00	167.50	1,218.00	0.00	52.80	20.00	1,440.00	3,086.30
"Potential" revenue ($)	0.00	0.00	1,920.00	0.00	336.00	0.00	2,010.00	1,218.00	0.00	52.80	240.00	1,440.00	7,216.80
Total subscribers													
Number of accounts	468	10	237	13	353	19	228	44	18	6	78	39	1,513
Number of tickets	862	22	514	30	742	41	553	124	40	15	188	166	3,297
Tickets per account	1.84	2.20	2.17	2.31	2.10	2.16	2.43	2.82	2.22	2.50	2.41	4.26	2.18
"Guaranteed" revenue ($)	1,295.00	314.70	1,285.00	627.50	2,041.20	1,218.00	1,808.00	4,774.00	176.00	792.00	810.00	9,585.00	24,726.40
"Potential" revenue ($)	15,540.00	314.70	15,420.00	627.50	24,494.40	1,218.00	21,696.00	4,774.00	2,112.00	792.00	9,720.00	9,585.00	106,293.60
Percentage of subscriber accounts (%)													
Male	31.06		16.35		25.36		17.70		1.50		8.03		88.10
Female	44.14		16.55		21.38		11.03		2.07		4.83		9.58
Corporate	0.00		22.86		8.57		57.14		2.86		8.57		2.31
Total subscribers in each seating level	31.59		16.52		24.59		17.98		1.59		7.73		–
Subscriber seats: MLG capacity													
Total subscriber seats	884		544		783		677		409				3,297
Total seats in MLG	3,031		3,076		1,554		3,784		1,021				12,466
% of subscriber seats	29.17		17.69		50.39		17.89		40.1				26.45

The limitations of city directories and census data must also be acknowledged. Historical census data are not a static reflection of an underlying reality, but are the result of human efforts that arise from the
"complex relationship of power and privilege between investigator and
subject."[8] For example, Ingrid Botting argues, in the context of her study
of domestic servants in Newfoundland, that the way in which census data
were collected and organized reflected gendered assumptions about
women's labour and "may have revealed more about the gender ideology of the dominant society than they did about the reality of men's and
women's lives in Newfoundland."[9] The content of city directories also reproduced ideological and methodological biases. "At their best," Harold
Carter and Roy Lewis note, directories "provide reasonable coverage of
towns on a systematic street-by-street basis, showing the name and type
of business performed in each building, or, for residential premises, the
occupation of the head of household."[10] Historically, however, city directories were not accurate renderings of entire communities, but were prepared for specific, often commercial purposes, which typically resulted in
"a bias in favour of cataloguing members of the middle class and towards
certain occupations."[11] The omissions common to city directories reflected dominant class, gender, and ethnic ideologies in urban settings.

Nevertheless, the Maple Leaf Gardens ledgers are a previously unex-
amined source of spectator demographics in the interwar years. Integrat-
ing ticket subscriber data with contemporary city directory and census
data creates a profile of a segment of the crowd at commercial hockey
games featuring the Toronto Maple Leafs during the 1933–34 NHL season. A detailed analysis of the ticket ledger from that season provides
a window into the identity of the hockey spectating crowd in interwar
Toronto – specifically its class, gender, and occupational character.

Maple Leaf Gardens Seating

The nature of Maple Leaf Gardens' seating – the differences in materials and proportions between seating sections – was discussed briefly in
chapter 2. But an examination of the ticket subscriber ledgers requires a
more detailed explanation of the arena's seating sections and their associated ticket prices. Seating ran the length of the ice surface on the east
and west sides of the arena, with each section painted or upholstered
(in the case of the padded red box and rail seats) a different colour. In
addition, there were some seats at the north and south ends of the rink.
The different seat sections were known popularly by their colour (e.g.,
the "reds," the "blues"), although when the arena first opened seating
vernacular also referred to tiers (i.e., first, second, and third tiers as one

Table 3.3. Maple Leaf Gardens, ticket prices, 1933–34

Seat section	Tier	Single-game ticket price ($)
Reds	Rinkside	2.20/2.50*
Side blues	First	1.75
End blues	First	1.40
Greens	Second	1.25
Greys	Third	0.75
Standing-room	At the back of the first, second, and third tiers	0.50

* Price varied depending on location.

moved higher up in the arena away from the ice surface). From those nearest to the ice surface moving up to the arena's rafters, seats were red, blue, green, and grey. Ticket prices and seat sections were directly correlated with proximity to the ice surface, that is, the seventy-five-cent grey seats were furthest from the ice and $2.20 and $2.50 box and rail seats closest (see Table 3.3).

From the rafters of Maple Leaf Gardens, the three tiers of seating (see Fig. 3.1) were configured in the following way. The third tier of the arena consisted of seven sections of grey seats on either side of the arena, each thirteen rows deep and between eighteen and twenty seats wide, with 1,516 seats on the west side and 1,515 on the east side.[12] These were all assigned seats; standing-room sections (see below) were the only general admission spaces in Maple Leaf Gardens. A mirror image of the third tier, the green second tier consisted of seven sections on both the east (1,520 seats) and west (1,556 seats) sides of the arena, each thirteen rows deep and eighteen to twenty seats wide. There were five sections of "side blues" on both the east (1,894 seats) and west (1,890 seats) sides of Maple Leaf Gardens, each fourteen rows deep and eighteen to twenty seats wide, as well as wedge-shaped sections of blue seats in each of the arena's four corners. There were also "end galleries" – as they were labelled on architectural drawings, although the seats were better known in spectators' vernacular as the "end blues" – that consisted of four sections, eight rows deep on the north (779 seats) and south (775 seats) sides of the arena.

Maple Leaf Gardens' most expensive seats – the reds – included four-row boxes, each row four seats wide, that were in front of the side blues. There were 392 box seats on each of the arena's east and west sides. The boxes in the arena's corners tended to be smaller and there were no box seats in either the north or south ends of the rink. By contrast, the

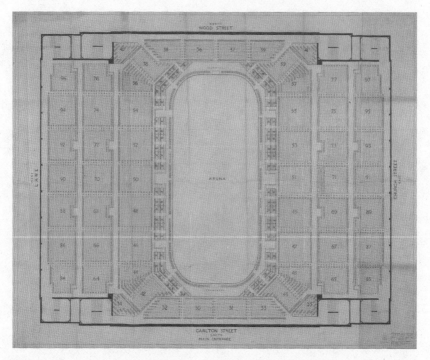

Fig. 3.1. The seating plan at Maple Leaf Gardens, taken from the architectural drawings prepared by Ross & Macdonald, 1931. (Ross & Macdonald fonds, Collection Centre Canadien d'Architecture / Canadian Centre for Architecture, Montreal)

rail seats (of which there were 237) ringed the entire ice surface. The closest seats to the action, the rail seats were in front of the box seats, separated by a promenade that offered access to all red seats. The rail seats positioned around the circumference of the ice surface were only interrupted by the two players' benches, on the east side of the rink, which were separated by eleven seats, the officials' area and penalty box on the west side, and goal judges on the north and south sides.

In contrast, the cheapest tickets for an evening spent watching NHL hockey in Toronto were the fifty-cent standing-room sections. In its original configuration, Maple Leaf Gardens had standing-room spaces between the first and second tiers (5'2" deep), between the second and third tiers (also 5'2"), and at the very top of the arena behind the third tier (6'7"), as well as standing room in the south end above the end blues, under the bandstand.[13] The box-office receipts from Maple Leaf Gardens for the last five seasons of the 1930s reveal that the arena's

Table 3.4. Fifty-cent admissions, Maple Leaf Gardens, 1935–40

Home game	1935–36	1936–37	1937–38	1938–39	1939–40
1	245	213	238	136	512
2	281	234	470	121	529
3	407	416	617	350	520
4	292	629	656	434	682
5	388	287	546	192	408
6	324	331	463	233	661
7	266	338	433	477	187
8	189	317	221	413	263
9	334	662	281	227	191
10	674	371	478	201	190
11	237	435	488	112	169
12	310	255	240	617	225
13	542	218	190	321	542
14	292	279	450	424	120
15	330	343	252	219	155
16	347	204	412	591	145
17	161	242	448	435	183
18	523	399	206	152	423
19	192	320	166	474	175
20	442	227	328	404	378
21	295	480	429	251	107
22	2,297	344	110	172	413
23	321	216	316	144	408
24	272	338	145	201	155
Average	333.22	337.42	357.63	304.21	322.54

Source: "Maple Leaf Home Games [by season]," F 223-3-1-60: NHL – Summary of Box Office Receipts, Conn Smythe Fonds, Archives of Ontario, Toronto, Ontario.
Note: Home game 22 from the 1935–36 season was not included in the calculation of average sales for that season. It was an "outlier," as that game was an occasion where all available seats at the arena were sold for discounted prices. In subsequent seasons, box-office receipts distinguished the fifty-cent admissions on such evenings from other discounted prices. (See the discussion of "booster" tickets in chapter 4.) The records did not make this distinction for this particular game.

standing-room spaces remained popular throughout the decade (see Table 3.4). Sales of fifty-cent tickets varied from game to game, from a low of 107 to a high of 682 in the 1939–40 season, but consistently averaged over three hundred standees per game for each of these five seasons.

Faces in the Crowd

Unlike the crowd at New York's Madison Square Garden, where stars of stage, screen, and sport were regularly and visibly in attendance, in Toronto well-known spectators tended to be businessmen as opposed to figures from the entertainment world, although musician and conductor Percy Faith subscribed to a pair of seats in the side blues.[14] More prominent were executives from many of the city's major businesses, including Harry McGee of Eaton's and Simpson's president C.L. Burton, who were joined among box seat holders by the president of another local retailer, Loblaws grocery stores. There were far fewer well-known female account holders. One exception was A.E. Marie Parkes, an important figure in student affairs at the University of Toronto, who subscribed to two seats in the $1.40 end blues.[15] Although she managed Canada's first women's Olympic team in 1928, it would be a stretch to label Parkes a prominent public figure in 1930s Toronto.

Other people in Maple Leaf Gardens' stands had connections to sport and entertainment in the city. Nathan L. Nathanson founded the Paramount chain of cinemas, which he sold to the American company Famous Players while assuming the presidency of their Canadian operations. On 13 December 1919, he had also been one of four men – with Charles Querrie, Paul Ciceri, and J.P. Bickell, the future president of Maple Leaf Gardens – who purchased the Toronto NHL franchise and renamed it the St. Pats.[16] This was the club Smythe and his backers, who included Bickell, purchased in 1927. Nathanson had box seats at Maple Leaf Gardens, while one of his co-owners in the St. Pats, Querrie, who managed the city's Palace Theatre, which advertised in Maple Leaf Gardens' programmes, had two pairs of seats in the side blues.[17] Jack Corcoran also had a pair of seats in the side blues, although his were complimentary. He was the manager of the Queen City Club, which in practical terms meant that he was responsible for staging the professional wrestling cards at Maple Leaf Gardens that competed in the Toronto marketplace in the early 1930s with Ivan Mickailoff's wrestling promotions at Arena Gardens.[18]

There were other spectators with direct connections to hockey, including Maple Leafs defenceman Red Horner and radio broadcaster Foster Hewitt, both of whom were listed in the ledger with a pair of seats in the side blues, the latter's being complimentary tickets available to Hewitt at no charge. Unlike the 1931–32 ledger, which included complimentary pairs of seats for every Maple Leafs player and head coach Dick Irvin, Horner was the only player listed in the 1933–34 ledger. This is not to suggest that players were not given access to seats during the 1933–34 season, only that they were not listed in the subscriber ledger.

Nevertheless, a review of the ticket subscriptions from the 1931–32 ledger (a record of the arena's inaugural season) reveals the interests to which Smythe and the Maple Leafs appealed in their first year of operation at their new home. Consistent with the pursuit of the preferred spectator, the composition of complimentary ticket holders during the inaugural season at Maple Leaf Gardens is evidence of Smythe's efforts to gentrify hockey spectating. Major political figures and bureaucratic institutions were granted free access to some of the Gardens' best seats. An entire box of eight seats along with two seats in an adjacent box were reserved for the mayor and board of control. Well-known federal member of Parliament and former Toronto mayor Tommy Church had two box seats reserved, while four box seats were set aside for the Lieutenant-Governor. The Ontario Athletic Commission (OAC, two seats), the fire marshall (two seats), and the amusement tax agency (six seats) – all of which had an interest in the operation of the arena – were seated in the side blues. The OAC tickets were eventually transferred into two box seats.[19]

Andy Lytle of the *Star* once noted that "no man in sport is more alertly aware of publicity's value than Smythe."[20] As a result, in anticipation of the contribution that press and radio coverage would make to the success of Maple Leaf Gardens, free access to the arena during its inaugural season was granted to all of the major media outlets, including national wire services such as Canadian Press (four seats), CN Telegraph (two), and CP Telegraph (two), and the four Toronto daily newspapers (*Globe, Mail and Empire, Star,* and *Telegram*), each with six seats. In addition, major sportswriters for each of the dailies – ten in total – were granted two complimentary seats. This list included Alexandrine Gibb of the *Star,* who penned "No Man's Land of Sports," a column on women's sport. W.A. Hewitt, who in addition to his duties at the *Star* also ran amateur hockey at Maple Leaf Gardens, was the only sportswriter with more than two seats and had an entire box of eight seats (see Fig. 3.2). All of the media tickets were in the side blue seats in adjacent sections 51, 53, and 55, on the east side of Maple Leaf Gardens. The only exception to this location, besides Hewitt's eight box seats, was *Star* sports editor Lou Marsh, who was allocated two box seats.

Not surprisingly, all members of Maple Leaf Gardens' executive and board of directors appeared in the 1931–32 ledger, some with complimentary seats and others with paid seats (see Fig. 3.3). Two seasons later, all five members of the executive of Maple Leaf Gardens' board were listed in the subscriber ledger and all five subscribed to box seats. President J.P. Bickell, a mining executive, purchased an entire box (eight seats) for the full season. Two of the Gardens' three vice presidents – McGee (Eaton's) and G.R. Cottrelle (Bank of Commerce) – each paid in advance for four box seats for the twenty-four-game season. The third vice president, E.W. Bickle, senior partner in a Toronto stock brokerage, received two complimentary box seats. The final member of

Fig. 3.2. *Toronto Star* columnist and amateur hockey administrator W.A. Hewitt, pictured here in 1942, had box seats at Maple Leaf Gardens. (*Toronto Star* Photograph Archive, Courtesy of Toronto Public Library)

the executive, managing director Conn Smythe was listed in the ledger with two "partial" box seats. The remaining members of the Gardens' board of directors were not so fully represented in the ledger, which is not to say that all of them did not find their way into the Gardens' seats for evenings of hockey spectating. Eleven of the seventeen directors were listed in the ledger, nine with box seats paid for a full season and two subscribed to "partial" ticket accounts in the side blues. None held accounts for seats in the arena's three least expensive sections. These men, and they were all men, were principals with important Toronto law firms, insurance companies, and brokerage houses or held senior executive positions with manufacturing enterprises such as oil companies and distilleries.

The *"Gardens" Executive*

Fig. 3.3. Maple Leaf Gardens executive board members, including chair J.P. Bickell, were all listed in the 1931–32 ticket subscriber ledger. (*Maple Leaf Gardens Programme*, 1931–32)

Mostly Male: Managers as Ticket Subscribers

Men, not all of them high-profile local figures or corporate executives, comprised the bulk of the crowd on any given game night at Maple Leaf Gardens. While these men may have purchased tickets and then been accompanied to games by women, the typical Maple Leaf Gardens crowd was predominantly male, as 88.1 per cent of the 1,513 subscriber accounts in the 1933–34 ledger were associated with male names (see Table 3.2). Nevertheless, an analysis of the ledger reveals the nuance that must be incorporated into such a characterization. The tickets of male subscribers were spread throughout the arena's five main sections: 31.1 per cent in the grey section, 16.3 per cent in the green seats, 25.4 per cent in the end blues, 17.7 per cent in the side blues, and 1.5 per cent in the red box and rail seats.

Of the 1,332 male account holders, 1,192 were also listed in the 1934 *Might's City of Toronto Directory*. Removing those men who were listed in the directory *without* occupational details as well as those subscribers who purchased multiple accounts leaves 1,068 unique male account holders whose professions or employers can be identified, allowing for a socio-occupational profile that contributes to a portrait of a "typical" male subscriber to hockey games at Maple Leaf Gardens. Furthermore, these men can be compared to the 1931 *Seventh Census of Canada*, which reported 170,693 male wage-earners in Toronto. Table 3.5 presents a breakdown of these men by occupational census category. The largest number of male Toronto wage-earners worked in manufacturing (22.3 per cent), followed by service jobs (15.1 per cent), labourers and unskilled workers (13.8 per cent), as well as occupations categorized as trade (12.6 per cent), transportation and communication (10.3 per cent), clerical (9.7 per cent), and building and construction (8.8 per cent). None of the remaining occupational categories constituted more than three per cent of male Toronto wage-earners.

The occupations of the 1,068 Maple Leaf Gardens' male ticket subscribers can be similarly categorized (also in Table 3.5). Much like the city's male wage-earning population, male subscribers worked most frequently in six occupational categories. Five of these – manufacturing, transportation and communication, trade, service, and clerical – were common to both ticket subscribers and the city's wage-earning population as a whole. The most marked discrepancy was among labourers and unskilled workers, who accounted for only 1.1 per cent of male ticket subscribers (as opposed to 13.8 per cent of the population of the city). This difference is made more significant by Victoria Bloomfield and Richard Harris's assertion that, in the 1930s, the Toronto city directory "identified about 50 percent *more* unskilled workers than did the census."[21] This is not to suggest that labourers did not attend games at Maple Leaf Gardens, but if they did, it is not surprising that with limited disposable income to attend games, which were not selling out, that these men did not purchase subscriptions in advance.

By contrast, the percentage of account holders in traditionally white-collar occupational categories was generally higher than that of Toronto's male population as a whole: trade (22.2 per cent of male ticket subscribers versus 12.6 per cent of Toronto's male labour force), service (16.6 per cent vs. 15.1 per cent), clerical (14 per cent vs. 9.6 per cent), and finance and insurance (6.6 per cent vs. 2.3 per cent), the latter being the sixth-most-common occupational category among male account holders. This pattern is consistent with overall economic conditions in the 1930s when, despite the prevailing economic depression, "white-collar jobs proliferated, especially in wholesale and retail trade and in the professions."[23] Predominantly working-class occupations were represented less often among male subscribers than in Toronto's male wage-earners: manufacturing (19.9 per cent vs. 22.3 per cent), building and construction (4.2 per cent vs. 8.8 per cent), and, as noted above, labourers and unskilled workers (1.1 per cent vs. 13.8 per cent). However, James Lemon notes that manufacturing operations in Toronto were curtailed by the Depression, "hitting a low point in 1933 and 1934," so the proportion of manufacturing wage-earners in the 1933–34 ledger may have reflected the industry three years after the 1931 census data were collected.[24]

Within each of these occupational categories, subscriptions were distributed among Maple Leaf Gardens' differently priced sections. Perhaps not surprisingly individuals with occupations in finance and insurance tended towards the more expensive seats. Subscribers who worked in manufacturing, trade, and service purchased accounts located throughout the arena. However, personal service job holders, such as janitors, watchmen, and caretakers along with clerical and transportation and communication workers, skewed towards the less expensive seats.

The implications of these differences are further revealed by adding another variable – average annual income – to the analysis (see Table 3.6). The aggregate annual income for individual occupations is included within the data in the 1931 census along with total number of employees in each sector, so that an average annual wage can be calculated. These figures were compared to the occupations held by ticket subscribers to establish an *estimated* average annual income, allowing both for any inconsistencies in the way subscribers were categorized and for the reality that individuals could not be expected to conform to a derived "average." The occupational categories where male ticket subscribers appeared less often than the proportions for the city as a whole earned less than the average male wage-earner. By contrast, occupational categories that were over-represented among male subscribers had average annual incomes higher than the Toronto average. Essentially, the ledger suggests that wealthier-than-average men in Toronto were more likely to be found among the crowd with subscriber tickets at Maple Leafs games.

Such distinctions are reflected in the estimated average annual income of male ticket subscribers, which was 57.8 per cent higher than the census average income of male wage- earners in Toronto, according to the 1931 census ($1,936 vs. $1,226). There were differences in income between the sections within Maple Leaf Gardens (see Table 3.7). The

Table 3.5. Occupational details, male ticket subscribers, Maple Leaf Gardens, 1933–34[22]

Census category and primary subcategory	1931 Census (total)	1931 Census (%)	Ledger (total)	Ledger (%)	$0.75 seats	$1.25 seats	$1.40 seats	$1.75 seats	$2.20 and $2.50 seats
TOTAL	170,693	–	1,068	–	334	183	259	195	97
Agriculture	1,451	0.85	0	0.00	–	–	–	–	–
Logging	86	0.05	0	0.00	–	–	–	–	–
Mining, quarrying, oil and salt wells	198	0.12	5	0.47	0	0	1	2	2
Manufacturing	37,997	22.26	212	19.85	54	29	46	62	21
Vegetable products	3,329	–	25	–	4	5	5	8	3
Animal products	3,847	–	22	–	2	4	7	7	2
Textile products	5,805	–	30	–	6	6	5	8	5
Wood products, pulp, paper, and paper products; printing and publishing	7,534	–	54	–	13	6	9	20	6
Metal products	15,163	–	67	–	26	6	18	12	5
Non-metallic mineral products	866	–	2	–	0	0	0	0	0
Chemical and allied products	616	–	5	–	2	0	0	3	0
Miscellaneous products	817	–	7	–	1	2	2	2	0
Electric light and power (including stationary enginemen)	2,480	1.45	31	2.90	14	8	8	1	0
Building and construction	15,007	8.79	45	4.21	18	4	9	5	9
Transportation and communication	17,576	10.30	103	9.64	53	18	18	11	3
Railway transportation	4,887	–	25	–	14	3	4	4	0
Water transportation	490	–	2	–	0	2	0	0	0
Road transportation	8,119	–	56	–	30	8	11	6	1
Other transportation and communication	4,080	–	20	–	9	5	3	1	2
Warehousing and storage	4,280	2.51	21	1.97	15	2	2	2	0
Trade	21,554	12.63	237	22.19	52	48	55	58	24

Finance, insurance	3,841	**2.25**	70	**6.55**	6	5	17	20	22
Service	25,840	**15.14**	177	**16.57**	56	34	49	25	13
Public administration and defence	3,031	–	25	–	14	4	7	0	0
Professional service	10,963	–	101	–	26	16	31	18	10
Recreational service	663	–	14	–	1	2	5	4	1
Personal service	9,381	–	34	–	14	11	5	3	1
Laundering; cleaning, dyeing, and pressing	1,802	–	3	–	1	1	1	0	0
Clerical	16,514	**9.67**	149	**13.95**	59	31	48	9	2
Other: labourers and unskilled workers	23,587	**13.82**	12	**1.12**	7	2	3	0	0
Unspecified	159	**0.09**	6	**0.56**	0	2	3	0	1

Table 3.6. Estimated average annual income, male ticket subscribers, Maple Leaf Gardens, 1933–34

Census category and primary subcategory	1931 Census (total)	1931 Census (%)	Average annual income ($)	Ledger (total)	Ledger (%)	Estimated average income ($)	Income differential (MLG vs. Toronto, %)
TOTAL	170,693	–	1,226.68	1,068	–	1,936.10	57.83
Agriculture	1,451	0.85	699.04	0	0.00	–	–
Logging	86	0.05	654.65	0	0.00	–	–
Mining, quarrying, oil and salt wells	198	0.12	1,059.60	5	0.47	3,500.00	230.31
Manufacturing	37,997	22.26	1,157.66	212	19.85	2,339.50	102.09
Vegetable products	3,329	–	1,198.95	25	–	3,196.34	166.59
Animal products	3,847	–	1,022.10	22	–	2,389.03	133.74
Textile products	5,805	–	964.65	30	–	2,181.80	126.18
Wood products, pulp, paper, and paper products; printing and publishing	7,534	–	1,325.33	54	–	2,743.34	106.99
Metal products	15,163	–	1,106.29	67	–	1,655.43	49.64
Non-metallic mineral products	866	–	1,602.66	2	–	4,311.03	168.99
Chemical and allied products	616	–	2,021.75	5	–	2,934.94	45.17
Miscellaneous products	817	–	1,311.51	7	–	2,243.24	71.04
Electric light and power (including stationary enginemen)	2,480	1.45	1,306.98	31	2.90	1,365.75	4.50
Building and construction	15,007	8.79	948.11	45	4.21	1,611.20	69.94
Transportation and communication	17,576	10.30	1,151.11	103	9.64	1,213.48	5.42
Railway transportation	4,887	–	1,586.39	25	–	1,488.38	-6.18
Water transportation	490	–	1,052.65	2	–	1,375.85	30.70
Road transportation	8,119	–	942.27	56	–	1,085.26	15.17
Other transportation and communication	4,080	–	1,057.13	20	–	1,212.62	14.71
Warehousing and storage	4,280	2.51	1,009.37	21	1.97	972.76	-3.63
Trade	21,554	12.63	1,685.64	237	22.19	2,234.45	32.56
Finance, insurance	3,841	2.25	2,779.59	70	6.55	3,524.78	26.81

Service	25,840	15.14	1,599.76	177	16.57	2,167.50	35.49
Public administration and defence	3,031	–	1,998.25	25	–	2,339.55	1708
Professional service	10,963	–	2,242.09	101	–	2,491.71	11.13
Recreational service	663	–	1,687.93	14	–	2,002.81	18.65
Personal service	9,381	–	86768	34	–	1,200.09	38.31
Laundering; cleaning, dyeing, and pressing	1,802	–	800.44	3	–	1,551.17	93.79
Clerical	16,514	9.67	1,183.68	149	13.95	783.12	-33.84
Other: labourers and unskilled workers	23,587	13.82	588.39	12	1.12	588.39	0.00
Unspecified	159	0.09	979.87	6	0.56	1,721.31	75.67

Table 3.7. Estimated average income by seat section, male ticket subscribers, Maple Leaf Gardens, 1933–34

Census employment category	Account holders	Estimated annual income ($): $0.75 seats	Estimated annual income ($): $1.25 seats	Estimated annual income ($): $1.40 seats	Estimated annual income ($): $1.75 seats	Estimated annual income ($): $2.20/$2.50 seats
Mining, quarrying, oil and salt wells	5	–	–	3,500.00	3,500.00	3,500.00
Manufacturing	212	1,094.98	2,016.65	1,890.54	3,414.67	3,631.26
Electric light and power	31	1,404.10	1,302.21	1,370.14	1,302.21	–
Building and construction	45	1,011.76	995.83	1,500.14	2,513.51	2,677.25
Transportation and communication	103	1,104.78	1,214.83	1,209.93	1,619.19	1,659.26
Warehousing and storage	21	935.35	1,066.28	991.89	1,140.67	–
Trade	237	1,529.68	2,046.53	2,176.76	2,757.27	3,005.99
Finance, insurance	70	4,505.96	3,505.81	2,666.96	3,616.71	3,227.62
Service	177	1,913.80	1,916.07	2,329.54	2,445.77	2,736.40
Clerical	149	786.88	790.52	744.76	901.06	947.42
Other: labourers and unskilled workers	12	588.39	588.39	588.39	–	–
Unspecified	6	–	860.81	2,008.15	–.	2,581.82
Total / estimated average annual income, by seat price ($)	1,068	1,299.04	1,667.74	1,781.60	2,841.96	3,046.71

estimated average annual income of male subscribers increased as one moved closer to the ice surface. Yet, in every section of the arena, the estimated average annual income of male ticket subscribers exceeded the city-wide average annual income of Toronto's male wage-earners: from $1,299 in the grey seats to a high of $3,046 in the box and rail seats.

Moreover, in all occupational categories, except warehousing and storage and clerical, male ticket subscribers had estimated average annual incomes higher than the census average. This was especially true of occupational categories, with the exception of clerical, that were over-represented among male subscribers: trade (32.6 per cent higher than the census average annual income for this occupation at $2,234), finance and insurance (26.8 per cent higher, $3,524), and service (35.5 per cent higher, $2,167). Even among under-represented wage-earning categories, which tended to be more working class, the estimated income of subscribers was significantly higher than the averages for these occupations: manufacturing (102.1 per cent higher, $2,339) and building and construction (69.9 per cent higher, $1,611). This is explained in part by the predominance of managers and business owner-operators among ticket subscribers in these industries.

Distinguishing between managerial and non-managerial positions among the occupations held by ticket subscribers further reveals the ways in which account holders were financially better off than Toronto's male wage-earners as a whole. In addition to considering job titles found in the city directory, it was assumed that clerical workers as well as labourers and unskilled workers were composed entirely of non-managerial personnel and that the men in the finance and insurance occupations along with the public service and professional service subcategories were "managers." Nearly 14 per cent of male wage-earners in Toronto in the 1931 census held managerial positions, while the vast majority of men (86 per cent) worked in non-managerial professions. By contrast, the occupations of nearly three times as many Maple Leaf Gardens subscribers (38.3 per cent) could be classified as managerial, as opposed to the 61.7 per cent who worked in non-managerial jobs. In typically working-class occupational categories, subscribers holding managerial positions represented a greater than average proportion of the jobs: manufacturing (41 per cent of subscribers vs. 5.5 per cent in the 1931 census), building and construction (33.3 per cent vs. 1.2 per cent), trade (35.9 per cent vs. 12.5 per cent), and recreational service, personal service, and laundering (25.5 per cent vs. 2.7 per cent). Not only were managerial personnel the more likely ticket subscribers among generally working-class occupational categories, managers and professionals also accounted for a majority of male ticket subscribers in the higher-priced seats, with accounts in the side blues and box and rail sections seating making up 51.8 per cent of managerial subscribers.

Managerial personnel had the means to afford Maple Leaf Gardens' most expensive seats. The 409 men in the ticket ledger who held managerial positions had an estimated average annual income of $3,222, more than two-and-a-half times greater than Toronto's average wage. Overall, male ticket subscribers had estimated average annual incomes substantially higher than Toronto's male wage-earning population, when "by January 1933, 30 per cent were jobless."[25] In part, it is the presence of men in managerial jobs, in numbers greater than the civic average, which marks spectating at Maple Leaf Gardens as a middle-class pastime. However, this generalization was more likely to be realized in the arena's two priciest sections than in other locations in the arena. Non-managerial personnel held the majority of the grey, green, and end blue sections, and more than 63 per cent of non-managerial subscriptions were located in the arena's two cheapest sections. The 659 men in the ticket ledger who worked in non-managerial occupations had an estimated average annual income of $1,137, *less* than the city-wide average of $1,226. So, while male ticket subscribers were by and large financially better off and more likely to work in white-collar occupations than male Torontonians as a whole, there were class distinctions *within* Maple Leaf Gardens. Among male ticket subscribers, Smythe's attempts to gentrify hockey spectating had occurred most clearly among the men in the more expensive side blue and red box and rail seats.

These same men can be identified not only by occupation, but also by employer.[26] The local businesses and corporations for whom male subscribers worked paint a portrait of Toronto as a centre of retail, transportation, and financial industries as well as the home to important public utilities, some of whose employees used the purchasing power of their incomes to spend their leisure time at what was the highest-profile entertainment enterprise in interwar Toronto. Forty-six of these businesses were represented among ticket subscribers by four or more employees.

The employer with the greatest number of subscribers was the T. Eaton Company (Eaton's department store) with thirty-nine male subscribers. Although Bloomfield and Harris raise the possibility of certain companies being over-represented in the Toronto city directory because "some companies submitted employee lists to the publisher and others did not," the predominance of Eaton's employees among subscribers is perhaps not surprising given the retailer's important place in the Toronto economy.[27] An October 1935 contest, organized through the YMCA, offered hockey tickets to Eaton's employees. The membership drive for Eaton's Young Men's Club included a notice in the company's newsletter offering "six tickets for professional hockey matches at Maple Leaf Gardens for the six members who sign up [the] most new members."[28] Eaton's flagship College Street department store was located one block west of the arena and the retailer played a significant role in the location and construction of Maple Leaf Gardens. Harry McGee was the only Eaton's executive listed in the ticket ledger, although his presence was likely a function of being a member of Maple Leaf Gardens' executive committee. The remaining thirty-eight male Eaton's employees who were subscribers were predominantly sales staff and garment workers.

Eaton's primary competitor for the retail and mail-order trade, Simpson's, had nine employees listed in the ledger. Its president, C.L. Burton, had been on Maple Leaf Gardens' original board of directors prior to the arena's opening in 1931. In 1934, he was also a member of the Toronto Industrial Commission, sat on the civic committee responsible for Toronto's centennial celebrations, and was still listed among Maple Leaf Gardens' box holders.[29] Birks-Ellis-Ryrie Jewellers – whose vice president, J.E. Birks, was also a director of the arena corporation – was the only other retailer with as many as five ticket subscribers among its employees (the jeweller also purchased a half-page advertisement in the arena programme).[30]

Prominent local manufacturing enterprises, such as Canadian National Carbon, Canadian General Electric, and American Anaconda Brass were also included among subscribers' employers, as were food and beverage producers and oil and gas companies. As well, the two local daily newspapers most disposed to offer readers considerable sports coverage – the *Telegram* (seven subscribers) and the *Star* (five) – had a number of employees listed among ticket subscribers. But, after Eaton's, the next greatest number of employees who were subscribers (twenty-three) worked for Toronto Hydro, the local electrical utility whose new Art Deco–inspired building opened in 1933 just west of Maple Leaf Gardens on Carlton Street (the construction of which is visible in the foreground of Fig. 3.4).[31] Its provincial counterpart, Ontario Hydro, had four employees who were ticket subscribers. Other public services that employed Maple Leaf Gardens' ticket subscribers included the Post Office and the Toronto Transportation Commission (TTC), the local streetcar service, each of which had fifteen employees listed in the ledger. The employees of other local bureaucratic services and utilities were also well represented: the customs house (six subscribers), as well as the city works department (nine), treasury (four), board of education (four), and gas company (four). Beyond the TTC, the transportation sector was an important employer in Toronto and the country's two major railways had numerous employees who, the ledger suggests, spent their leisure time as hockey spectators: Canadian Pacific Railway (sixteen) and Canadian National Railway (ten). The telegraph service of Canadian National accounted for another four ticket subscribers, while the primary telephone service, Bell, had ten employees listed in the ledger.

F.K. Morrow, a director of Canadian National, subscribed to four box seats. While he sat on Maple Leaf Gardens' board, Morrow was also a director for the Bank of Toronto, and financial services firms were common employers of ticket subscribers. Three firms – Dominion Bank, Imperial Life Assurance, and Manufacturers' Life Insurance – each with nine employees, were the most frequently represented financial services companies in the ledger, and the president of Dominion Bank paid in advance for a season's worth of two seats on the east rail. The prospectus

Fig. 3.4. Maple Leaf Gardens (c. 1934), with the construction of the new Toronto Hydro building visible in the foreground. (City of Toronto Archives, Fonds 1244, Item 3185)

intended to raise money for the nascent arena project listed Maple Leaf Gardens' three bankers as the Canadian Bank of Commerce, Dominion Bank, and Bank of Nova Scotia.[32] Consequently, not only did nine Dominion Bank employees subscribe to tickets, the Maple Leaf Gardens ledger included three Bank of Nova Scotia board members and two Canadian Bank of Commerce directors (including the bank's president and chairman of the 1929 Royal Commission on Radio Broadcasting, Sir John Aird), as well as Victor Ross, vice-president of Imperial Oil and a director of the Toronto General Trusts Corp., which was listed in the same prospectus as Maple Leaf Gardens' registrar.[33]

Six individual subscribers held accounts for ten or more seats. Four of these six men were a senior partner at a stock brokerage; the presidents of a dairy and an auto dealership; and the manager of major Canadian distillery. For these men, in addition to providing an opportunity for socializing, such significant ticket purchases may have been a business expense, a perk for employees, or an incentive for clients. The other

Fig. 3.5. Local camping advocate Taylor Statten (pictured here in 1943) subscribed to a large number of seats at Maple Leaf Gardens. (Archives of Ontario, International Press Limited Fonds, C 306-0-0-3474)

two men who had substantial ticket holdings present interesting possibilities about the composition of the crowd at Maple Leaf Gardens. One was Taylor Statten, the organizer of one of Toronto's better-known boys' summer camps, Camp Ahmek, and the only one of the six men whose seats (thirteen in total) were all in the same section, the end blues (see Fig. 3.5). Perhaps his tickets were used during the winter by campgoers, which would suggest the presence of young spectators (a topic that is considered in chapter 4).

The final individual who held a large number of seats was the father of Maple Leafs defenceman Alex Levinsky. Abraham (Abe) Levinsky, whose occupation was listed in the city directory as printer at a local company,

Dominion Printing, held seven ticket accounts that totalled twenty seats. These were located throughout the greys, end blues, and side blues. The younger Levinsky was not only a well-known local athlete, he was also Jewish. His father was among the unknown number of Jewish patrons who attended Maple Leafs games. Former spectators, including Tom Gaston, recall Abe Levinsky for the role he played in the origin of his son's nickname, claiming that the father would yell that's "mine-boy" every time the younger Levinsky touched the puck, and the nickname stuck.[34] Nevertheless, it is unclear what impact having a Jewish defenceman on the Maple Leafs with a vocal father in the stands had on the composition of the crowd. The reasons why Abe Levinsky purchased so many tickets remain unknown: Were they for Jewish community members who wished to watch his son play, did he intend to resell them, or did his printing company use them as a business development investment? It seems possible – indeed likely given their status as the largest non-British-origin immigrant population in the 1931 census – that Levinsky was not the only Jewish spectator at his son's games.[35] At least four male ticket subscribers in the 1933–34 ledger appear to be Jewish, based upon an assessment of their last names (e.g., Lebovitz). Three of these four men were listed in the ledger with anglicized last names (which appear in their original spelling in the city directory) – although it is unclear whether these anglicizations were self-declared or initiated by the ledger-keepers – including Messrs. Elite (rather than Israelite), Fagan (Feigenbladd, whose first name was also anglicized), and Small (Smollner).

The multiple Statten and Levinsky ticket holdings point to the ways in which ledger subscriptions are evidence of men socializing together. The average male ticket account holder in Toronto subscribed to 2.1 seats during the 1933–34 NHL season (see Table 3.2). The seats-per-account average was lowest in the grey seats (1.8 tickets per account) and highest in the $2.50 red box and rail seats (2.4).[36] Men who subscribed to only one seat were more likely to be found among the upper reaches of Maple Leaf Gardens. While single-seat accounts represented only 14.1 per cent of all male subscriptions, more than half of these (95 of 188 accounts) were located in the least expensive seats. This is not to suggest that these subscribers attended hockey games by themselves. Rather, socializing was common in the uppermost sections of Maple Leaf Gardens, where, more frequently than anywhere else in the arena, individuals paid solely for their own ticket (as opposed to buying tickets for themselves and a companion). Nevertheless, even in the grey seats, two-seat accounts represented the majority (71.5 per cent) of subscriptions.

Combining the employment details included in the city directory with the seat locations associated with each subscriber account listed in the ledger allows for a tentative portrait of workplace socializing to be drawn. The evidence is suggestive of co-workers attending Maple Leafs games together. Throughout Maple Leaf Gardens, there were examples of pairs of people – most often men – who worked for the same company, occasionally even in the same position, who subscribed to seats that were adjacent to or nearby one another within the arena. It is impossible to say for certain whether employees of the same organization who had subscriptions for Maple Leaf Gardens seats that were adjacent to or located near one another actually attended games together. Nonetheless, in the grey seats, there were two Eaton's stockkeepers with adjacent single seats in section 90, two stenographers from the *Toronto Star* with adjacent single seats in section 84, and two optometrists from Eaton's as well as a proofreader from Eaton's, all with adjacent pairs of seats in section 89. The green seats included three employees of Bell Telephone with adjacent pairs of seats, while in the end blues there were two sales managers with Standard Brands who each subscribed to two seats, side by side. Finally, the side blues included two Canadian National Railway yardmen with adjacent single seats.

In total, there were fifty-seven examples of this trend in the 1933–34 ledger, twenty-eight of which were co-workers subscribing to adjacent seats, another thirteen with seats in front of one another, and finally sixteen examples of people employed by the same company with seats near one another. There is an important pattern in these examples that is reflected in all fifty-seven cases as well as in the subset of twenty-eight adjacent-seat co-worker accounts. The majority were located in the cheapest seats at Maple Leaf Gardens. Fourteen of the twenty-eight adjacent-seat co-worker accounts were located in the grey seats. Among all fifty-seven co-worker accounts, 52.9 per cent were in the greys, with another 25.5 per cent in the greens, for a total of forty of the fifty-seven account-pairs in Maple Leaf Gardens' two least expensive sections. The predominance of cheaper tickets among all of these cases suggests that this form of socializing took place on a shared-cost basis among working-class acquaintances.

The socializing patterns that existed among co-workers stood in contrast to the socializing and ticket purchasing habits of presumably wealthier spectators. The ways in which socializing through spectating differed according to ticket price and social standing were on display in those parts of the arena where two-seat subscriptions were *not* the norm. The subscriptions for central box and rail seats ($2.50 reds) that were paid in full were the sole location in Maple Leaf Gardens where two-seat accounts were not the majority among subscribers. There were eighteen accounts of four seats or more among the thirty-five "full" box and rail accounts purchased by men. (By contrast, only 5.6 per cent of the grey-seat accounts and 6.9 per cent of the green-seat accounts were for four or more seats.) These men who could afford to pay hundreds of dollars in advance for hockey tickets to the Gardens' most expensive seats were far more likely than men sitting in other locations in the arena to sponsor large social groups attending Maple Leafs games.

These wealthier subscribers were also likely to socialize outside of the workplace and were connected through a variety of social networks to Toronto's most prominent citizens. These connections were detailed in the *Blue Book*, Toronto's social register, which listed the members of the city's most exclusive social, sport, and political clubs.[37] These were the social networks into which Suzanne Morton noted that working-class men were "certainly not invited."[38] In addition to club memberships, the *Blue Book* included the names, addresses, and occupations of each person listed, which makes possible a comparison with data from the subscription ledger. Such cross referencing reveals that ninety-nine of the approximately 3,500 people listed in the 1934 *Blue Book* were also Maple Leaf Gardens ticket subscribers during the 1933–34 NHL season. Collectively these ninety-nine subscribers – ninety-two men and seven women, a ratio similar to that of the entire ledger – purchased 113 ticket subscriptions (some subscribers were associated with more than one ticket account) totalling 335 seats, an average of 3.4 seats per subscriber. The seats connected to these accounts were located throughout Maple Leaf Gardens, although they were concentrated in the arena's more expensive sections: 46 per cent in the red box and rail seats, plus another 34.5 per cent in the side blue seats.

The ninety-nine subscribers who appeared in the *Blue Book* had well-formed social networks that extended beyond Maple Leaf Gardens' choice seats. The ninety-two men held 460 club memberships among them, an average of five per subscriber, while the seven women had fourteen club memberships. The *Blue Book* also listed the spouses and adult-age children of the people it profiled. The ninety-nine Maple Leaf Gardens subscribers who were also listed in the *Blue Book* had seventy familial relations whose club memberships were also detailed in the social register. These relations were predominantly wives of male Maple Leaf Gardens account holders (sixty-one), however there was also one husband of a female subscriber and four mothers and four fathers of account holders. Spouses and other relatives are an important addition to a portrait of spectators. If spectating was a predominantly social activity, these people may well have attended games at Maple Leaf Gardens in the company of ticket subscribers. The seventy relatives of the ninety-nine Maple Leaf Gardens subscribers shared 202 club memberships: five men with fifteen memberships and sixty-five women with 187 memberships. In total, these 169 people had 678 memberships in over fifty different Toronto clubs, as well as a number of out-of-town clubs, stretching from Montreal to the US to London, England. Eight clubs counted more than twenty-five Maple Leaf Gardens subscribers and relations on their membership rosters.[39] The most popular was the Granite Club, a sport and social club, with sixty-two members, followed by the Royal Canadian Yacht Club with forty-three members. Golf and country clubs were also popular, but Toronto's elite gentlemen's clubs, such as the National, York, Canadian, Toronto, Empire, and Albany clubs, were also well represented.

There were two father-son pairs, as well as two members of Toronto's Gooderham family, well known for their distillery business, who both subscribed to Maple Leafs tickets and were also listed in the *Blue Book*. In addition, while Smythe did not come from a moneyed Toronto family, he sought well-connected backers both when he purchased the city's NHL franchise in 1927 and when he financed his new arena in early 1931. As a result, all the members of the Maple Leaf Gardens executive – notably excluding Smythe – appeared in the *Blue Book*, as did ten of the eleven Maple Leaf Gardens board members who, as noted, were also listed in the 1933–34 ledger.

It was not only in the most expensive seats that groups of people chose to socialize with one another at hockey games. In a number of instances, family members subscribed to seats at Maple Leaf Gardens. There were nine examples in the 1933–34 ledger of men who shared the same last name and lived at the same address holding ticket accounts for adjacent seats or seats near one another (e.g., in front of one another). This is not to claim definitively that these people were necessarily family members and/or that they attended hockey games together, although the evidence is certainly suggestive of this: three of the nine examples were for adjacent single seats, suggesting that these individuals attended Maple Leafs games together. Additionally, five of these "family" ticket purchases were in the grey seats, with one each in the other four higher-priced sections. There were also three instances of homeowners and their boarders both subscribing to seats at Maple Leaf Gardens. In two of these cases, the renter and landlord were not sitting together, but in the third they subscribed to tickets in front of one another in the greys. Again, these examples suggest that the cost of social outings was shared among men who sat in Maple Leaf Gardens' least expensive seats. But they are also evidence of the ways in which hockey spectating was a social occasion, one that for people living under the same roof may have been aided by the at-home sociability provided by the increasing availability of the radio in the 1930s. Listening on the radio created an aural familiarity with Maple Leaf Gardens and created, in the memories of many former spectators, a desire among friends and family to attend games and see the new arena in person.

There are other instances of potential family members purchasing ticket subscriptions at Maple Leaf Gardens but not sitting together. This is the case in four instances where individuals who shared the same last name and address were seated in different sections of the arena. There were a further four instances of two family members, neither living together nor sitting near one another at Maple Leaf Gardens, subscribing to tickets. Two of these four cases appeared to be a father and son both working in the family business, while the other two pairs were members of two of Toronto's better-known families: the Airds and, as noted, the Gooderhams

In a similar vein, there were also seventeen instances in the ledger of men who lived near to one another on the same street subscribing to tickets at Maple Leaf Gardens that were adjacent to or nearby one another within the arena. As with family members, there is no way of confirming for certain that these neighbours attended games together – indeed it may have been a coincidence that neighbours ended up with seats near one another – but the pattern is interesting nonetheless for what can be inferred about the social nature of hockey spectating. Of these seventeen instances, however, eleven were neighbours each subscribing to a *pair* of seats, which may further indicate that hockey spectatorship at Maple Leaf Gardens was an occasion for heterosocial bonding: two heterosexual couples socializing with one another.

Of these seventeen examples, six were in the grey seats, five in the greens, four in the end blues, two in the side blues, and none in the box and rail seats. The predominance of cheaper tickets among these cases might be, as above, an example of this form of socializing taking place on a shared-cost basis among acquaintances. While these seventeen examples are suggestive of a trend, these figures do not include those neighbours who lived on the same street, went to games together and engaged in the social activities such as travelling to Maple Leaf Gardens together and perhaps having dinner together before games, but did not sit together. Nor are instances of neighbours who lived on adjacent streets and went together to and/or sat together at Maple Leafs games included here. There were likely examples of both of these cases contained within the Maple Leaf Gardens ledgers – they are just harder to tease out.

It is worth remembering that while sport spectating offered an occasion for male sociability, the majority of Maple Leaf Gardens' male accounts holders, at every price level, paid for two seats. Nearly three-quarters (74.3 per cent) of all the male subscriber accounts were for two seats.

With the exception of the box and rail paid-in-full accounts, at none of Maple Leaf Gardens' price levels did two-seat accounts represent less than 58 per cent of all male accounts. Presumably those men who actually used their subscribed seats purchased two tickets so that they could take a companion, male or female, to games with them.

Corporate Toronto in the Stands

Toronto's business community was not only represented by individual employees among Maple Leaf Gardens subscribers. In each ledger, there were also ticket subscriptions associated with a company rather than a person. By the mid-1930s Toronto had become the national centre of finance and industry, with transactions on the Toronto stock market exceeding those of the Montreal market for the first time in 1932.[40] It is not surprising then that Smythe's new arena attracted spectators from Toronto's corporate community, who bought tickets themselves or in the name of their company. Of the 1,513 subscriptions in 1933–34, thirty-five were listed in the names of twenty-four different companies. These accounts represented 195 seats, as the average "corporate" account of 5.6 seats was considerably larger than the average individual subscription of 2.2 seats. The majority of these were located in the greens and side blues (see Table 3.2). Eight corporate accounts subscribed to more than four seats, including one account for five seats and two others for six seats. Five corporate accounts, however, purchased twelve or more seats.

Given the debate with Eaton's prior to the construction of Maple Leaf Gardens over the impact of the new arena on the local commercial district, it is worth noting the ways in which this neighbourhood supported the new venture. While no employer was associated with more individual ticket subscriptions than Eaton's, the largest single ticket holder, corporate or individual, in the ledger was the Happy Day Pharmacy with sixty seats, including one subscription for forty seats in the greens and another for twenty seats in the side blues. Not only was this pharmacy located next to Maple Leaf Gardens, it was also operated by Maple Leafs defenceman and team captain (and Smythe's partner in his sand and gravel business) Clarence "Happy" Day – although what use Day or his pharmacy made of sixty seats to each Maple Leafs game during the 1933–34 season remains unclear. Similarly, Love & Bennett, a sporting goods retailer located within the arena with a storefront east of the main Carlton Street entrance, had an account for six end blue seats and advertised in the arena programme.[41] United Cigar Stores rented the prime storefront at Maple Leaf Gardens' southeast corner (the northwest corner of Carlton and Church Streets) and one of the retail chain's vice presidents was also a ticket subscriber. He was joined in the side blues by a salesman for a beauty parlour supplier located next to the arena on Church Street.

Besides the Happy Day Pharmacy, other large corporate accounts included Canada Bread Co. (twenty-four seats), McNamara Construction Co. (seventeen seats), and Alfred Rogers Co. Ltd. (sixteen seats). Alfred Rogers was a major shareholder in Maple Leaf Gardens, the president of both Canada Building Materials and St. Mary's Cement, and "just about the top man in the business and social world of Toronto."[42] The Elias Rogers Co. Ltd., which sold coal for domestic use in Toronto, and whose president was also Alfred Rogers, had a half-page advertisement in the 1933–34 *Maple Leaf Gardens Programme*.[43] A final corporate account holder with a large cache of tickets was General Motors, which had twelve seats in the first row of the side blues, immediately behind the box seats. This was one of only two complimentary corporate accounts – the four front-row side blues held by O'Keefe's, a local brewery, being the other.[44] General Motors' significant gratis ticket holdings were unsurprising as the automobile manufacturer was, in the early 1930s, the lead sponsor of the national radio broadcasts of hockey games at Maple Leaf Gardens, which were also broadcast locally on radio stations CFCA and CKCW, and featured Foster Hewitt.[45] By the time its seats listed in the 1933–34 ledger would have been occupied, "the national General Motors broadcasts were reaching over a million listeners."[46]

Female Subscribers and the Consumption of Leisure

That some of these listeners were women is confirmed by Barry Broadfoot's oral history of Depression-era Canada.[47] A considerable number of women also passed through Maple Leaf Gardens' turnstiles to watch games in person. Nevertheless, how many women attended hockey games and the degree to which commercial hockey offered women an opportunity to socialize with one another, beyond accompanying a male partner or family member, has received little consideration.

Of the 1,513 subscriber accounts listed in the 1933–34 ledger, 145 were associated with "obviously" female given names (e.g., Elizabeth or Mary) or preceded by the title "Mrs." or "Miss" (account holders with a given name that could not be clearly attributed to a presumed gender identity, e.g., Leslie, were not assumed to be female). At 9.6 per cent of the ledger total, female account holders clearly accounted for a significantly smaller proportion of subscribers at Maple Leaf Gardens than their presence in the city as a whole, where women were more than 51 per cent of the population.[48] These 145 accounts were located throughout the arena (see Table 3.2) and, if subscribing translated into spectating, female spectators occupied a variety of locations and price points within Maple Leaf Gardens. The portrait of female spectators that follows is based upon the 66 of these 145 women whose names appear in the city directory *with* occupational details. As married women were often omitted from the city directory, this is quite possibly a snapshot of single working women who appeared in the stands at Maple Leaf Gardens during the 1930s.[49]

The 1931 census lists 68,064 wage-earning women in Toronto, who earned an average annual income of $721 – significantly lower than the male average of $1,226. Veronica Strong-Boag argues that "there were in reality two separate labour markets distinguished by sex."[50] In such a context, ticket subscriptions were likely more onerous for wage-earning women than for employed men. This might explain why the average number of tickets purchased by female subscribers (1.9) was lower than the average for male subscribers (2.1). There was also a higher percentage of single-ticket accounts among female subscribers (23.5 per cent) than male (14.1 per cent). While this might suggest that women were attending hockey games on their own – or at least not always in the company of companions who had purchased tickets for them – it is not possible to distinguish between leisure and labour (i.e., women buying tickets for other people, perhaps partners, family members, or employers) for female ticket subscribers based on ledger data alone.

The vast majority of Toronto's wage-earning women held positions that the census classified within one of three occupational categories: service (33.9 per cent of female wage-earners), clerical (31.7 per cent), and manufacturing (17.8 per cent); see Table 3.8. Fewer female subscribers at Maple Leaf Gardens held manufacturing jobs (12.1 per cent) than among the female wage-earning population as a whole (17.8 per cent). Service occupations (21.2 per cent vs. 33.9 per cent) evidenced a similar discrepancy. These differences in what were largely working-class occupations were offset by the predominance of clerical occupations among female ticket subscribers (53 per cent vs. 31.7 per cent of city-wide female workers). The most prominent job titles among female subscribers were stenographer (ten subscriber accounts), teacher (ten), clerk (ten), secretary (six), bookkeeper (five), and sales clerk/saleslady (four). Of these, only teachers were not classified as clerical workers; teaching was categorized as a service occupation.

The small number of manufacturing workers and preponderance of clerical and service employees suggests that female subscribers were financially better off than the average Toronto working woman, when considering their earnings. The average income for female clerical workers in Toronto in the 1931 census ($918) was considerably higher than

Table 3.8. Occupational details and estimated average annual income, female ticket subscribers, Maple Leaf Gardens, 1933–34

Census category and primary subcategory	1931 Census (total)	1931 Census (%)	Average annual income ($)	Ledger (total)	Ledger (%)	Estimated average income ($)	Income differential (%)
TOTAL	68,064	–	721.76	66	–	971.73	34.63
Agriculture	12	0.02	433.33	0	0.00	–	–
Manufacturing	12,132	17.82	569.96	8	12.12	950.20	66.72
Vegetable products	968	–	553.31	0	–	–	–
Animal products	689	–	554.57	0	–	–	–
Textile products	7750	–	565.94	4	–	556.65	–1.64
Wood products, pulp, paper, and paper products; printing and publishing	1,474	–	612.28	3	–	1,245.01	103.34
Metal products	856	–	568.57	1	–	1,640.00	188.44
Non-metallic mineral products	32	–	553.13	0	–	–	–
Chemical and allied products	94	–	643.62	0	–	–	–
Miscellaneous products	269	–	533.83	0	–	–	–
Building and construction	23	0.03	452.17	0	0.00	–	–
Transportation and communication	2,233	3.28	825.79	2	3.03	795.33	–3.69
Other transportation and communication	2,233	–	825.79	2	–	795.33	–3.69
Warehousing and storage	1,779	2.61	483.64	1	1.52	569.47	17.75
Trade	6,077	8.93	698.88	5	7.58	735.57	5.25
Finance, insurance	102	0.15	1,395.10	0	0.00	–	–
Service	23,067	33.89	636.46	14	21.21	1,288.99	102.52
Public administration and defence	46	–	1,626.09	0	–	–	–
Professional service	5,715	–	1,265.63	11	–	1,462.82	15.58
Recreational service	39	–	784.62	0	–	–	–
Personal service	16,280	–	419.13	3	–	651.61	55.47
Laundering; cleaning, dyeing, and pressing	987	–	526.14	0	–	–	–
Clerical	21,556	31.67	918.34	35	53.03	918.74	0.04
Other: labourers and unskilled workers	723	1.06	460.86	0	0.00	–	–
Unspecified	71	0.10	492.96	1	1.52	492.96	0.00

that of manufacturing employees ($569) and service workers ($636). Moreover, the sixty-six female account holders had an estimated average annual income of $971, 34.6 per cent higher than the average annual income of Toronto's female wage-earning population. However, female subscribers earned only 50.2 per cent of the incomes of male subscribers, less than the 58.8 per cent Toronto's female wage-earners took home as a percentage of male incomes (which also reinforces how well off male ticket subscribers were relative to the population as a whole).

Despite the distribution of Toronto's female wage-earners into manufacturing, service, and clerical jobs, a look at the specific positions held by women workers in 1931 Toronto reveals their concentration in certain occupations. Table 3.9 lists the twelve occupations in which more than one thousand female wage-earners were employed. These specific occupations accounted for more than three-quarters of all female wage-earners in the city and they reveal the importance of occupational categories whose prominence is understated by aggregated occupational category data. Trade (8.9 per cent of wage-earning Toronto women in 1931), transportation and communication (3.3 per cent), and warehousing and storage (2.6 per cent), while not the predominant occupational categories among wage-earning females, included occupations (saleswomen, telephone operators, and packers, wrappers, and labellers) in which more than nine thousand Toronto women worked. Similarly, the vast majority (80.3 per cent) of female subscribers at Maple Leaf Gardens for whom occupational details were available worked in these same occupations. However, the positions among this dozen in which female subscribers were *not* employed reveals the ways in which the women who purchased ticket subscriptions were considerably more middle class than working women in Toronto as a whole. Consider the service occupations represented (teachers) and absent (domestic servants, waitresses, nurses) among female subscribers. With an average annual income of $1,519, teachers earned more than double the average female wage and were the third most common census occupational category among female subscribers.

Clerical occupations were not as well paid as teachers, but they earned more than the average female working wage. Nevertheless, historians have highlighted the ghettoization of women in clerical jobs and the feminization of this work in the early twentieth century.[51] Women held 45.1 per cent of clerical positions in Canada in 1931 – an increase from 14.3 per cent in 1891 and 32.6 per cent in 1921 – at a time when they accounted for only 17 per cent of the workforce. In 1931, "49 per cent of all head office employees of Manufacturers Life were women," two of whom were among Maple Leaf Gardens' female subscribers in 1933–34.[52] It is

Table 3.9. Common professions, female wage-earners, Toronto, 1931

Specific census occupation	Primary occupational category (secondary, if applicable)	Female census wage-earners	Avg. annual income ($)	Female MLG subscribers
Stenographers and typists	Clerical	11,690	909.57	15
Domestic servants, not elsewhere specified	Service (personal service)	10,212.	364.16	0
Other clerical (office clerks)	Clerical	5,753	911.12	14
Saleswomen	Trade	5,495	652.79	4
Bookkeepers and cashiers	Clerical	3,864	959.52	6
Sewers, sewing machinists – shop, factory	Manufacturing (textile goods)	3,644	521.76	1
Teachers – school	Service (professional service)	2,632	1,519.15	10
Telephone operators	Transportation and communication	1,947	795.33	2
Waitresses	Service (personal service)	1,682	455.71	0
Packers, wrappers, and labellers	Warehousing and storage	1,664	476.44	0
Housekeepers and matrons	Service (personal service)	1,475	472.47	1
Nurses – graduate	Service (professional service)	1,203	1,001.41	0
Total	–	51,261	–	53
% of relevant population	–	75.31	–	80.30

possible that subscribing to hockey tickets fell within the remit of clerical responsibilities. An examination of clerical employment among female subscribers who worked at businesses where tickets might be used by their employers or the businesses' clients and where the businesses' addresses were associated with ticket accounts revealed at least three instances where tickets might have been purchased by women as part of their daily labour and were perhaps not used by these women. These examples included two secretaries in doctor's offices and one secretary at British American Oil.

Nevertheless, as Bloomfield and Harris observe, "an especially large number of female clerical workers were single."[53] Rather than purchasing tickets as part of their daily labour, the presence of these women in the ledger might be an indication that they were spending disposable income and leisure time on hockey spectating. Their location within the arena, as well as their presence, is also revealing. Of the 35 clerical workers who purchased ticket subscriptions, nearly half (sixteen) were for seats in the cheapest section,.the grey seats. These women were the most likely candidates among female ticket subscribers to have purchased hockey tickets for their own leisure and they did so at a price range commensurate with the earning power of clerical jobs. In fact, nearly 45 per cent of all female accounts were located in the greys. There were sixty-four subscriber accounts for grey seats listed in women's names, more than in any other section. Of these sixty-four accounts, eighteen were for single seats, which mitigates to some degree the possibility that these ticket accounts were an indication of women performing domestic labour by purchasing hockey seats for themselves and their spouses or other relatives. After the greys, the greens and end blue seats were the next two most common sections among female subscribers (16.7 per cent and 21.5 per cent of all female subscribers, respectively), whereas the more expensive sections, the side blue seats (11.1 per cent) and the red box and rail seats (6.9 per cent), featured the fewest female subscribers. With the possible exception of the standing-room spaces, women were regular attendees throughout Maple Leaf Gardens.

Observations about occupational categories are further nuanced by considering the specific employers of Maple Leaf Gardens subscribers. Eleven of the sixty-six female subscribers listed with occupational details worked in local Toronto public and secondary schools, with two women each teaching at Central Technical School and Orde Street Public School. The largest single employer was, as with male subscribers, Eaton's department store, with ten female subscribers (recalling Bloomfield and Harris's assertion that certain employers may have been over-represented in the city of Toronto directory). Another two accounts were held by women who worked for Eaton's retail competitor, Simpson's. These department store employees worked in both sales and factory jobs. The predominance of clerical and secretarial work among female subscribers was also reflected in the number of women who held ticket subscriptions and also worked for insurance companies (seven), doctor's or dentist's offices (three), and Bell Telephone (two). No other workplace accounted for more than one female ticket subscriber.

Within the ledger, there is evidence to suggest that women such as these may have attended Maple Leafs games together *and* sat together in the uppermost sections of Maple Leaf Gardens. The only instance in the entire ledger of one subscription co-listed with the names of two people was for two unmarried sisters, one of whom was a teacher, who lived together. It is not unreasonable to conclude that using the pair of tickets in the green seats was part of their recreational lives, either as a pastime they shared or by taking other friends to Maple Leaf Gardens. There is additional evidence to suggest that women chose to watch hockey games in one another's company. There were three instances of pairs of female accounts that were associated with women who resided near each other on the same Toronto street also having seats located near to one another, and in two of these cases the seats were adjacent, indicating that these neighbours likely attended games together. One of these two included accounts in the names of two married women who might have purchased their pairs of tickets for themselves and their husbands so that the two couples could attend games together. But in the other instance, two single women were account holders, one with a pair of seats and the other with one adjacent seat. In another case, two women who lived at the *same* address each subscribed to single seats that were adjacent to one another in the grey seats. Not only did these women share the same residence, perhaps as boarders, they were also both sales clerks at Eaton's department store. There are four other instances in the ledger of female account holders who also worked for the same institution subscribing to adjacent or nearby seats. Two of these four pairs of women were also employees of Eaton's. The other two pairs of co-workers were also revealing of the ways in which Maple Leaf Gardens was host to female socializing. These four women were all teachers – as noted, two each taught at Central Technical School and Orde Street Public School. The subscriptions of these four women accounted for nine seats, seven of which were in the same row in the grey seats, with the other two located in the row in front of them. These single women might have attended games together as an example of hockey spectating as a female social activity.

Ticket accounts such as these recall Joan Sangster's assertion that women's social peer groups, similarly to those of working-class men, were often formed in the workplace.[54] The average of nearly two seats per account and the fact that the majority of female subscribers (66.9 per cent) purchased two seats suggests that for them spectating was a social pastime. Although it is possible that some women purchased tickets as paid labour or domestic duties – for example, purchasing subscriptions for men who might not have had the time during the workday to travel to the arena and make their own ticket purchases – it seems clear that other women attended games at Maple Leaf Gardens as part of their leisure consumption, at times in the company of female companions.

Nevertheless, women represented a significant minority of the crowd at Maple Leaf Gardens in the mid-1930s and purchased fewer than 10 per cent of all ticket subscriptions in the 1933–34 season. It is unwise to make sweeping conclusions based on sixty-six female subscribers who purchased tickets to an arena that sat more than twelve thousand spectators. Furthermore, these sixty-six subscriptions were fewer than half of those associated with female account holders in the 1933–34 ledger. The reality is that many women who attended hockey games at Maple Leaf Gardens likely did so accompanying men who provided tickets for them.

Conclusion

Despite the important contribution of spectators to the success of commercial sport in the first half of the twentieth century, their demographic composition has proven an elusive subject for historians. To contribute to redressing this absence, this chapter has focused on a detailed analysis of the 1933–34 Maple Leaf Gardens ledger. Toronto's interwar hockey crowd was "mostly male," as men represented 88.1 per cent of account holders. Male subscribers worked more frequently in white-collar occupations than the men in Toronto's wage-earning population overall, and those who did work in blue-collar industries were more likely to occupy managerial jobs. On the basis of this occupational profile, male subscribers had an estimated average annual income of $1,936 – 57.8 per cent higher than the average income in 1931 Toronto ($1,226) – when the annual cost of living in 1930 had been estimated at $1,430. By the time that the 1933–34 Maple Leaf Gardens ledger was being compiled the economic situation was likely worse for the average Toronto wage-earner, making subscriptions to hockey tickets a luxury for many. The significant gap between general wage levels and the estimated average annual income of account holders suggests that many hockey subscribers, if not all spectators, were financially better off than the average Torontonian.

While better-off Torontonians could budget the funds required to subscribe to seats, we know little about single-game ticket purchasers. Nevertheless, a distinction can be made not only *between* ticket subscribers and Toronto's population, but also *among* ticket subscribers, with an important factor being the nature of employment (i.e., managerial/professional versus non-managerial) within occupations. A similar pattern is evident among female account holders in the arena's three cheapest sections, where their financial standing improved as their seats moved closer to the ice surface. Within all seat prices, the estimated average annual income of female account holders was substantially greater than the city-wide average for female wage-earners of $721.

Despite Smythe's explicit efforts to link his new venture to notions of feminine respectability, the revenues that made the enterprise a financial success were provided, by and large, by men. While many women attended games as the guests of male ticket purchasers, the women who subscribed to seats were similarly middle class. The majority of female subscribers for whom occupational details were available worked in clerical and service positions, and had an estimated average income of $971, 34.6 per cent higher than the city average for wage-earning women. Clerical work, despite having become an occupational ghetto for women in the interwar years, was still better paying and more common among ticket subscribers than domestic service or manufacturing jobs in the needle trades. Despite the overall middle-class status of spectators, as one moved down through Maple Leaf Gardens' stands closer to the ice the estimated average annual income and the frequency of managerial or professional employment among ticket subscribers increased.

While men and women with greater incomes could afford increasingly more expensive seats, differences in social class held between sections, for the most part, regardless of occupational category. These patterns are revealing because attempts to gentrify the spectating experience did not relax socio-economic boundaries. In fact, Smythe's attempts at selling respectability may have relied on them, with the patrons of the more expensive seats modelling attire, behaviour, and indeed aspiration. However, the 1933–34 ledger portrays the audience at Maple Leaf Gardens for only one particular season and even then only identifies a portion of the crowd, because it highlights only those customers who could afford ticket subscriptions. The identity of those people who, for example, purchased single-game tickets or lined up for standing-room sections remains somewhat hidden. Moreover, the ledgers can only tell us so much about the experience of spectating, an experience not only of watching hockey, but of engaging with the community of other spectators. This is because beyond their class, occupational, and gender identities, spectators ultimately entered Maple Leaf Gardens to watch a game. It is to this experience, understood through the memories of former spectators, that we turn in chapter 4.

Chapter Four

Community in the Stands

Having examined the efforts made by Conn Smythe and his board of directors as well as Maple Leaf Gardens' architects to locate, design, and operate their new arena in such a way as to construct a preferred spectator, it remains to consider how these efforts were received and what the experience of the new building was for spectators. While chapter 3 considered who spectators were at Maple Leaf Gardens in the 1930s, this chapter reflects upon what their attendance at Maple Leafs games meant to them. Questions of who occupied the space give way to inquiries into why people chose to spend their time spectating. How was Smythe's appeal to feminine notions of respectability received by spectators, especially those who had attended games prior to 1931? Did the building of Maple Leaf Gardens change the ways in which people spectated? Men and women might have responded to the new arena in different ways, recognizing also differences among men and among women. How did class and gender identities intersect within this space? Men attending with other men and men escorting women were both located throughout the arena. But did where they sat and who they sat next to affect their experience of spectating? How did men's spectating practices fit into their public lives, whether they were joined by their wives and girlfriends as Smythe had hoped or in the company of male friends and family members? What was women's experience of the space? Did it differ if they accompanied a male escort or attended with a group of female friends? At root, why did people choose to spectate at Maple Leaf Gardens and socialize with others?

To address such questions, this chapter introduces this book's third evidentiary pillar, a series of interviews with former Maple Leaf Gardens' spectators and employees, whose memories build upon the conclusions drawn from the archival material and ticket subscription ledgers upon which previous chapters were based. These memories

Table 4.1. Interviews conducted with or about former spectators at Maple Leaf Gardens

Interviewee (pseudonym)	Other details
Claudia	–
Colin	–
Donald	–
Emily	–
Ernest	–
Flora	–
Frank	–
Grant	Subject of interview was Lillian (grandmother)
Harry	–
Howard	Interviewed with Olive (spouse)
Irene	–
James	–
John	–
Katherine	–
Lawrence	–
Marjorie	Interviewed with Nancy
Nancy	Interviewed with Marjorie
Olive	Interviewed with Howard (spouse)
Stuart	–
Vic	–
William	Subject of interview was Patricia (family's domestic servant)

paint a picture of the spectator experience at Toronto's then-new arena. Interviews were conducted with (or about) twenty-one former spectators, whose names are listed in Table 4.1. Consistent with standards of research ethics, these people are referred to by pseudonyms, but for the sake of clarity they are cited by these first names, while the written recollections of others are associated with full names or their last name only.

With the exception of two interviews, all twenty-one of the discussions conducted in connection with spectating at Maple Leaf Gardens focused on the interviewees' own experiences of the arena in the 1930s. In the other two cases, interviewees recounted the spectator experiences of a family member or close acquaintance. In all, the interviews capture the experiences of twenty-one people, eleven men and ten women, all white. Given the chronological distance, most of these people were adolescents or young adults when they first visited Toronto's new arena. However, three of the interviewees worked at Maple Leaf Gardens during the 1930s, and a fourth played for the Maple Leafs hockey club in the years before the Second World War.

While extremely rich sources, these interviews have limitations as historical evidence. One challenge in studying the experiences of spectators in the 1930s at Maple Leaf Gardens is that the building remained a cultural touchstone in Toronto until its closing in 1999. Inevitably people's memories of the 1930s are filtered through subsequent experiences of the arena and the nature of modern spectating. Additionally, few of the people interviewed had rarely, if ever, turned an analytical eye towards their spectating. In their estimation, understandably, there was little reason to. Many noted that they were too focused on the game they were watching to have thought critically about what was going on around them.

In spite of such issues, interviews of this nature are a valuable resource. Two of the primary methodological benefits of oral history – giving voice to traditionally silent historical actors and providing details of everyday life – are important to the study of spectators.[1] While oral history, as Linda Shopes observes, "is inevitably an act of memory," this need not be an evidentiary weakness.[2] It is not the job of the historian to confirm or disprove the recollections of interview participants. As Alessandro Portelli argues, any "discrepancy between fact and memory ultimately enhances the value of the oral sources as historical documents." Memory is not the poor cousin of "fact," but rather "an effort to make sense of crucial events of history" and the process of making sense helps to uncover the meaningfulness of an event as seemingly everyday as watching a hockey game. As Portelli concludes: "Beyond the event as such, the real and significant historical fact which these narratives highlight is the memory itself."[3] Indeed, the late Canadian novelist Paul Quarrington described his Maple Leaf Gardens memories as "a jumble of facts and feelings, often contrasting, even contradictory." Yet, he continues, "everyone sees and remembers things differently … I am not an expert on any facet of the Gardens except what the building means to me."[4]

What Maple Leaf Gardens meant to the people interviewed for this book is the foundation upon which this chapter is built. It sketches out the "typical" experience of a hockey spectator in 1930s Toronto, using the recollections of former spectators, buttressed by contemporary press accounts. It catalogues the spectating experience in the 1930s, following the pattern of an evening at Maple Leaf Gardens: from preparing for the game and arriving at the Gardens, to acquiring tickets and entering the arena, to taking a seat (or standing) and engaging with the both the spectacle on the ice and other spectators.

The people experiencing a game on any given night were likely more diverse than the crowd suggested by the demographics of those who could afford ticket subscriptions. Following the characterization of an evening spent watching hockey at Maple Leaf Gardens, this chapter proceeds to explore what spectating meant to spectators, specifically the ways in which the practice offered an opportunity for socializing with family, friends, partners, or co-workers. Considering how spectators understood the space they were entering is the first step in foregrounding the spectator experience. As elsewhere, issues of social class and, in particular, gender relations are highlighted for the ways in which they contoured the experience of watching commercial sport.

A Night at the Gardens

James recalls that Toronto in the 1930s "was known as the city of homes and city of churches." A man whose wife was a former Radio City Music Hall Rockette chorus line dancer, James regretted that in Toronto "there were no bars, no night life to speak of." Maple Leaf Gardens became a focal point of much of the city's social life. The arena was Toronto's largest public meeting place and Irene recalls that "it was the only place for big things [events] to come to." As a result, the building held an important position in Toronto's public consciousness, and its opening was much anticipated. Nancy recalls the excitement in Toronto as Maple Leaf Gardens was being erected: "This building was going up and nobody knew what it was going to be." Once it was finished, Howard remembers a civic landmark that "wasn't just a drowsy old building sitting up some side street" (which may be an oblique reference to Arena Gardens on Mutual Street). Indeed, Maple Leaf Gardens "was lit up like the Taj Majal." There was, however, the potential for expectations to be set too high. Donald remembers "one of the fellows from our hockey team," who went to Maple Leaf Gardens. "I said, 'what did you think of the Gardens?' and he said, 'oh, nothing really, just ordinary.' And I was more disappointed than he was 'cause I'd built it up so much in my mind." Howard recalls first entering the Gardens' third tier of seats: "you turned around and looked at the Gardens and everything you heard and read and saw about it and there it was down there, this little oval. [laughing] You know, it seemed just like a little toy oval."

Arriving

Making his new building visible and accessible had been important issues for Smythe during his negotiations with the T. Eaton Company in 1931 concerning the location of the new arena. He would later recall that his insistence on the lot at the intersection of Church and Carlton Streets was based in part upon the public transportation routes that serviced the intersection: "I thought right on Carlton would be better. There were street cars on Yonge, a block away, another line on Carlton, another on Church."[5] The Toronto Transportation Commission (TTC), which in 1921 had centralized the city's streetcar and bus service, had, by 1930, "over 250 miles of track and almost 1,300 vehicles and that year serviced about 200 million passengers over twenty-six different routes."[6] Although ridership peaked in 1929 at more than two hundred million passengers annually, bottomed out in 1933, and barely reached 150 million by the end of the decade, public transportation remained an affordable way to get around Toronto.[7] Indeed, with "an average fare of a little more than 6 cents (with free transfer privileges), TTC fares were among the lowest on the continent."[8] Not surprisingly, a considerable number of spectators travelled to Maple Leaf Gardens in the 1930s using public transportation. As James recalls, "you [would] take a streetcar to the Maple Leaf Gardens and think nothing of it" (see Fig. 4.1).

The ability of public transit officials to handle not just arrivals to Maple Leaf Gardens but departing spectators as well was praised by the media. The *Globe* editorial page, linking crowd management at the new arena to Toronto's civic standing, noted of the Gardens' first evening of hockey that "Police and Transportation Commission officials are being congratulated on their successful handling of traffic problems created by the vast crowd of people assembled for the opening of the new arena." The TTC officials, who could not "say when the hockey contest would end," came in for special praise for their capable management, as "T.T.C. cars seemed to appear instantly from all directions ... and literally swooped down for their passengers when the first rush out of the arena was observed."[9]

Not all opening-night patrons arrived via one of the nearby streetcar lines. Yet in the surrounding neighbourhood, noted the *Globe*, "there were not great open spaces, such as at the Exhibition Grounds, for the parking of cars." Traffic officials, like their TTC colleagues, ably dispersed the opening-night crowd as "cool heads were in command, with well-trained men prepared to carry out prepared plans."[10] Tom Gaston, his father, and his older brother were among the spectators who travelled to the game by car that November 1931 evening. Gaston recalled that "Dad knew there would be a lot of traffic that night, so we parked at a tire shop owned by one of his friends. It wasn't far to walk to the Gardens from there."[11] Similarly, Vic remembers that he "used to take my dad's car ... [and] park on Jarvis Street," east of the arena. Automobile access was important, because Maple Leaf Gardens attracted a crowd from a wide geographic area. For their first visits to the arena in the 1930s, Donald's family travelled from Lindsay, northeast of Toronto; Frank and his brothers drove in from Kitchener, to the west; and Ernest and his father came from Whitby in the east. All three of these communities were more than an hour's commute from Maple Leaf Gardens by means of transportation available in the 1930s.

Fig. 4.1. An exterior view of Maple Leaf Gardens, including the streetcar
that stopped outside the arena and the United Cigar Store on the corner of
Church and Carlton Streets, as the Maple Leafs prepared to host the New York
Americans (14 March 1939). (City of Toronto Archives, Globe and Mail fonds,
Fonds 1266, Item 57299)

Nevertheless, many of the former spectators interviewed for this book
who arrived on public transportation sat in the less expensive green and
grey seats and, moreover, viewed this as a typical experience shared by
most hockey patrons. According to Harry, spectators eschewed driving
to the Gardens "'cause parking wasn't the best down there." But for Lawrence, the "TTC was the main transportation" because "in the thirties,
there wasn't as many cars then." Nancy has similar memories: "The Depression was on at that time and there wasn't many people had cars." She
recalls attending a famous 1933 playoff game, which ended in the sixth
overtime period after a goal by the Maple Leafs' Ken Doraty. When those
spectators who stayed until the game's late conclusion exited Maple Leaf
Gardens they were greeted by "about ten or twelve streetcars all lined
up waiting to take the crowds away." The journey home that evening
for Nancy and her father was no small undertaking: "We had to take
two streetcars and a bus to get home. Well, it must have been after two
o'clock by the time we got home."

Hockey spectators who were prepared to embark on such a lengthy and involved round trip–outing viewed an evening at Maple Leaf Gardens as an important social occasion and often dressed accordingly. The expectations of the appearance of the respectable spectator were often met. Harry recalls, "you couldn't go scruffy," and James concurs, "we'd go in suits, and shirts and ties of course." Grant remembers that for his grandmother, Lillian, "it was very important to dress up" for her weekly Saturday night visits to the Gardens. What Lillian called her "fancy clothes," Grant recalls, "were meant for going out to the hockey game and then she made a big point about how well dressed they [she and her companions] all were." Despite these recollections, other spectators assert that how they were attired was a relatively minor component of their attendance at hockey games. Emily wore the "winter clothing that I had at that time" and was just happy "to get out of the nursing uniform." Men have similar memories. Harry notes, "I had a tie on and maybe a windbreaker," and Howard just "put on my camel hair coat."

Expectations of dress varied depending upon a spectator's location within Maple Leaf Gardens. Lawrence, who was on the staff at Maple Leaf Gardens during the 1930s, remembers that "People in the red section – that's the most expensive seats – they would all come very well dressed." Peggy Moxton remembered her parents dressing up on the nights that they used their rail-seat tickets. Her mother "always dressed for games in a woman's suit with a frilly white blouse and, I remember so well, a hat of velvet pansies."[12] However, Flora recalls that, in the grey seats, "they just wore their ordinary clothes," and Marjorie concurs that "in the cheapies, no, [you] didn't dress up." Flora remembers that her father "always wore a tie" to Maple Leaf Gardens: "Most men did in those days." This extended well beyond the arena. "We all wore shirts, suits, and ties in those days," recalls James, and men would "put on a fedora to go down to the store or go downtown," remembers Ernest. Similar prescriptions held for women. Katherine remembers that "we used to wear a hat and gloves." She "wore slacks in the house, but I never went out with them on." In fact, "you wouldn't think of even going downtown without proper dress." Watching hockey at Maple Leaf Gardens fit within these expectations of public display and, Lawrence suggests, "as a general rule, most of the people who came to the games wore their best."

Many people who spent an evening at Maple Leaf Gardens incorporated dinner beforehand into their night's plans, which is why during the 1930s games did not start until 8:30 p.m. Spectators "would go out to early dinner and be all duded up and then they'd come to the Gardens, or they'd come all duded up and then go out afterwards," remembers Colin, who was himself more likely to go out for fish and chips with his other teenaged friends after a game. This recognition that hockey spectators' dinner routines accompanied getting "duded up," suggests that an evening out on the occasion of a Maple Leafs match was more likely among the Gardens' better-off patrons during the Depression, and former spectators who sat in the box seats recall patronizing some of Toronto's more exclusive eateries before games. Flora and her family dined at the King Edward Hotel, while John and his family went to the University Club. He remembers the routine that accompanied evenings spent at Maple Leaf Gardens: "We'd go to the University Club, share a bottle of Mumm's amongst us, have dinner, and be in our seats in time for the game to start. And that's what the other people in the boxes would do. They'd go out someplace for dinner and make a whole evening of it."

Nevertheless, spectators who sat in a variety of locations throughout the arena enjoyed similar experiences, different from that of John's family more in degree than kind. Katherine and her husband, who "might end up in the greens or greys, right up on top," dined before Maple Leafs games at "Murray's on Front Street, almost near the Royal York [Hotel]." Other spectators ate much closer to Maple Leaf Gardens, at the restaurant on Carlton Street, opposite the arena's main entrance. This included Frank and his older brothers, who "if we were there early we often went in the Gardens' restaurant … they had in the lobby … Just next to the ticket booth was a little coffee shop."[13]

Regardless of how they were dressed or how they got there, as spectators approached Maple Leaf Gardens for an evening's hockey game they were confronted with a variety of sights and sounds.[14] Nancy remembers seeing "scalpers outside selling the tickets," while Howard vividly recalls arriving at the arena for the first time:

> Coming in, outside there 're all these people milling around. I said to my dad, "what are all these guys doing?"
>
> "They're selling tickets." [whispering] You know, ticket scalpers.
>
> 'Course I didn't have a clue what the business was. And I said, "Daddy, what are all these guys selling all the tickets outside the Gardens for?" My dad explained to me in words of one syllable that they were scalpers. I didn't know what a scalper was at that point.

Entering

Hopeful spectators who arrived at the arena without tickets, and who chose not to patronize scalpers, sought out more "respectable" ways to gain entrance to the evening's game. The most common sight outside the Gardens in relation to ticket purchases were the people waiting for standing room only general admissions to go on sale (see Fig. 4.2). In addition to the crowds that mingled outside the Gardens, many spectators entered the building's main entrance to visit one of the two ticket offices

Fig. 4.2. A line-up outside Maple Leaf Gardens to purchase tickets to a playoff game, c. 1932. (*Maple Leaf Gardens Programme*, 1932–33)

in the lobby to collect their subscribed tickets or to enquire as to which seats – possibly uncollected subscriptions – were still available. They entered a lobby that was anything but grand. For spectators, the lobby was a space primarily to be moved through as they sought access to their seats within the arena proper (see Fig. 4.3). Outside of Frank's memory of visiting the Maple Leaf Gardens coffee shop, few former spectators recalled spending any significant time in the arena lobby. Nevertheless, the lobby was also where spectators waited, as former Maple Leafs player Stuart recalls, to attempt to get autographs from players (see Fig. 4.9).

Despite the culture of middle-class respectability with which Smythe sought to cloak Maple Leaf Gardens and, more specifically, attendance at events hosted there, transgression of these expectations was immediately apparent upon entering the building. Not only did scalpers patrol the sidewalks outside the arena, they were also "always" to be found within the Gardens, according to Colin. The *Telegram* noted of one March 1937 game that "Before the game scalpers were in the lobby trying to get rid of blue tickets for one dollar."[15] This was not the only economy to make its home in Maple Leaf Gardens' lobby. Ernest's "memory is of big, burly men," in the lobby, "passing the money back and forth … I guess they had bets on the first goal

Fig. 4.3. The turnstiles in Maple Leaf Gardens' lobby as captured by a *Globe and Mail* photographer for a meeting (15 March 1939) of the short-lived Leadership League, started by the newspaper's owner, George McCullagh. (City of Toronto Archives, Globe and Mail fonds, Fonds 1266, Item 57310)

and the outcome and that sort of thing." These were not illicit exchanges, as they were "quite well known and even recounted in newspapers," according to Ernest. From the opening of the Gardens in 1931, the press commented on "the boys in Peacock Alley" who "didn't know where to congregate for their Woolworth wagering" and were searching for their "place" within the culture of the new arena.[16] By January 1937, gamblers took bets in the lobby and had found a home within the arena, as "the boys in the wagering ring" could be found "on the east side behind the blue section."[17]

Regardless of their presence – and perhaps even because of a transgressive thrill associated with being around them – gambling and profiteering did little to quell the excitement that Torontonians in the 1930s felt at the prospect of their first visit to the new arena. Donald recalls "I don't think I slept [the night] before I went there." So excited was the thirteen-year-old on the occasion of his first visit to Maple Leaf Gardens that, while at dinner at the restaurant across from the arena before the game, "my father said I was continually walking up to the front and

Fig. 4.4. Toronto hockey spectators new to Maple Leaf Gardens discovered an arena space larger than any they had encountered before, pictured here in the second period of a Maple Leafs versus Boston playoff game, 30 March 1933. (City of Toronto Archives, Globe and Mail fonds, Fonds 1266, Item 29464)

looking out the window to see that the Gardens didn't disappear." Ernest recounts the story of his friend who, upon walking into Maple Leaf Gardens asked "where's the ice?" because "he got in the doors and he expected the ice to be right there" like in the small-town rinks around which he had grown up. Once inside the turnstiles, Donald remembers "the rustling crowds, everyone in motion, the noise of the streetcars, the crowds going in through the gate and meeting the programme vendors," of which he noted, "of course, you had to have a programme."

Nevertheless, while people remember the lobby and other congregational spaces, it is their first impressions of the inner arena space that former spectators most frequently recall. Howard first experienced Maple Leaf Gardens through "a young guy's eyes getting boggled by the sights of this sort of famous emporium that you'd heard all about; it's like going to Buckingham Palace." Emily remembers that "Maple Leaf Gardens seemed to be immense," although what was impressive to James was both "the size of the place and the fact that it was packed with people" (see Fig. 4.4).

It was not just the people, but the seats they filled, that struck Tom Gaston. They "were so bright. And everything smelled new – I'll never forget it."[18]

Taking a Seat

Gaston, his brother, and their father looked down from their vantage point in Maple Leaf Gardens' least expensive seats upon the largest indoor space in Canada. Below them were three tiers of seating (including their own) as well as boxes and a row of rail seats closest to the ice surface. Considering these sections from the Gastons' viewpoint as they looked down on opening night from the third tier is fitting as Maple Leaf Gardens was designed to focus its inhabitants' attention down towards the ice.

The Gastons sat in the seats furthest from the ice, the arena's third tier (the "greys"). The distance of the grey seats from the ice stands out in the memory of former spectators. Harry notes that, in the years prior to the installation of escalators at Maple Leaf Gardens (which occurred in 1955), "you used to have to walk up to the greys, 100, 101 steps, and come down about 20 steps." There were similar accessibility issues throughout the arena (see Fig. 4.5). Harry goes on to recall that "my aunt and uncle," who took him to hockey games, "were getting up in age in those days and they did it," walking up and down the stairs. Howard remembers his father, who had a sustained a serious leg injury during the First World War, happily struggling up the stairs to the third tier at Maple Leaf Gardens, but adds, "you thought you never were going to get there." The *Telegram* worried that the "boys in the back sections certainly look as if they are up on the moulding and we trust none of them give way to vertigo," while Emily recalls wishing that the boyfriend who took her to hockey games would "spend a bit more" and purchase better seats. Her concerns were related to the view of the game from the grey seats: "we'd get up to see [the action on the ice] from where we were sitting 'cause we were so bloomin' high up." Frank also recalls: "I had seats in the greys and they were, it was a long way up. Like it was tough to see ... You could see the plays, but it was tough to see the players."

It was from the second tier – in the first row of the greens – that Smythe regularly watched his hockey team play. John, who often sat with Smythe, recalls that "from this viewpoint," Smythe "could see the games developing." The print media were accorded a similarly good vantage point from which to report on Maple Leafs games. The press were important to Smythe's respectability project and the new arena housed members of the media in a press box located at the front of the second tier on

Fig. 4.5. The stairs that the majority of spectators had to climb to reach their tier of seats, pictured here before a performance by the Metropolitan Opera in the 1950s. Those spectators in the seats furthest from the ice had to navigate multiple staircases. (City of Toronto Archives, Fonds 1257, Series 1057, Item 6941)

Maple Leaf Gardens' east side.[19] The accommodations were the envy of the media that travelled with teams visiting Maple Leaf Gardens. As the Montreal *Gazette* noted, "Toronto's newspaper fraternity is well accommodated in the new amphitheatre, the large press box being situated just behind the first section of seats. It affords a splendid view of the ice. A press room, completely equipped, is also given over to those who chronicle events for the sports pages."[20]

Directly in front of the press box, the first tier of seats, painted the Maple Leafs' team colour, blue, ran along either length of the ice surface as well as along the north and south ends of the rink. Despite John's claim that Smythe found the first row of the side greens to be his preferred location, Bruce Hunter remembers his grandfather, Bryce Beverly Hunter, recounting the story of touring Maple Leaf Gardens with Smythe while the arena was under construction. The two men "selected what they both thought were the best seats ... first row end blues right over visitor goal ...

balcony front ... no one in front, never had to look around anyone, close enough to hear!! the action, high enough to see play develop and the other end."[21]

By contrast, John asserts that "the worst position for seeing a hockey game is the one that the coach has [at ice level] because when something happens everyone stands up and he can't see what's going on." Regardless, spectators' perceptions of the red box and rail seats closest to the ice, to say nothing of their price, marked these spaces as Maple Leaf Gardens' preferred locations. "Well," notes Vic, "the reds had cushions," and Grant remembers that his grandmother "talked about 'fancy people,' as she would say," who were "very dressed up and sitting ... closer to ice." Spectators more accustomed to sitting in less expensive seats remember visits to the box and rail seats as a special event. Donald sat with his father and his father's friends in the rail seats. These were not located right against the boards. Rather, as Donald remembers, "there was actually a rail in front of you." These seats offered "a clear view," he recalls. "There was no heads in front of us." But for Peggy Moxton's parents, this meant "no barrier in front to deflect flying pucks," which is why "the rail seats were terrible seats to watch the game," in John's estimation.[22]

John also recalls that "a lot of my friends went down and paid seventy-five cents for standing room behind the greys." The advantage of these spaces was that the Gardens had "this huge dome with no columns in it," so that in standing room, "every view was unobstructed" – except perhaps by someone standing in front of you. Frank remembers that inside Maple Leaf Gardens there was "a big steel gate" barring access to the standing-room sections. "It was an organized line 'til they opened the gate [laughing]." He goes on to note: "I think the standing room went in at seven o'clock [p.m.] and you lined up about six thirty, quarter to seven, and when they let the standing room in everybody ran and got up." Ernest remembers that "a big sight was to see people get standing room tickets and then rush in and try to get the best location to watch the game." Standing-room culture had its own "hurry up and wait" ebb and flow. The waiting in line and mad dash up the Gardens' stairs to grab a preferred location were capped off each game night by a further hour of loitering in anticipation of the players taking the ice, unable to move for fear of losing a choice vantage point. "The games were started at 8:30 [p.m.]," recalls Frank. "I'm not sure if we got in at 7:00 or 7:30, but I know you had to be there for at least an hour before."

As the game was in progress, the men in the standing-room section – and it is remembered as an almost entirely male space – stood two or three deep. Frank recalls that, as a boy, "I got in the front row." But the rest of the spectators would "have to find containers to stand on and the tallest ones were always at the best advantage," remembers Ernest. "They'd improvise and try to find something to elevate themselves and be able to see over the fedoras of the people in front of them." As with patrons throughout the arena, standees developed their own spectating behaviours, practices, and strategies. While there was access to standing room via all four corner stairways in Maple Leaf Gardens, Frank remembers that he and his brothers entered from Carlton Street and "turned left. Left is the way we always went up to the standing room. Now I would think it went up both ways, but ... we always got into the line that we went up the left side." Getting the best possible vantage point was also a product of experience. Frank asserts that "the ideal spot for standing room was at the end." Running up the stairs to find a space was one strategy, but it helped if you knew where you were headed. As Frank recalls, "A lot of people went along the side, but you had to go [up] one more [flight of stairs] to get up to the ends. So the people that knew where they were going there wanted to get up to the ends [and] took that one more turn to get up to the end zone ... If you didn't mind standing that was a lot better place to watch the game than from the greys."

Beyond the Game

Once patrons were in their seats, there were some elements of the spectating experience that all of them shared. They sat within an arena that, even though on opening night "management also made a mistake in turning on too much heat," was still "a cool place."[23] James recalls that those women who wore evening dresses to Maple Leaf Gardens "must have had some outer wrappings around them," while the *Star* noted that a Mrs. A.L. Ross "plans to attend the opening game warmly clad in a royal blue Poncho."[24] In a facility whose social meaning was tied so overtly to feminine cultural values, it is worth noting that these concerns over climate highlight women's comfort. Music was another of the creature comforts offered in Smythe's new ice palace. Frank recalls standing "right under the bandstand" where the national anthem was played, while Gaston has a more vivid memory: "Every time the Leafs stepped onto the ice to start the game or a new period, the organist would play 'The Maple Leaf Forever.'"[25]

The music that welcomed the Maple Leafs back onto the ice to begin each period also signalled the end of intermission, which former spectators experienced in different ways. Both Ernest and Harry remember men from the arena staff pulling barrels of water and carrying brooms and scrapers to re-surface the ice between periods, however the former recalls that during intermissions "music blared and the crowds filled the hallways," while the latter asserts that "nothing happened between periods." Yet spectators were capable of entertaining themselves. Frank remembers that "between periods, up in the blues and that, there'd be somebody with balloons and they'd start bouncing those balloons around … See how long they could keep 'em going." However, intermissions held fewer opportunities for excitement for standing-room patrons as hard-earned vantage points had to be safeguarded, so "you pretty well had to stay there," Frank recalls. These spectators were not the only ones who remained in the arena during intermission. Even though Marjorie does not "remember them putting on entertainment during an intermission," those people who did remain in their seats were occasionally entertained by on-ice ceremonies, such as the presentation of the Velma Springstead Award – also known as the "Rose Bowl" of the Women's Amateur Athletic Federation – to Noel MacDonald of the Edmonton Grads basketball club, recognizing her as Canada's premier female athlete, during the second intermission of a February 1939 game between the Maple Leafs and Boston Bruins.[26] William Kilbourn recalled his more maudlin first visit to Maple Leaf Gardens in the 1934–35 season. He described a first-intermission ceremony that honoured the memory of former Chicago Black Hawks goaltender Charlie Gardiner, who died on 13 June 1934: "As if it was not enough excitement for an eight-year-old boy to see his first period of NHL hockey, the vast cavern was darkened at intermission, and a small black box (with ashes in it? or was it a shrunken head?) was set out under a spotlight on a little stand at centre ice. A trumpeter sounded Last Post, and after a minute's silence, Reveille."[27]

In the concourse areas of Maple Leaf Gardens during intermissions, "you'd find a lot of little clusters all discussing the pros and cons of what happened in the previous period." One reason that spectators left their seats during intermissions, continues Howard, was to "go down and get food or refreshments" (see Fig. 4.6). Although these memories are perhaps influenced by more recent experiences, Donald suggests that "the concession business wasn't big in those days" and John calls them "pretty primitive … I mean you could get a Vernor's Ginger Ale between periods but it [the concession stand] wasn't very attractive." Nevertheless, concession sales were important enough to the economy of the 1930s arena that three of the people interviewed for this book worked at Maple Leaf Gardens selling food, beverages, or programmes. Lawrence remembers the items he sold while walking up and down through the stands: "Peanuts, popcorn, apples, Cracker Jacks, chocolate bars, chewing gum. All confectionaries." Additional items were for sale at the concession stands in the concourse areas that Claudia and others staffed, and from which Ernest's father purchased an ice cream bar for his son that was still memorable seventy years later.

Fig. 4.6. The concourse area (at ground level, with directions to box and rail seats), where many spectators congregated between periods, pictured here on 12 April 1955, when the newly installed escalators at Maple Leaf Gardens opened. (City of Toronto Archives, Fonds 1257, Series 1057, Item 7426)

Colin and his brother "sold the programmes around the box [seats] and rails." They worked for a year at Arena Gardens on Mutual Street before joining the new arena's staff as young teenagers. They were among the approximately seventy people – "a lot of them were fairly old," Lawrence recalls – who sold programmes, food, and other concessions both in the stands and at stalls located in the Gardens' corridors. Lawrence summarized his routine as a Maple Leaf Gardens' concessionaire: "between periods we sold the stuff we had and then once the game started, we sat down and watched the game." Similarly, Colin's honest assessment of his and his brother's commitment to their programme-selling jobs is that "our main interest really was watching" the Maple Leafs play. The pair would "sell programmes 'til about five or ten minutes after the game got started, then we'd ... find a spot around the Gardens somewhere." Noting that "there was lots of seats that were empty in those days," the two teenagers would "hang around the boxes and rails, 'cause the ushers they all knew us. So, they would let us find a spot and not bother us."

One beverage that was not for sale at Maple Leaf Gardens, or any other non-licensed public establishment in 1930s Toronto, was alcohol.[28] This is not to suggest that beer and other spirits did not find their way into the Gardens. John Moor, who once played cornet in the Toronto Irish Regiment band at the Gardens before joining the arena staff and moving up to supervisor of ticket takers, recalled "a drunken senior hockey fan who staggered to his seat and promptly passed out. 'At the end of the game, I woke him up and told him it was time to go home. "When's the game start?" he asked me.'"[29]

Regardless of what fans were consuming, the need to relieve oneself was often a desire satisfied during intermission. The nature of the restroom facilities – including the oft-remembered stainless-steel troughs – still stands out in the memories of male former spectators. Harry recalls the "big trough" that served as a urinal: "I've never, ever seen anything like that other than [at] Maple Leaf Gardens." Vic remembers "it was like an eave," so that "all the urine went downhill, you see, so the little guys [would] be down at one end. So, it suited everybody [laughing]." Beyond heeding nature's call, Flora recalls what she believes was the most common reason for spectators to leave their seats during intermission: "Oh, you went out and had a cigarette, but you had to go outside. Not outside but out of where the ice was. They wouldn't allow you to smoke where the players were playing." Former spectators recall the designated lounges as well as smoke-filled lobbies and corridors where, as Ernest notes, "smoking was so common."

Surroundings such as these attracted some well-remembered patrons. The *Globe* noted in March 1932 that two hundred Montreal fans were travelling to Toronto on "a special excursion train" for that evening's Canadiens–Maple Leafs game "decked out in red caps and sweaters," suggesting that fans of visiting teams may have formed identifiable groups within the Gardens' crowd.[30] Nevertheless, well-known celebrities attending Maple Leafs games do not feature prominently in either spectators' remembrances or popular legend. Famous Torontonians who did attend games, notes Lawrence, "were down in the red seats … and I'd be working up all over the top of the building, so we wouldn't see them too often."

Yet, certain spectators did capture the imagination of regular patrons. Gaston remembered "an elderly fan named Edith Mitchell who always used to send apple pies to the players. They used to call her 'Apple Annie.'"[31] Colin recalls her as a somewhat more combative personality: "she'd give the players she didn't like, she'd give 'em hell. If she happened to be there and see them before the game she'd give 'em hell and she'd give 'em hell after the game." But perhaps the best-known individual spectator was John Arnott, the owner of a gas station in Toronto's west end, who John recalls as "a guy on the end blue that had a marvellous voice that could fill the whole Gardens." Arnott supported Maple Leafs centre Pete Langelle in a very unique way, as he "would yell from the greens, 'COME ONNNNNNNNNNN, PETERRRRRRRRRR!' The crowd would go wild."[32] Note how Arnott shifts in geographic memory from the end blues to the side greens, as though his was a voice from above that could not be precisely located. After Langelle left the club in the mid-1940s, Arnott switched allegiances to Ted "Teeder" Kennedy and cries of "C'mon Teeder" echoed through the Gardens. Arnott, however, is remembered as much for timing as for volume, as his bellowing enlivened a hushed atmosphere. "He always waited until there was silence," recalls former Maple Leafs player Stuart, "just before a faceoff or something and the fans ... were quiet, and that's when he made his big statement. You could hear him all over the rink."

From the Drop of the Puck

Despite the sensations and distractions that surrounded them, spectators were most focused on the game taking place on the ice, and Arnott offers a useful starting point for examining the nature of this engagement. Was he a noisy iconoclast within a sea of Smythe's respectable preferred spectators or was he just one example, one that has survived within Maple Leaf Gardens' popular lore, of boisterous, individual spectatorship? On the most general level, spectators recall the crowd possessing what Lillian called "a very lively spirit." In certain circumstances, the atmosphere at Maple Leaf Gardens was described as "frenzied." On the occasion of the Maple Leafs eliminating Boston in the 1936 NHL playoffs, the *Globe* – which was encouraged by Smythe and his staff, as all Toronto newspapers were, to report events from the Gardens in the breathless tones typical of the era – noted that "Maple Leaf Gardens last night was no place for fans with heart trouble. It is doubtful if the building ever before reverberated to the swells of such excitement crazed vocal efforts. The Leafs had asked for support from the crowd, and they certainly were given it; given it in a manner that showed what Toronto fans, critical as they become at times, think of their team in the final analysis. The crowd scene matched the game spectacle itself as hockey's frenzied fandom reached new heights of enthusiasm."[33]

Such a scene fit perfectly within the respectable "enthusiastic support" that Maple Leafs president J.P. Bickell had requested of Toronto's hockey patrons from the very first night at Maple Leaf Gardens (see Fig. 4.7).[34] Spectators, Ernest recalls, "would cheer

Fig. 4.7. Spectators celebrate Ken Doraty's third-period goal in a playoff game versus Boston (30 March 1933). Two games later, Doraty scored the series-winning goal in the sixth overtime period. (City of Toronto Archives, Globe and Mail fonds, Fonds 1266, Item 29471)

appropriately, at appropriate times, when the Leafs would get a goal or get a scoring chance." Howard agrees that "there was no rowdiness in those days. It was very respectful ... They cheered, but very modestly." While Harry recalls "hollerin'" occurring only at specific moments: "It was more or less a goal scored, they hurrayed." The establishment of a respectable spectating environment – perpetuated by convention and emulation – may explain why spectators have a difficult time recalling Toronto fans in the 1930s booing, barracking, or generally venting their displeasure. Donald recalls that "I think there was some booing. I don't remember individual cases of it. But later in the Gardens I remember fans, one fan near me, years later, like twenty or thirty years later, singling out a player and just settling on him the whole game because he was a defenceman that was having a bad time and would cough up the puck a lot. But I don't remember anything like that in the thirties."

Basketball coach Percy Page "was struck by the dead atmosphere in the Gardens," telling the *Telegram,* "There was very little cheering, to my surprise."[35] Similarly, former Maple Leafs player Stuart remembers spectators in Toronto being "sedate" compared to audiences in other NHL cities, while, during his time as a concessionaire, Lawrence recalls, "hardly any noise at all whatsoever. Fifteen thousand people and you'd think you were in church; there's very little noise." Yet, akin to the tales of Arnott, he also remembers that there were "maybe five or ten people with loud voice[s] ... [and you] could hear them all over the ice." Indeed, even those spectators who remember the atmosphere at Maple Leaf Gardens as somewhat reserved had experiences that undermine these general characterizations. John notes that while "Toronto crowds were considered to be less demonstrative than those in other cities," this "wasn't my experience ... where I was sitting, because there was always somebody yelling at the referee or yelling at the players."

Spectators were involved with the spectacle at Maple Leaf Gardens in ways that pushed the boundaries of what was considered respectable. They were engaged with action on the ice, but also with each other. Colin recalls that "the only games I'd go to would be the Boston [Bruins] and [New York] American[s]," because he had friends playing for both teams. On the evenings those teams played in Toronto, he actively rooted for the visitors. "Well then I'd be sitting there," he remembers, "and this guy, a real hot Maple Leaf fan, he really got hot about me going in there cheering for every club but the Leafs. Oh, we used to get into some pretty good arguments." Nevertheless, "I never saw any fights at the Gardens." The behaviour of spectators might change, however, if they felt their on-ice allegiances threatened. At a March 1935 game, the Maple Leafs' Red Horner was involved in an altercation with Boston's Babe Siebert in the penalty box. Rather than remaining a passive observer, one "indignant spectator ... aroused Siebert by shouting invectives at him," noted the *Globe.*[36] The *Star* also remarked that Siebert "was roused again to berserk rage by a spectator who cursed him."[37] This particular patron was a man, but female spectators were also vocal in their support of the home team, often in ways that might have challenged the presumed norms of feminine respectability on which Smythe hoped to capitalize. From the opening night at Maple Leaf Gardens, the *Telegram* observed that female spectators "wanted to cheer and raise general 'whoopee.'"[38] The paper's women's sports columnist, Phyllis Griffiths, echoed these sentiments, noting that "the fair ones put the O.K. stamp on the new arena" and predicting that "it is a certainty that soprano shrieks and squeals will be prominently included in the Leafs rooting brigade this winter."[39]

But spectators at Maple Leaf Gardens did more than use their voices
while interacting with the spectacle they were paying to watch. They
participated in physical ways that further challenge portrayals and expectations of a respectable, perhaps passive, observer. Long-time radio
and television broadcaster Foster Hewitt observed that "when a rumpus
started and the players clashed, many spectators stood up and blocked
the view of others."[40] Spectators would often take advantage of the opportunity to vent their frustration during a fight by throwing objects onto
the ice. The most common projectile was that evening's programme.
Donald's first visit to Maple Leaf Gardens was memorable because of an
altercation between Horner and Boston's star defenceman, Eddie Shore:
"a great fight ensued and down came the programmes from the spectators." Sitting in the rinkside seats, Donald jumped over the rail and
collected his first childhood souvenir by claiming one of the many programmes discarded by disgruntled spectators. He is still unsure "whether
the spectators threw them in derision, in disagreement over the fight, or
just in the whole excitement of it all."

Programme tossing often followed a referee's decision that went against
the home team. On occasions such as these, most officials responded as
referee Ag Smith did during a January 1937 game, when he "refused
to change his mind despite the burning words that poured upon him
from assembled Leafian choristers."[41] The referee's decision to disallow
a Toronto goal "was the signal for a wild verbal outbreak by the Leafs and
their supporters ... Programs flew into the air and their [sic] was quite a
delay before the arguing subsided, the ice was partially cleared of paper,
and play resumed."[42] Spectator frustrations with officials infrequently es-
calated to physical violence. After a February 1935 game, "an irate fan
attempted to attack Referee Bill Stewart, and was promptly ejected from
the Gardens by a hu[s]ky man in blue." While the *Globe* continued that
"this particular spectator evidently takes himself too seriously," at times it
was the men on the ice who took the intervention of spectators into the
proceedings "too seriously."[43] Long-time NHL referee Bill Chadwick recalled an evening at Maple Leaf Gardens where a spectator "sitting right
along the sideboards, was giving me an awful verbal beating ... he even
held my referee's sweater and prevented me from jumping quickly back
into the action." When the same man held Chadwick's sweater again, the
frustrated referee "swung backwards with my hand, the hand that had
my whistle in it, and caught my tormentor hard, right in the mouth, with
the whistle. There was some blood and a cut, of course, and the poor guy
needed stitches."[44] Only afterwards did Chadwick realize that the man
used a wheelchair – the rinkside locations being the only spaces in the
Gardens that could accommodate wheelchairs.

Fig. 4.8. Rail-seat spectators often found themselves in the middle of skirmishes between players, as seen here at a playoff game between the Maple Leafs and Montreal, 27 March 1945. (City of Toronto Archives, Globe and Mail fonds, Fonds 1266, Item 95475)

It was not uncommon for spectators in the rail seats to find the game impinging upon their space (see Fig. 4.8). Colin "saw the odd one get hit with a stick or a puck," while the *Globe* reported that at a November 1934 game, "One man was knocked out, but he was a spectator, not a player. The high stick of a Detroit player speeding along the east boards struck a rail-seat occupant in the face. The 'fan' slumped to the floor, blood spurting from his mouth, and was carried away so quickly by ushers that only those in the immediate vicinity noticed the incident."[45] The proximity of rail-seat spectators to the action on the ice – recalling that there was only a short distance between the rail and the rink boards – also meant that spectators could impose themselves upon the game. The Siebert-Horner fight from March 1935, mentioned earlier, "started when a fan dashed down from a box seat and started mixing things with Siebert."[46]

Yet former player Stuart reveals that interactions between players and spectators could also be respectful and cordial. He recalls that he would

Fig. 4.9. Spectators greet players as they arrive for game 2 of the Stanley Cup finals versus Chicago (5 April 1938). (City of Toronto Archives, Globe and Mail fonds, Fonds 1266, Item 50617)

regularly be recognized in public as a member of the local hockey team in the late 1930s and that people would stop him on the streets of Toronto to talk about the Maple Leafs. Autographs were a favoured souvenir of an evening at Maple Leaf Gardens. Stuart remembers that people would "wait and we'd shower and so on and come out. And we'd be confronted and asked for an autograph" in the Gardens' lobby. Harry confirms that spectators would, "stand outside the Maple Leaf dressing room and watch them going in and out ... You always got down there early too for that purpose" (see Fig. 4.9). These interactions with the many elements of the spectacle – whether deferential or disruptive, deemed respectable or not – were important components of people's enjoyment of the spectating experience.

Distinctions in the Stands

Despite this portrayal of a "typical" night at the Gardens – and the evidence from ticket ledgers that suggests a predominantly male, upper-middle-class audience – the Maple Leaf Gardens crowd was not homogenous nor was the experience of the arena the same for all spectators. Before examining the meanings spectators took from the experience and the social bonds to which time at Maple Leaf Gardens contributed, it is worth considering how former spectators understood the people with whom they were sharing the space. Centring the spectator experience requires acknowledging that in any given seat, on any given night, a ticket holder was defined by multiple intersecting identities.

Tickets to games at Maple Leaf Gardens, especially during the Depression, were not equally accessible to all. As Nancy remembers, "wages were terribly low. I worked for Eaton's [earning] $12.50 a week." Her father subscribed to two seats in the greens, but his subscription soon lapsed as it "was a problem in those days to scrape up the three-fifty," the cost of the two tickets for each game. Faced with these realities, Maple Leaf Gardens' management experimented with ways to sell as many seats as possible, to both generate revenue and foster the impression that events at Maple Leaf Gardens were among the most popular tickets in town. The success of these efforts was reflected in the fact that during the Depression gate receipts continued to rise after ticket prices were reduced slightly in the 1933–34 season.[47]

One tactic was the sale of "booster tickets," which offered low-priced admission to games that had not sold out. For such tickets, patrons only had to pay the entertainment tax to obtain entry to the arena. Vic's uncle knew an employee in the Maple Leaf Gardens' ticket office, which got him access to booster tickets. "Cost me sixty cents for two tickets," Vic remembers. Table 4.2 offers evidence of the importance of booster tickets and other discounts to the financial success of Maple Leaf Gardens during the 1930s. These types of tickets contributed to the perception that the arena was doing a booming business. The decreasing number of booster tickets sold through the decade was evidence of their lessening importance to the bottom line as the economic situation began to improve; the increase in booster ticket sales in the 1939–40 season is likely evidence of the effect that wartime conditions were having on Maple Leaf Gardens' box receipts. In 1944, Maple Leafs acting manager Frank Selke wrote to Smythe that "we did sell out thanx [sic] to a judicious sale of green Boosters to Dunlop Rubber Company and 800 to Manning pool."[48] In addition to selling booster tickets, there were a number of games at Maple Leaf Gardens each year during the late 1930s, typically four to five per season, when all unsold seats in the arena were put up for sale at discounted prices (e.g., fifty cents, seventy-five cents, and $1.25). While these ticket sales strategies helped the hockey club weather the effects of the Depression, these efforts not only contributed to the bottom line, but they also likely changed the composition of the crowd in attendance.

Table 4.2. Booster tickets sold per game, Maple Leaf Gardens, 1935–40

Home game	1935–36	1936–37	1937–38	1938–39	1939–40
1	1,675	216	190	96	63
2	1,674	262	282	69	102
3	135	317	939	68	64
4	631	272	*250*	110	316
5	285	·536	250	397	112
6	359	572	250	148	–
7	318	545	274	111	126
8	335	*280*	**1,029**	137	216
9	369	–	7	96	101
10	378	247	2	125	134
11	2,043	**1,236**	*86*	1,821	126
12	410	**1,231**	735	92	131
13	1,007	–	**1,159**	408	–
14	518	**1,200**	–	257	2,080
15	1,554	259	462	396	988
16	400	629	369	–	481
17	3,229	**1,386**	–	–	963
18	368	–	558	1,015	*15*
19	3,765	318	**1,147**	–	1,687
20	407	374	480	–	–
21	468	–	–	311	4,443
22	–	41	349	438	–
23	590	462	–	868	109
24	976	–	460	209	306
Average	951.91	546.47	463.90	358.60	628.15

Source: "Maple Leaf Home Games [by season]," F 223-3-1-60: NHL – Summary of Box Office Receipts, Conn Smythe Fonds, Archives of Ontario, Toronto, Ontario.
Notes: (1) The games indicated in italics are those evenings when *all* unsold tickets were put up for sale at discounted prices. (2) The games indicated in bold were evenings designated in the box office records as "shareholders' nights."

Another promotional scheme further diversified the crowd – on one night per season, at least (see Fig. 4.10). Each year, the Maple Leafs' final Saturday home game before Christmas was set aside as "Young Canada Night." Children under age fifteen were admitted free when accompanied by a ticket subscriber. As early as the Leafs' second season at Maple Leaf Gardens, the *Mail and Empire* noted that "more than 3,000 youngsters have obtained tickets for to-night, but there is still room for more."[49] Archival records indicate that Young Canada Night attracted 4,121 children on 25 December 1937; another 2,849 on 24 December 1938; and 2,529 on 23 December 1939.[50]

While Harry recalls that "there'd be a few thousand kids on [Young Canada] Night," the usual crowd at Maple Leaf Gardens was "mostly

Fig. 4.10. Young spectators were, at times, prominent among the crowds at Maple Leaf Gardens. (City of Toronto Archives, Fonds 1257, Series 1057, Item 7500)

adults ... It was a much older crowd." The typical starting time for games of 8:30 p.m. was perhaps incompatible with large groups of young spectators, as was Smythe's attempt to frame spectatorship as a respectable heterosocial pastime, which might have precluded kids attending. So, although eleven of the twenty-one Maple Leaf Gardens' attendees interviewed for this book went to games at the arena before their eighteenth birthday, it is remembered as a largely adult space. Ernest was one of those child spectators and he is "certain there were lots of kids there, but my memory is of big, burly men." Similarly, Howard first attended as a child but recalls "not an awful lot of kids," even though "there were other kids with their parents."

Spectators who gained entry to Maple Leaf Gardens through booster tickets or other discounts likely altered the composition of the crowd that was suggested solely by considering the demographics of ticket subscribers. A more financially diverse crowd also reflects the experiences and assumptions of former spectators. Colin recalls the box and rail seats being populated by people who "didn't go to the operas ... [but] had money." They were the "hoi polloi of the city." By contrast, in Lawrence's estimation, "once in the cheaper seats, you got the cheaper kind of people," based upon "what they were wearing and the way they handled themself and the way they spoke to you or answered you." He continues his economic geography of Maple Leaf Gardens' seating: "In the blues, people were pretty well off and people in the greys, they were lucky to be there."

Lawrence was not alone in his experience of the crowd at Maple Leaf Gardens, where observations of how people handled themselves conflated social class and norms of public behaviour. "The people up at the top," Flora asserts, "couldn't afford tickets down in the reds." There was some truth in this assumption. For some spectators, in fact, even securing seats in the greys was a "special occasion" (Marjorie) or "birthday treat" (Howard). Some former spectators assumed that the cheapest seats were home to the most demonstrative spectators, while fewer assumptions were made about the composition and behaviour of the crowds in the first and second tiers. In memory, these were liminal spaces. The upper seats in the second tier (greens) were often associated with the grey seats, while the patrons in the first couple of rows of the side blues (first tier) were often characterized similarly to spectators in the red box seats immediately in front of them. The distinctiveness of two sections – grey and red – led them to be most often remembered. The green and blue seats, however, held the faceless majority that populated most Maple Leafs games.

Not only did Colin associate the box seats with Toronto's "hoi polloi," he also asserts that "the Jewish guys" were "up in the blues ... working their action there," as bookmakers. Even Selke worried to Smythe, in January 1944 while the latter was serving overseas during the Second World War, that defenceman Babe Pratt had spent too much time consorting "with a lot of tinhorn gamblers last season[,] Jews and Italians[,] and it was reflected in his play."[51] Racialized stereotypes such as these are among the few memories spectators have of the ethnic composition of the hockey crowd in the city, 81 per cent of whose inhabitants were identified in the 1931 census as having British ancestry. Recalling Abe Levinsky's considerable subscription ticket holdings, there is no evidence to suggest that any Jewish or Italian spectators in attendance at Maple Leaf Gardens would necessarily have been bookmakers. These two populations were the largest ethnic groups in the city not of British origin. Their communities were hardly as invisible as memories might suggest. Nevertheless, Nancy remembers that hockey spectators were predominantly "British," in part, Flora asserts, because interwar Toronto was "very Scotch, Irish, English."

Class and Gender Commingling in the Stands

There is considerable evidence to suggest that spectators chose to spend their time and disposable income during the Depression on admission to Maple Leaf Gardens – regardless of their circumstances – because hockey games were an opportunity for socializing with friends, family, and colleagues. The subscription ledgers suggest that this was primarily a male audience (and a relatively well-off one, at that). However, the predominance of male ticket subscribers should not lead to the assumption that hockey spectating was solely a male pastime. Moreover, the presence of women in the stands at Maple Leaf Gardens is not the only reason to examine the gendered nature of spectating. As Ava Baron asserts, "gender is present even when women are not." In the context of writing working-class history, she argues, "there has been little attention given to how male workers are constituted by gender and to how work and the workplace have been structured around masculinity."[52] A similar focus can be paid to leisure spaces, after "dislodging man as the universal subject."[53]

"He and His Wife Had Season's Tickets": Men Socializing at the Arena

Interrogating men's presence in Maple Leaf Gardens builds upon the ways in which spectating was socially and historically constructed, recognizing that men's experience of the arena and its spaces was not universal. This includes considering men's experiences socializing both with other men and with women, while foregrounding gender as a relational construct. Michael Kimmel argues that, at times, "men define their masculinity, not as much in relation to women, but in relation to each other."[54] Within such a context, men's awareness of women's presence in Maple Leaf Gardens can be understood both as a masculine response to the feminine, but also in terms of the ways in which men's behaviour with other men was affected by the presence of women. As Kimmel notes, "Women are not incidental to masculinity, but they are not always its central feature, either. At times, it is not women as corporeal beings but the 'idea' of women, or femininity – and most especially a perception of effeminacy by other men – that animates men's actions."[55]

Examinations of men's sociability by Canadian historians have focused primarily on working-class culture. Rooted in the notion that "at the core of masculinity in Western capitalist societies is the importance of work," these analyses have highlighted the workplace as a site where homosocial bonds were formed.[56] "Through waged work," Joy Parr argues, "boys learned manliness; they mastered disciplines and discriminations, ways of appraising their work and one another." Days spent in the factory or workplace meant different things for men and women, as these "were lessons males alone might learn. Girls did not learn womanliness through their paid employment."[57] Culturally constructed differences existed between all men and women, but as Suzanne Morton observes of a working-class neighbourhood in interwar Halifax, "class differences remained important."[58]

Such differences are brought into clearer relief by Craig Heron's examination of public drinking in late nineteenth and early twentieth-century working-class Hamilton. Heron incorporates age into his analysis and considers the ways in which life course influenced male sociability. "Bachelors generally preferred the company of other men" while enjoying "a vibrant leisure-time culture" that included "vaudeville and movie theatres, and skating and roller rinks." Marriage, however, was accompanied by "the responsibilities and constraints of domesticity."[59] The social lives of married men ran the gamut from time spent at home or on excursions with the family to escapes to licensed drinking places. The latter course, however, remained firmly within working-class culture as the legislation of public drinking establishments "allowed male wage-earners … to use the new gathering places as major sites of homo-social leisure."[60]

One institution that provided opportunities for men of diverse economic circumstances to interact and socialize was the local fraternal organization. Judith Fingard notes that membership in these organizations provided men "respectability and defined their masculinity," while Lynne Marks adds that "social life among lodge brothers served to reinforce masculine bonds."[61] Organized sport provided another venue through which men socialized, yet class barriers were frequently maintained in these activities. Participation in sport offered men opportunities to socialize with one another, although often on a class-exclusive basis. Sport as a site of homosociability "was characteristic of men across all classes," notes Morton, "though the activities were usually class based."[62] In the late nineteenth century, membership in sport clubs was primarily the purview of middle-class men, due to the strictures of amateurism and the pursuit by middle-class reformers of strategies such as rational recreation.[63]

For the most part, observations about male sociability and sport focus on athletic participation rather than on spectating. Indeed, the promoters of rational recreation – organized physical activity put to social reform ends – often directed their efforts at the idleness they associated with sport spectating. Woodcraft Indians founder and Boy Scouts of America president Ernest Thompson Seton blamed "spectatoritis" for "turning 'such a large proportion of our robust, manly, self-reliant boyhood into a lot of flat-chested cigarette-smokers with shaky nerves and doubtful vitality.'"[64] Spectating came under such an attack not only because middle-class reformers saw it as disreputable, but also because it was so very popular, especially at professional baseball games in the US. Despite the efforts of reformers such as Seton and Lord Baden-Powell, originator of the Boy Scouts, participation in sport – "as athletes or spectators" – Morton argues, remained an important site for the promotion of working-class culture.[65]

While the unsavoury elements that gravitated towards commercial sporting events in the late nineteenth century led to spectating being sullied by association, by the interwar years, entrepreneurs such as Smythe were designing and operating new facilities in ways that broadened the appeal of spectating – or, at least, made it a more respectable pastime for a wider cross section of men. At the same time, Kimmel notes, "fraternalism had lost much of its luster by 1925. Membership declined precipitously, and many organizations folded." The same desires for homosociability as a way "to ground their manhood and to dispel those gender anxieties moved from separate clubs outside the world of work to the corporation itself and to male bonding within the work world as well as in the world of leisure."[66]

The importance of Maple Leaf Gardens in Toronto's social scene and the variety of price levels at which entry could be gained meant that the new arena became an important institution for men in the city during the interwar years. As Morton has noted of Halifax during the economic downturn of the early 1920s, and which was also true of Depression-era Toronto in the 1930s, "economic dislocation made many working-class men feel particularly vulnerable and hence created anew the experience of a gender crisis."[67] This further enhanced the value of public spaces where men could socialize together, even ones such as Maple Leaf Gardens that also catered to heterosocializing and, to a lesser degree, women socializing with other women. While men of all social classes did not intermingle while within the arena, many of them viewed Maple Leaf Gardens as a central public site in their social lives. "It was a man's place in those days," Howard remembers.

Data from the 1933–34 ticket subscription ledger suggest ways in which the practice of hockey spectating can be understood as an element of male sociability for a variety of men in interwar Toronto. This includes evidence in Maple Leaf Gardens' least expensive seats – the greys and the greens – that co-workers attended Maple Leafs games in one another's company. These seats were home to subscribers who are better classified as middle class rather than working class (although single-game ticket purchasers may well have fit the latter description). For some of these men, spectating at Maple Leaf Gardens may have been an extension of the social bonds they formed at work. "Leisure and work were not completely distinct," Morton notes in the context of company sports teams in interwar Halifax, an argument that could be extended to watching as well as participating in sports.[68] For others, attendance at a public site "that had recognized status in the community" may have conferred upon them a respectability that Fingard identified among fraternal orders that welcomed members of marginalized populations in interwar Halifax.[69]

While the age of the former spectators who were interviewed for this book – many of whom went to Maple Leaf Gardens in the 1930s as adolescents – precludes them from sharing their own stories of adult sociability, some recall hockey games as an occasion where business relationships were nurtured. Katherine went to Maple Leafs games in the company of her husband, who was an accountant with McIntyre Porcupine Mines for over forty years. Throughout the 1930s, J.P. Bickell, the president of McIntyre Porcupine Mines, was also the president of and a significant shareholder in Maple Leaf Gardens. As well, Olive remembers that her sister did not go to games with her brother-in-law "if he had a customer that had to go." Other men may also have used spectating as a way to entertain clients, including Smythe, whose business contacts found their way into Maple Leaf Gardens' stands. William John McAnally's trucking company, McAnally & Son, "hauled sand and gravel for the building of Maple Leaf Gardens" and McAnally "had tickets for the hockey games at the Gardens," remembers his grandson's wife, Dorothy McAnally.[70] She goes on to recount the ways in which McAnally's business relationship with Smythe evolved into a social one: "He did know Hap Day, King Clancy and Connie Smythe. He did travel on road trips with them." Similarly, Bryce Beverly Hunter and Smythe "both had cottages at Lake Simcoe and I believe my grandfather looked after Connie's insurance arrangements," recalls Hunter's grandson, Bruce.[71]

Maple Leaf Gardens was not only a gathering place for men socializing with other men. If hockey spectating was a social activity, women were often the companion of choice for male ticket purchasers (see Fig. 4.11). This is not to suggest that men and women had identical spectating experiences, even if they attended together. And the assumptions male spectators had about the masculine nature of spectating are revealed through their characterizations of female spectators, as discussed below. Yet the arenas of the interwar years created new spaces, much as Heron suggests of licensed drinking places after the end of Prohibition, for a "new kind of public heterosexual socializing in couples."[72] While Hamilton's working-class men would gather after work, they were often joined later in the evenings by their spouses at local establishments, where the assembled gatherings "seem to have been

Fig. 4.11. Many former spectators recall Maple Leafs games as an opportunity for an evening out for heterosexual couples, although the typical crowd was overwhelmingly male. (City of Toronto Archives, Fonds 1257, Series 1057, Item 7507)

made up primarily of married couples."[73] At the other end of the economic spectrum, Vic remembers of Maple Leaf Gardens that "people that would have a pair of tickets would [be] ... usually men and their wives, especially in the box seats."

In keeping with these patterns, and the age of interviewees, many former spectators – located throughout the arena's different sections – recall men attending with a spouse or child. Donald (sitting in rail seats), John (box seats), Ernest (side blues), Nancy (greens), and Howard (greys) all recall attending their first games at Maple Leaf Gardens in the company of their father. Lawrence worked as an employee at the arena, but his memory is that "in a lot of cases men and women came together." Indeed, Katherine only remembers going to games in the company of her husband; Marjorie ("my very first date was there") and Emily began their careers as hockey spectators being taken to Maple Leaf Gardens by their boyfriends; and Irene recalls of her next-door neighbour in a west-end Toronto neighbourhood: "he and his wife, they had season's tickets ... They had a subscription for years." Male spectators had similar experiences. Vic took his girlfriend, while James went with his wife. Olive went to her first game with her sister's boyfriend (her future brother-in-law), who was typically accompanied by Olive's sister. Although Emily recalls that she and her boyfriend "never ever went with anyone else ... just the two of us," this heterosocial experience was often shared with other couples. Both Katherine and James – who sat in different sections – also remember attending games with their spouse and other husband-and-wife couples.

"A Fashion Show in the Stands"? Female Sociability and Hockey Spectating

While women often attended sporting events in the company of male escorts, they also appeared in the stands at Maple Leaf Gardens in ways that both affirmed and challenged the prevailing image of the female spectator. The notions of feminine respectability that informed Smythe's attempts to reimagine sports spectating in Toronto were intended to make the practice of spectating more respectable, but not necessarily to attract more female spectators. Yet, women in interwar Toronto – primarily middle-class women – not only went to hockey games to fulfil gender stereotypes and become a part of what one former female spectator at Maple Leaf Gardens called the "fashion show in the stands," but often attended with other women, finding hockey spectating, as men did, an opportunity for socializing with family and friends.

Historians have focused extensively on women's place in Canadian society in the late nineteenth century and the years before the First World War, as well as in the interwar years. Much of this scholarship has emphasized the increasing fluidity between the public and private realms and women's roles and opportunities within each, and indeed has challenged such a binary construction.[74] When it comes to consumption, the emphasis has been on women shopping for the domestic economy or their pursuit of beauty ideals that were constructed and communicated by the emerging mass media and the burgeoning advertising industry. The department store as a feminine space of consumption has been central to much of this scholarship. There has been less exploration, however, of Canadian women as consumers of commercial amusements and entertainments in the interwar years.[75]

Women were, however, at least in urban settings in English Canada in the interwar years, consumers of entertainment, including, but not limited to, movie houses and dance halls. In a study of working women in

1930s Toronto, Katrina Srigley characterizes leisure as either informally organized non-commercial activities (e.g., gathering to play music or listen to the radio), social events that revolved around church groups, or commercial amusements such as movies.[76] Joan Sangster also argues that women's consumption of commercial leisure in the 1930s centred predominantly on movies and shopping. These events were usually the focal point for women's socializing with one another and focused on products and services related to beauty and romance, including movies that advocated heteronormative ideals, as well as domestic management.[77] In addition to the popularity of shopping and movie-going for women, baseball stadiums and hockey arenas across North America were home to audiences that counted female fans among the paying crowds. Beginning in the late nineteenth century, primarily in baseball, there was an instrumental element to women's participation within sport crowds. Sport entrepreneurs viewed female customers as a "purifying" force in the face of the unruly nature of largely male crowds in the belief that the presence of women would engender more respectable behaviour from men. Such discourses, however, only served to reinforce middle-class notions of femininity that proscribed women's public consumption of entertainments.

Little has been written to suggest that women actively chose to be spectators at commercial sporting events in North America. Yet it is worth recalling Franca Iacovetta and Mariana Valverde's admonition that "there is a great deal more to Canadian women's lives than work, the family, and formal politics."[78] While women were certainly present in Smythe's building, how should we think about them? What did their presence signify? At the outset, it is illustrative to consider the ways in which the recollections men have of women spectators reflected dominant narratives of the female spectator.[79]

Women present at Maple Leaf Gardens were often depicted as overly emotional, as disinterested bystanders, or both. Andy Lytle of the *Star* noted that at one March 1935 game a "girl who made one of the red box seats look like a queen's throne played with a broken link in her arm bracelet most of the second period." This portrayal – which appeared on the same page as a photograph of Maple Leafs stars Busher Jackson and Charlie Conacher each kissing their wives, an image that also reproduced heteronormative ideals – captured the presumed ennui of the female spectator: "When her escort arose and peered excitedly down the ice for a better look at a jam, she looked up boredly and asked: 'Where's the fire, ducky bumps?'"[80]

Other men who were spectators at Maple Leaf Gardens in the 1930s also acknowledge women's presence in the crowd in a way that reaffirms these stereotypes. Ernest remembers that "a lot of women fans and a lot of women attended the games ..." Without stopping, he goes on to assert that they were most likely there as companions of men: "I don't know what the ratio would be, male to female, but I think a lot of the men certainly took their wives." He finishes this thought by placing women within their traditional gender roles both geographically and figuratively: "Mind you, on Saturday nights if they didn't go to the game the women would gather in the kitchen and make tea and cookies and the men would gather around the radio and listen to [broadcaster] Foster [Hewitt] and the Leafs game and all the socializing would take place after the game."

Ernest was not the only former spectator to characterize women present in Maple Leaf Gardens as primarily the companions of men. It was a rare sight, in Colin's memory, to see a woman at Maple Leaf Gardens who was *not* there in the presence of a man. "The only ones who were there by themselves," he remembers, "were the ushers, the usherettes." James is slightly more generous: "My impression is men and women were both there, although there may have been sections, the cheap seats at the ends of the Gardens, which were mostly male."

How then, in the light of such portrayals, should we consider women's experiences as hockey spectators, as consumers of commercial entertainments such as professional hockey in the 1930s? The stories from and of women who attended games at Maple Leaf Gardens in the 1930s do affirm traditional notions of women's gender roles in the interwar years. Lillian recalled that going to hockey games "was a big occasion. We all dressed up. It was very social." Her grandson, Grant, remembers that for Lillian, "it was a fashion show in the stands." In the early 1930s, Hewitt and his technicians went in search of voices in the Gardens' stands that were interfering with the radio broadcast. These voices belonged to "a couple of young ladies." They "deduced this, in our Sherlock Holmes manner, from the voices themselves and from the fact that their dialogue involved hats, styles, bargains, shopping trips and social gossip."[81] The conflation of women's participation in spectating with an interest in fashion was evident from the opening of Maple Leaf Gardens. The *Star*'s women's sports columnist, Alexandrine Gibb, advised female spectators in advance of the first game of the latest in spectating fashions, the "royal blue Poncho": "It has all the earmarks of being a suitable garment for a hockey game in a rink where the heat is turned off so that the ice won't melt."[82]

There were other elements of women's spectating experiences that reflected the patriarchal nature of both the arena and the larger society that congregated within it. When women accompanied men to Maple

Leaf Gardens, societal norms dictated that it was the man who determined where the couple sat. Emily rued that she had to watch the Maple
Leafs from "away the heck and gone up quite high," but her boyfriend
at the time "couldn't afford front-row seats." Proscriptions outside the
arena also affected women's spectating. Single women in the interwar
years were expected to exchange their jobs in the labour force for domestic responsibilities upon getting married.[83] Lillian did not just leave a
job, she also had to give up hockey spectating. Having regularly attended
games every Saturday night in Toronto between 1926 and 1938 following
her emigration from Scotland – meaning she spent five years spectating at Maple Leaf Gardens' predecessor, Arena Gardens – she married
a man in 1938 who was the chief engineer of a blast furnace at a steel
manufacturer in Hamilton. The couple moved to Hamilton after their
wedding and Lillian's days as a regular Maple Leaf Gardens spectator
were over. "When she moved to Hamilton, and if you asked her what she
missed," remembers her grandson, Grant, "it was going to the Gardens."

The memories of female spectators challenge prevailing conceptions
of them as sport consumers. Not only do female spectators need to have
their presence within the arena acknowledged as more than merely the
companions of men, the assumption that women were not hockey fans
themselves, and indeed that men were the "true" fans, needs to be recon-
sidered. Emily remembers, in a story not dissimilar from Lillian's experience, that when she married a man who "wasn't much of a hockey fan,"
she stopped going to games. However, before assuming a stereotypical
narrative, Emily recalls from whom she acquired her love of hockey: "It
all started with my mother ... who was an enthusiast." Emily grew up
in a small town about 150 km north of Toronto. Her father spent win-
ters away from his family working at a remote logging camp in northern
Ontario. On Saturday nights during these months, Emily would accompany her mother as they visited a neighbour's house, because that family
had a radio, and the assembled group would listen to the hockey game.
She can still recite Foster Hewitt's introduction to his broadcasts. Other
women have similar stories, reinforcing the role of the radio in shaping the spectator experience. Marjorie asserts that, although she went
to Maple Leaf Gardens with her husband, she "was interested in hockey
long before I met my husband" because her family listened to Hewitt's
broadcasts on the radio: "Saturday night was hockey night ... I don't
remember anything else."

Such passions were not reserved for radios in living rooms. Women
with access to financial resources and/or geographic proximity to Maple
Leaf Gardens attended games in person. Harry recalls squeezing into the
benches in the grey seats, between his aunt and uncle, and remembers

that "my aunt was right into hockey." She was not alone. The Gardens was home not only to female spectators in the 1930s, but to women who were interested, knowledgeable, committed fans. Griffiths of the *Telegram* asserted that, at the arena's opening, "a few of the feminine forces were on hand simply because it was a social event, but 99 per cent came because they are ardent supporters of the Big Boy Blues."[84] Claudia and Patricia, who worked as a concessionaire at Maple Leaf Gardens and a household domestic, respectively, were representative of the many women in Toronto working in service jobs in the 1930s. But it is clear that both went to hockey games because they enjoyed the entertainment:

> Claudia: I used to sneak around the end of the bench and watch. But I wasn't supposed to. But I did ... There was another girl at the [concession] stand ... I didn't leave her alone. The other girl she was, "Go and watch it. I don't want to watch it. I don't like hockey." "Oh," I says ... I'd go and watch the game all night.
>
> William (speaking about Patricia): She used to take sisters, usually ... She had four or five sisters. So she would take one of them ... She was right into the game. She knew it very well.

Like Patricia and her sisters, some women went to hockey games with one another as an opportunity to socialize. "Women used to go. Weren't afraid you know like to go, a couple of women together," remembers Marjorie. "'Cause my sister and I ... we used to go together and never think anything of it." Yet while scholarship has discussed the ways in which women socialized with one another during the 1930s, there has been little suggestion that women's consumption of commercial amusements extended as far as attending professional hockey games together. The memories of female former spectators encourage such a (re)consideration of women's historic presence in predominantly masculine sport spaces and women's willingness to choose to consume this kind of commercial amusement together. Considering women as hockey spectators reveals that women were consumers in non-traditional ways and that they consumed public entertainments such as sporting events without necessarily being preoccupied with the stereotypical priorities of beauty and domestic management. Such a history of women's lives as social consumers in the 1920s and 1930s continues to be written. As Wright notes: "The study of consumer culture is a rich site for research into gender relations apart from the more common subject areas of work and family."[85]

An especially "rich site" for this research is Maple Leaf Gardens' upper reaches, the grey seats, the section of the arena furthest from the ice

Fig. 4.12. Female spectators were found throughout Maple Leaf Gardens, including in the third-tier grey seats (pictured here on 26 March 1947), often in one another's company. (Archives of Ontario, Fonds 4485, Item 26)

surface that the memories of male spectators recall as a predominantly masculine space, populated almost exclusively by men. Harry believes that there were "not too many" women in the grey seats, even though when he attended games with his uncle he was sitting in a subscriber seat usually occupied by his aunt. In fact, Lillian recalled to her grandson, Grant, that "a large portion of the crowd up in the greys were women" (see Fig. 4.12). The story of Lillian and five of her friends is evidence of this counter-narrative. Of these six women, some were married and some single (so their fandom cannot be dismissed as a courting ritual), three were sisters, and three worked at Eaton's. Every Saturday night they went to Maple Leafs games together and sat in the greys. They did this from 1926 to 1938, so their fandom preceded Smythe's attempt to attract women and gentrify his business with the building of Maple Leaf Gardens in 1931. For Lillian and her friends sitting in the greys was a badge of honour, evidence that they were serious about their spectating. As Grant recalls,

She went every Saturday night. And she said, "We always sat in the greys …
It was a big occasion. We all dressed up. It was very social. Everyone enjoyed
seeing the same people." … She was very interested in the social aspect …
and that there were a lot of women in the greys, which is where she sat … She
always made a big point of telling us she sat in the greys, up in the nosebleeds.

The story of Lillian's and her friends' Saturday-evening routine, as
well as Patricia's practice of taking one of her sisters with her to Maple
Leaf Gardens, points at hockey spectating as a social practice for women
and makes clear that women in 1930s Toronto were more than accesso-
ries to the city's male hockey fans. When asked if she went to games in
the 1930s with her husband out of a sense of marital duty, Katherine is
quick to respond: "Oh no, I enjoyed it." Located throughout Maple Leaf
Gardens, female spectators were passionate and engaged participants, as
Emily is quick to add when asked if she would cheer out loud, "and roar,
you know."

"It Was Like Old Home Week": Socializing in the Stands

While many spectators entered Maple Leaf Gardens in the company of
the companion(s) with whom they would share the experience, they and
others joined a wider community when they took their seats. Katherine says that "it was like old home week … when we'd go to the hockey
games." Flora also remembers that her father "got to know all the people
[sitting] around him." A similar sentiment seemed to prevail throughout
the arena. Among patrons in the box seats, John asserts, for example,
that "the people down in the southwest corner would know people that
lived in the southwest corner and they would have a little social group
going together." Meanwhile, in the greens, "most of them were subscribers around us," remembers Nancy, "and we used to, when we'd go in,
greet each other: 'Hello, how are you tonight?' And you know we knew
them all, most of them." Even in the standing-room sections, which were
general admission and thus seemingly a more likely place to find yourself
standing next to a stranger, "you'd get to know the people around you
'cause you were standing there for an hour before the game and everybody were Leaf fans basically," asserts Frank. He continues: "I remember
different games. We'd see people down in there that we knew. There was
some fellows from Listowel [a town 160 km northwest of Toronto] that
we were staying with one time that we knew and you just, if you got there
you'd kind of get to know some people."

These communities extended beyond Maple Leaf Gardens' stands.
John recalls of spectators that "one way or another, they would share the

experience other times other than Saturday night at the Gardens." He developed relationships with spectators who sat nearby: "So you got to know them and you know them in areas other than because they were bodies that happened to be sitting next to you impersonally." Often these social groupings reflected the ways in which talking about what happened on the ice was also a meaningful element of the sociability of spectating, even while the game was not on. As noted earlier, many spectators would leave their seats for the arena's concourse areas during intermissions and, Howard remembers, "you'd find a lot of little clusters all discussing the pros and cons of what happened in the previous period." Beyond the walls of the arena, the rhythms of spectating for Donald were "go to the game, watch the game, go home and talk about the game."

Gardens' patrons were also corporally involved while following the action on the ice. Emily remembers rising out of her seat in the greys to observe the play below, while newsreel footage of the Maple Leafs' 1939 home opener shows people in the crowd rising and sitting to get the best possible view as play moves from one end of the ice to the other.[86] Throughout the arena, spectators shared an embodied experience, often spending their evenings in Maple Leaf Gardens in physical contact with one another. The standing-room sections were at times crowded two or three rows deep, recalls Frank, so that "you couldn't go anywhere." While in the grey seats, with their hard wooden benches, spectators, Harry remembers, rarely leaned back. This was in part to get a better vantage point, but also, Harry asserts, because the excitement of the game kept entire sections of spectators "always awake … You were always forward. You know you were always looking over." And "when a goal did score," recalls John, who was sitting in the expensive box seats, "I, like everybody else in the Gardens, leaped up and cheered."

Despite Percy Page remarking on "the dead atmosphere in the Gardens," as noted earlier, many others found watching hockey in person to be an exhilarating experience. One fan writing to the sports editor at the *Globe and Mail* remarked on the "hollering fun": "It is all a matter of excitement, and the big crowd enjoy the show … its [*sic*] good for the lungs and helps the merry-go-round to get merrier."[87] The pleasure that spectators took in the excitement of the play on the ice, the ways in which they reacted in concert with it, and the meaningfulness they derived from sharing these experiences with others were the central features of this "hollering fun" (see Fig. 4.13). Nancy's experience as a spectator "was exciting, all the people around and everything." It was in "the people around" that many spectators found the enjoyment of spectating. Tom Gaston remembered the people with whom he shared section 94 in the Gardens' grey seats. For him, the collective rituals mattered. Each

Fig. 4.13. A community of spectators excited for game 1 of the Stanley Cup finals versus Chicago (5 April 1938). (City of Toronto Archives, Globe and Mail fonds, Fonds 1266, Item 50589)

time "The Maple Leaf Forever" was played, "we made up our own words, and sang them proudly to the tune each time the organist played it." It was a shared experience for him and his neighbours. "Oh boy, we had a lot of fun."[88]

Conclusion

In preparation for a typical evening watching hockey at Maple Leaf Gardens, spectators had to dress for an appearance in public – which would have taken little thought for many – and decide how they would get to the arena. Once there, with games starting at 8:30 p.m., many incorporated into their evening a meal at any one of a number of establishments located near Maple Leaf Gardens. Upon entering the arena, spectators shared the same lobby space before finding their way to seats or standing-room spaces. As the game commenced, the spectating experience affected all the senses, with former spectators recalling the sounds of organ music and memorable fans, the sights of the arena ice and Foster

Hewitt's gondola, and the smells of cigarette and cigar smoke in the arena's lounge areas and concourses. The latter spaces were popular during intermissions, as were food and beverage concessions. Overall, however, what spectators most recall is watching the game unfold on the ice and the people with whom they shared that experience.

For many, this experience was a social one. While the nature of sociability varied by gender and social standing, more often than not people entered Maple Leaf Gardens with one or more companions intending to share an evening watching hockey in one another's company. Although many spectators recall their focus being taken up by the game action unfolding on the ice below or in front of them, spectating occurred in both homosocial contexts (men attending with men, and women with other women) as well as heterosocial ones. The memories of former spectators that have formed the basis of this portrait of the spectating experience suggest homosocial bonding was often accompanied by performances of hegemonic forms of masculinity or femininity, while heterosocializing was tied to heteronormative performances of sociability. It is to this more theoretical framing of the spectator experience, as well as a consideration of the success of Smythe's respectability project, that the analysis turns in the final chapter.

Chapter Five

The State of Smythe's Respectability Project

On the occasion of the closing of Maple Leaf Gardens in February 1999, a considerable amount of ink was used by the local and Canadian press to memorialize the sixty-seven-year-old arena.[1] The dominant theme of this media coverage was that Toronto was losing a significant civic landmark (although the building was not scheduled for demolition), a place around which the city's social life had circulated since the Depression. As the Maple Leafs prepared to move into their modern, new arena, another theme emerged: "The Gardens was built for people who wanted to watch what was happening on the ice (or the floor below), people who didn't expect a level of comfort equivalent to their arm chair at home, who didn't expect a range of gourmet options beyond hot dogs and popcorn, who didn't have a million other leisure options to lure them away."[2] Sportswriter Stephen Brunt captures here the nostalgic belief that Maple Leaf Gardens represented an earlier, less commercial era, when spectators expected fewer in the way of creature comforts. But this is sentimental hindsight. Maple Leaf Gardens was certainly "built for people who wanted to watch what was happening on the ice," but, as we've seen, "comfort" – in the context of the interwar years – was very much top of mind for the arena's designers and owners. Elsewhere in the same 13 February 1999 issue of the *Globe and Mail* another columnist remembers the Gardens not as a hallmark of a simpler age, but as its own state-of-the-art facility, where "Spectators no longer had to worry about spit raining down on them from the balconies, an ever-present hazard at the old arena. They were warm for the first time."[3] This too is its own form of nostalgia – given that photographs of the "old arena," Arena Gardens, do not suggest balconies from which spit could rain down (see Fig. 1.10) – but it is certainly closer to the rhetoric that accompanied the opening of Maple Leaf Gardens in 1931.

From the building's opening, the local press played a central role in fostering such narratives. Sportswriters were not only complicit in marking the boundaries of respectable spectatorship but also encouraged citizens to patronize Maple Leaf Gardens. W.A. Hewitt remarked that, thanks to Maple Leaf Gardens – where he was also employed to organize amateur hockey – "Toronto now can lay claim to the finest building of its kind on the continent."[4] Bert Perry of the *Globe* also boasted that "Toronto had at last blossomed forth into major league ranks to the fullest extent."[5] However, such civic achievements came with attendant responsibilities for the city's entertainment consumers. "Toronto sportsmen have done their part," noted the *Globe*'s sports editor, Mike Rodden, "and now it is up to the fans and players to do theirs."[6] J.P. Fitzgerald of the *Telegram* was even more direct. While the new arena was "one of the best rinks in the world," he observed, "it remains to be seen whether Toronto as a city has kept up with Toronto as a hockey centre."[7]

The location of Maple Leaf Gardens, its design, and operation highlight in significant ways the respectable, civilized middle-class Torontonian for whom the building was intended. This was the anticipated audience of Conn Smythe's efforts to gentrify spectating. However, the pursuit of revenues was seemingly paradoxical. Having set the boundaries of respectability in the stands, Smythe (and, to be fair, other NHL owners and managers) would do what they could to present a spectacle on the ice (fast, physical, and occasionally violent) that was appealing – and hopefully profitable – because it offered the tantalizing possibility of transcending these very same boundaries.

Yet, as Colin Howell identifies, sport spaces, much like sport itself, are "contested territory."[8] Architects and building operators could intend their spaces to be used by spectators in particular ways, but there were ample opportunities for people in the crowd to resist these strictures and spectate as they chose. Throughout the 1930s, incidents of spectators becoming involved in altercations with players, officials, or each other received comment in the popular press. The spectacle was rarely to blame for such events; rather, spectators would have to be better behaved. Following an altercation between Maple Leafs players and fans at New York's Madison Square Garden in 1931, the *Telegram* was moved to remind potential spectators in Toronto that "Whatever justification there may be for players to take the odd crack at each other in the heat of play there is none for spectators to butt into the argument and much less than that to start any fracas with players."[9] The frequency of such admonitions suggests that these were not isolated incidents. As a consequence, regardless of how a space is conceived, the people who inhabit the space define its existence as lived space, as Henri Lefebvre suggests.[10]

The spectator within Maple Leaf Gardens did as much to define the nature of the space as Maple Leaf Gardens did to shape the spectator.

Building upon this observation, this chapter concludes the examination of hockey spectators – viewed through the building and operation of Maple Leaf Gardens in the 1930s – by reflecting on Smythe's respectability project in three ways. First, in considering the promotion of respectability, this chapter examines how the ways in which Maple Leaf Gardens was designed and operated reflected how classed and gendered notions of respectability were tied to commercial profits. Second, it considers the ways in which Smythe and the Maple Leafs both encouraged and profited from transgressions of respectability. Any relaxing of respectability points at the ways in which an analysis of space that identifies the intended audience only tells half the story. Thirdly, this chapter explores how Smythe's respectability project was received and the ways in which it was resisted by spectators. In pursuing these three interrelated themes, this chapter offers a theoretical perspective, grounded in the empirical findings of the previous four chapters, to frame the experience of the historical sport spectator.

Promoting Respectability

From its opening, Maple Leaf Gardens hosted a wide variety of events. These included boxing and wrestling cards, the six-day bicycle races that were common at North American arenas in the interwar years, as well as ice shows and a variety of other organizational meetings.[11] Each of these attracted crowds whose class and gender composition would have been different from the Maple Leafs' audience. While Colin remembers that ice shows at Maple Leaf Gardens "got a classier crowd all over the rink for that than you did for the hockey even," he cautions, "the hockey was a classy enough crowd." This assessment reflects Smythe's success in marking Maple Leaf Gardens as a site of respectable consumption that attracted a preferred spectator, one who was both respectable and respectful (see Fig. 5.1).

The organizers of Canada's many nineteenth-century agricultural and industrial exhibitions pursued similar aims. Beyond organizing and displaying the modern world, exhibitions, notes E.A. Heaman, "disseminated the upper-class values of their organizers."[12] The largest of these fairs was Toronto's Industrial Exhibition, which Keith Walden argues was an institution used by the city's elites to shape cultural values, promote confidence in new industrial processes in the wake of the decline of craft production, and stimulate (and legitimate) consumer desires for the products of this new industrialism. Social order was promoted through

Fig. 5.1. In building Maple Leaf Gardens, Conn Smythe, pictured here at his desk, sought to imbue spectating with an air of respectability. (Archives of Ontario, Conn Smythe Fonds, F 223-1-1-1)

carefully constructed displays and the attention paid to their organization. Exhibitions were "calculated not just to impress, but to elicit specific types of responses."[13]

These examples call to mind Michel Foucault's conceptualization of the disciplinary institution, which he based upon Jeremy Bentham's Panopticon, a 1787 model of a "modern" prison. Bentham designed a carceral space that left its inhabitants open to surveillance at any time yet also hidden from both one another and the observing power. Unsure of whether they were being watched or not, inmates were left in "a state of consciousness and permanent visibility that assures the automatic functioning of power."[14] The disciplinary tool was the architecture itself, which became "a machine for creating and sustaining a power relation independent of the person who exercises it."[15] Foucault contends that the metaphor of the Panopticon can be extended to understand the functioning of power relationships in everyday life. Similar disciplinary mechanisms occur in a variety of institutional settings, where the design and operation of space controls and communicates the operation of power, without the overt use of force, to create rational, productive bodies. These bodies, in turn, enhance the surveillance of the disciplinary institution by watching one another, so that, in Foucault's configuration, an incarcerated prisoner "who is subjected to a field of visibility, and who knows it, assumes responsibility for the constraints of power."[16]

While Foucault formulated these ideas around carceral spaces, the museum (and other cultural institutions, such as arenas) operated in an appreciably different manner. As a space of display and exhibition, the museum did not try to hide disciplined bodies from one another, as in the Panopticon. The nineteenth-century museum sought to reveal these bodies to one another, making power public and "forming a technology of vision which served not to atomize and disperse the crowd but to regulate it, and to do so by rendering it visible to itself, by making the crowd itself the ultimate spectacle."[17] Notions of visibility and performance are central to the ways in which Maple Leaf Gardens' management worked to construct the preferred spectator. An element of this was contained within the building's design, but as with the museum, "this was not an achievement of architecture alone."[18] The museum, and by extension, the arena, was a "performative environment in which new forms of conduct and behaviour could be shaped and practised."[19]

Public spaces – including sport spaces – are never neutral. Power relations, "which construct the rules, define the boundaries and create spaces with certain meanings in which some relationships are facilitated, others discouraged," mark out who is included and excluded from such spaces.[20] The spaces of cultural institutions such as nineteenth-century museums and exhibitions were designed and operated in such a way as to create settings for the acting out (and replication) of respectable bourgeois culture. In this way, "the most important exhibit at the fair was the audience," while "the space of the museum was also an emulative one; it was envisaged as a place in which the working classes would acquire more civilized habits by imitating their betters."[21] But it was not just other spectators who dictated what was to be emulated. At Eaton's College Street department store in Toronto, "class distinctions were organized through a particular arrangement of goods and people within the store in which the indiscriminate mixing of merchandise and shoppers from various classes was avoided as much as possible."[22] This was not an isolated case within institutions of middle-class consumption. Within the culture of late nineteenth-century New York theatre, "Vaudeville houses were built to attract middle class families for good 'clean' fun in grandiose, luxurious palaces. These fabulous architectural temples were designed to instill in the audience a sense of embourgeoisement ...

The managers appealed to the mass audiences' ostensible desires to learn manners and proper behavior, including speech, and to enhance upward mobility."[23]

One consequence of these new sites of middle-class respectability was that they created spaces for the public consumption of entertainment by women. Turn-of-the-century department stores combined "gracious appointments," "lavishly displayed merchandise," and a "range of services designed to make consumption more than just a process of procuring goods."[24] These amenities were designed to "equate purchasing with a genteel style of life, to make the department store the women's equivalent of a men's downtown club."[25] Similar processes of reform also took place in the theatre, where, as a substitute for racier entertainments, such as burlesque, "vaudeville houses provided a space for hetero-social attendance."[26] Despite this, thanks in part to residual Victorian morals, women, especially unescorted women, remained in the minority among spectators.

This notion of "hetero-social attendance" points to the other interests at stake in the creation of spaces respectable enough for women. While the department store was a "feminine" space, other cultural institutions promoted middle-class respectability and "safe" environments for women not solely to encourage female consumption of entertainment. At local fairs, "women were a hook to lure in the men."[27] Ladies' departments, for example, were incorporated by exhibition organizers in the hope that female fairgoers would be accompanied by men. Similarly, "the primary target of the museum's reforming intent was the working-class man."[28] Middle-class reform attempts to lure men away from corrupting influences such as the tavern and into "cleansed" public spaces co-opted women to these efforts. From the museum to the public park to the public library, "women were held to exert a civilizing influence through their mere presence in both embodying and enjoining a gentleness of manners."[29] Individually, women "were expected to elevate the men in their lives" and "as a social force were to elevate society by exercising domestic virtues."[30] Half a century later, sport entrepreneurs such as Smythe still sought to invoke the presumed respectability that female spectators would bestow upon buildings such as Maple Leaf Gardens. This was consistent with an earlier "pattern in which women, in being welcomed out of the 'separate sphere' of domesticity to which their naturalization had earlier confined them, were accorded a role in which the attributes associated with that sphere were enlisted for reformatory purposes – as culture's instruments rather than its targets."[31]

Nevertheless, mixing presumed notions of middle-class femininity with male sociability did not always go uncontested. Take the example of public transit in Toronto during the 1940s. Smoking on the city's streetcars was restricted to the rearmost seats in each car. This space was "by custom a male preserve, a rolling men's club" where "men gossiped about the weather, politics, exotic travel experiences, and the transit service."[32] Non-smokers kept to the front of each tram, spaces that became "female." Moreover, ridership varied over the course of the workday and struggles ensued over how space was occupied and defined. Male "smokers" dominated the morning and evening rush hours, while female "shoppers" were more common during off-peak hours. As public transit faced unprecedented overcrowding during the Second World War, these two archetypes "competed for physical space ... redefining the meaning of public space and the appropriate behaviour within it for 'ladies and gentlemen.'"[33]

Maple Leaf Gardens cannot be extracted from these cultural circumstances, especially as its design and operation sought to capitalize on classed and gendered notions of respectability. Unlike other contemporary arenas – such as Madison Square Garden, which was primarily conceived as a boxing venue – Toronto's new arena was planned from the outset with hockey spectating in mind. It was designed not to separate spectators in different sections, but rather to ensure that they commingled. Although they could not move between the three tiers of seats while in the arena, all spectators used the same entrances and gathered in the same lobbies. (Gallery seats in New York's Madison Square Garden, by comparison, were accessed through doorways on the side of the building separate from the main entrance.) Those with the best seats – rinkside rail seats or box seats – entered the main arena at ground level from the lobby. All other spectators climbed the same sets of stairs to reach whichever of the arena's three tiers was home to their particular seat. In an environment that sought to promote propriety, all spectators at some level inhabited the same space. What's more, the design of the arena, not surprisingly, focused attention downward on the ice surface below. Spectators in the less expensive seats also found within their field of vision the inhabitants of the most expensive seats – those spectators most likely, one presumes, to model respectability.

Henning Eichberg uses an inverted pyramid as a metaphor for the stadium and argues that, in modern sporting spaces, the base of the pyramid views the top.[34] Indeed, Marjorie remembers that "if you sat in the cheaper seats, you always looked down to see what they [spectators in the more expensive seats] were wearing." The knowledge of how one dressed or behaved at a game at Maple Leaf Gardens, or in any public space, was learned from those who occupied the space with you. While perhaps apocryphal, two long-time Maple Leaf Gardens' staff recalled

Fig. 5.2. For some, patrons in the box seats, including this couple pictured at a playoff game vs. Detroit on 26 March 1947, were the model of respectable spectatorship. (Archives of Ontario, Fonds 4485, Item 26)

that "Smythe could insist that male customers in the box seats wear ties, holding a threat of cancelled season tickets over their heads."[35] Nevertheless, Vic notes that "if I'd gone down there [to Maple Leaf Gardens] in a sweater or something, I would've felt out of place." In aspirational terms, he recalls, "it was the environment that made you behave. You were with the upper crust and you wanted to sort of be like that" (see Fig. 5.2).

The preferred spectator was valuable not only in maintaining respectability but in modelling the correct behaviours for others. If fandom is a "simultaneous form of communication and identity building" – the former directed at others, the latter an expression for oneself – the implications of the pyramid metaphor can be understood by incorporating Pierre Bourdieu's notion of symbolic capital, one of a number or "capitals" that can be accrued, along with economic, cultural, and social capital.[36] This is grounded in Bourdieu's concepts of *habitus* (broadly speaking, people's socialized demonstration of their beliefs, habits, and tastes) and *field* (the "objective social reality" in which habitus-capital positions reflect power relations).[37] The articulation of habitus, capital, and field connects the economic motives of sport entrepreneurs in the 1920s to the shift in cultural tastes with which they hoped to imbue spectating. As Bourdieu notes, "the accumulation of symbolic capital" includes "the acquisition of ... an image of respectability and honourability."[38]

Bourdieu argues that habitus and capital dictate people's sporting and sport consuming practices, with people of different habitus-capital identities (i.e., the ways in which people's tastes are reflected in the benefits they accrue) taking up different pastimes and entertainments.[39] How then to account for spaces such as the arena where multiple habitus-capital positions are present, often demarcated by different sections within the arena and different ticket prices? When do different identities opt for the same cultural practice? Bourdieu, in his consideration of film, asserts that "different groups consume the same film in different ways."[40] However, what about the consumption of the same cultural practice by different groups in *similar* ways? The concept of field – a semi-autonomous frame within which different habitus-capital identities have their own logic – is useful in explaining how different social groups can engage with the same cultural practice. Other considerations of sports spectating have employed this theorization in fairly static ways. These studies have taken demographic data that characterize spectators and looked for correlations to levels of economic, cultural, and educational capital.[41] They were, in essence, snapshots in time. In employing Bourdieu's theoretical framework within the arena in a more dynamic way, spectating not only reflects the capital(s) that accompanied spectators into the arena, but also reflects the kinds of "benefits" that spectators hoped they would accrue from spectating.[42]

In interwar Toronto, the symbolic capital available from spectating in this modern space was not something to be brought to the practice but something to be gained from aspiring to be a part of it. Recall Vic's desire "to sort of be like that." This aspirational notion reflects the memories of former spectators at Maple Leaf Gardens, where there were comparatively limited differences in spectating practices, behaviours, and expectations between the building's three tiers. The different ticket "price points" of the arena, which were segregated within the architecture of the space, can be used to make assumptions about different habitus-capital identities. Patrons in the box seats talked about an evening at the hockey game in Toronto being an event for which dressing for an evening out and a formal dinner were typical components. Former spectators who sat in Maple Leaf Gardens' most inexpensive seats recalled the Depression and the expense involved in going to see games, but they too highlighted the importance of Maple Leafs games as "events" in their social lives and they also often incorporated visits to local restaurants into their spectating experiences. While they may have possessed different habitus-capital identities, people in the least expensive seats aspired to realize the same symbolic (e.g., prestige and respectability) and social (e.g., networks of friends and colleagues) capital from attending hockey games in the 1930s that some of Toronto's wealthier citizens achieved in the box seats and their experiences were different more in degree than in kind. If one group of spectators was modelling respectability, another was perhaps aspiring to emulate them. In this sense, the symbolic capital available from spectating was realized from adhering to the expectations of the preferred spectator and being part of the environment Smythe endeavoured to create.

Relaxing Respectability

Olive remembers that her first game as a spectator at Maple Leaf Gardens was the annual Young Canada Night. "They commented on the young people being there growing up to be hockey players," she remembers. "And I said, never [laughing]. I wasn't going to be a hockey player. Girls didn't play hockey then." Olive's story – based as it is on her memories of an evening spent sitting in the first row behind the box seats, in the company of an executive from a Toronto manufacturing concern – is a useful reminder that Smythe, in invoking notions of feminine respectability for his new arena, had not sought to feminize the practice of hockey spectating (nor the game itself) but to gentrify it, providing male spectators with an environment to which they *could* take their wives and girlfriends. This is not the only paradox revealed in the operation of Maple Leaf Gardens' respectability project.

Foster Hewitt recalled that at Maple Leaf Gardens "the frenzied cheering of many thousands is so concentrated and the excitement spreads so rapidly, that no one can escape it."[43] Andy Lytle of the *Star* concurred: "Don't tell me a hockey spectator doesn't have fun. He gets everything on the menu and the service is wonderful!"[44] The contents of this "menu" reflected the belief that hockey spectators' passions were aroused by the prospect of physical, even violent altercations on the ice. This, the argument went, was one of the sights that attracted patrons to the NHL's new arenas in the late 1920s and 1930s. In 1933, the *Globe*, trying to shape rather than reflect opinion, argued that "Patrons of hockey do not attend games that they may witness fist fights between the players; the game is the thing."[45] However, such opinions of spectators' lack of interest in fisticuffs may have been in the minority. In reporting on a game during the 1936–37 season that included a ten-player brawl, the *Globe and Mail* reminded its readers: "Don't think the crowd didn't enjoy the fight."[46] Two years earlier, Hewitt contemplated hockey's popularity with spectators: "Dazzling speed and frequent change are only two reasons for hockey's popularity; the prevalence of physical danger is another ... even in twentieth-century mobs there still lurks an earnest desire to see men in perilous situations ... Assuredly, hockey does tend to satisfy that blood-spilling yearning."[47]

One explanation of this apparent paradox, between the nature of the crowd (with the attendant expectations of how it would comport itself) and the on-ice spectacle to which it was witness, is that this was the most profitable state of affairs for Maple Leaf Gardens' management. Despite Smythe's attempts to create a space where middle-class respectability was acted out, he was often the very reason such efforts were undermined. In a 1937 game at Maple Leaf Gardens, Smythe transgressed the boundaries he had worked so hard to impose and "added to the entertainment in the third period when he dashed out on the ice and joined in the argument over [Maple Leafs winger Bob] Davidson's disallowed goal."[48] This was not an isolated incident: "A week ago he [Smythe] reached over and grabbed [referee Babe] Dye. Saturday he couldn't reach [referee Ag] Smith so he hopped the boards and let loose a verbal barrage."[49] Two years earlier, "a very heated gentleman [presumably Smythe] scrambled over the boxes, rushed to the ice and was restrained from clambering on to the ice, by Ed. Bickel [*sic*]."[50] Although *Telegram* columnist Bobby Hewitson wondered, "How Conny gets away with this without being fined is a mystery," Maple Leaf Gardens' patrons often protested alongside Smythe's antics, as one could often "see his gray fedora through the mob scene bobbing and weaving and quivering in strong sympathetic agony."[51]

Off the ice, Smythe regularly used the media to generate rivalries with and foster spectator antagonism towards other clubs in the hopes that fans would flock to see how this "hatred" played out on the ice (see Fig. 5.3). The press was complicit in such strategies by adhering to what J.P. Fitzgerald of the *Telegram* called the "time-honored angle" of publishing "advance notices dwelling on grudges and promising roughness as an appeal to the general rather than to the regular hockey public."[52] Before a Maple Leafs game versus the Montreal Canadiens, Selke antagonized his team's opponent in the press. "What effect it had if any," Selke wrote to Smythe, "other than to annoy [Montreal coach Dick] Irvin and create a rough game which the fans enjoyed and which our boys won I do not know." Actually, Selke (and, by extension, Smythe) was fairly certain of the financial efficacy of such tactics: "our attendance has jumped

Fig. 5.3. Conn Smythe surrounded by members of the Toronto media, including Lou Marsh of the *Daily Star* and Bert Perry of the *Globe* (1926). (Archives of Ontario, Conn Smythe Fonds, F 223-3-2-1)

since [Maple Leafs coach Hap] Day and I spluttered a bit [to the press] – the team has improved and we have the fans talking on the streets for the first time this year."[53]

Smythe's most famous rivalry was with the Boston Bruins and his counterpart there, Art Ross.[54] Their mutual antipathy was well documented and widely known. The *Mail and Empire* noted that "there has always been quite a feeling between the two clubs," while *Hush* observed that "Conny Smythe and Art Ross are not going to harmonize that popular ballad 'Just Friends.'"[55] The infamous December 1933 incident where Leafs star Ace Bailey was badly injured by the swinging stick of the Bruins' Eddie Shore, although it took place in Boston, gave Fitzgerald an opportunity to rail against hockey promoters and their "press ballyhoo ... appealing to the public as a rowdy rough-house affair." Hockey, he continued, "can add nothing in its attractiveness as an entertainment by an appeal to the lower instincts of players or spectators."[56] Nevertheless, his colleague at the *Telegram*, Ted Reeve, noted that the possibility of violence on the ice and the excitement it provided the crowd ensured that "business at the turnstiles was better than ever." Reeve observed, tongue in cheek, that "customers have become so plentiful that ... One rinksider, for instance, was given his cut for the play-offs right in the first period and, almost before he started to bleed, his seat had been sold to three other people" (see Fig. 5.4). Reeve went on to note, lyrically, the economic benefit of stirring up the crowd in the ways that Smythe and Selke did:

> When hockey gets gentle it goes dead,
> As no one is crushed through the ribs or the head,
> And when it grows gentle the crowds they grow small,
> So where would be shinny with no brawls at all?
> What? No brawls at all?
> No, no brawls at all!
> Oh, where would be hockey (hold it),
> With no brawls at all? (at all, at all).[57]

Reeve's poetry highlights an important contradiction. Maple Leaf Gardens may have been built with the preferred respectable spectator in mind, one whose behaviour would be emulated by others within the arena, but as an entertainment business in the Depression it needed more than anything to sell tickets. Indeed, Selke wrote to Smythe in 1944, "hockey is a bigger thing than playing and winning games."[58] Filling all the seats at Maple Leaf Gardens often meant relying on the very customers the Maple Leafs sought to reform, what Fitzgerald in the *Telegram*, as noted earlier, called "the general rather than ... the regular hockey public." In a similar way, Eaton's College Street store, even in its attempts to attract the carriage trade, could not ignore working-class shoppers – although the creation of "bargain basements" certainly marginalized them.[59] At Maple Leaf Gardens, all manner of fans were welcome: the respectable, those labelled unrespectable, and those who enjoyed transgressing that boundary – provided they were paying customers.

Maple Leaf Gardens' staff also contributed to the relaxation of respectability. Colin recalls that his father, who also worked at the Gardens, would "go up into the office and there was a door into the blues" where "the odd friend would be out[side] that door. Dad would open it and let them in. Then they had to find a seat or find a spot to stand." His colleague, Claudia, worked at a concession stand that served the red box and rail seats. The bulk of her business was transacted in the intermissions between periods. Yet, while the game was in progress, she "used to sneak around the end of the bench and watch. I wasn't supposed to. But I did." She was not the only person within Maple Leaf Gardens to "sneak

Fig. 5.4. Spectators rise out of their seats to get a look at an altercation between players in a tense playoff game between the Maple Leafs and Boston (24 March 1938) that the home team won 1–0 in double overtime. (City of Toronto Archives, Globe and Mail fonds, Fonds 1266, Item 50393)

around." Ernest remembers that junior hockey players who played Saturday afternoon at the Gardens would often try to find ways to get into that evening's Maple Leafs game. "They'd go into the men's rooms and hide in the stalls or any little cubicle they could find to hide out," he recalls, "before the workmen came around and shooed them all out of the building."

Resisting Respectability

While Maple Leaf Gardens' president J.P. Bickell may have urged "enthusiastic" but respectable "support" from his patrons in a message published in a 1931 Maple Leaf Gardens' programme, spectators cheered in a variety of ways, at times loud, boisterous, and occasionally at odds with expectations of respectability (see Fig. 5.5).[60] Their emotions were often displayed by tossing the very programmes in which Bickell's request had been written onto the ice. Such an enjoyment of the space – to

Fig. 5.5. Spectators were engaged in the drama unfolding before them and often found ways to voice their displeasure. (City of Toronto Archives, Fonds 1257, Series 1057, Item 7502)

say nothing of the commingling of well-dressed box-seat patrons with "tinhorn gamblers" and ticket scalpers – affirms that the space of Maple Leaf Gardens was defined in a significant way by the spectators who inhabited it.[61] Or, as Lefebvre suggests, "the social relations of production have a social existence to the extent that they have a spatial existence," contending that these social relations of production "project themselves into a space, becoming inscribed there, and in the process producing the space itself."[62]

One explanation for the demonstrative nature of the hockey crowds that Colin called "classy enough" was that this label may have applied to distinct components of the audience. That is, the better-off patrons in the box and rail seats might have been perceived to be bringing class to the crowd while customers in the grey seats of the third tier added their vocal cheers and perhaps tossed the occasional programme. Certainly an element of the public felt uneasy about the valorization of hockey's physicality. Professor Thomas Loudon of the University of Toronto offered his confident opinion to the *Star* on the violent state of the game: "If people wanted things like that stopped, they'd be stopped, I feel sure ... Spectators like the excitement. I know what I'd do if a fight like that developed; I'd put them in jail."[63] While it might be assumed that similar viewpoints were common in Maple Leaf Gardens' more expensive seats, it is worth remembering that many of the altercations between spectators and players that were reported in the press took place closest to the ice, involving those spectators who could afford this vantage point (recalling the letter to the editor with which this book began).

Such an apparent dichotomy was reflected in the fraternal orders and other places where men congregated in the late nineteenth century. Lynne Marks argues that "two masculine ideals coexisted in these associations: the responsible, respectable breadwinner and the rowdy rough."[64] It is within this context that the paradox of Maple Leaf Gardens' spectators who occupied the most expensive seats nearest the ice and who were also, if press reports are an accurate guide, most often engaged in transgressive behaviours, including cursing at or becoming physically involved with the action on the ice, can be understood. These were men desiring on the one hand the respectability conferred by the public consumption of entertainment (where their outlay of disposable income was visible), while on the other hand enjoying the pleasure of an aggressive and at times vulgar masculinity that came from watching a physical contest while socializing with other men.

Other spectator practices seemingly more resistant of the respectability project, which was intended to reduce undesirable elements such as rowdyism and gambling, were themselves not absent at Maple Leaf Gardens. Ticket scalpers, another potentially undesirable element, graced the neighbourhood of the Gardens and shaped the experience of spectators entering the arena. Smythe may have advertised his building as a respectable home of commercial entertainments, but these activities had a history that predated Maple Leaf Gardens and, perhaps out of economic necessity, Smythe had to accept all the subcultures associated with hockey spectating, even if they compromised his respectability project. This was evidenced by the absence of any prominent campaigns to rid the arena of either ticket scalping or gambling.

Moreover, actual spectator practices worked at times to confound the pursuit of social capital. In his theorization of everyday life, Michel de Certeau contends that everyday life can be experienced in ways that disrupt the dominant order without altering it. Such experiences are made meaningful by "mak[ing] use of the cracks that particular conjunctions open in the surveillance of the proprietary powers."[65] The consumption of the products of the dominant culture in this way is its own tactical production. In the case of historical hockey arenas, some spectators found ways to create meaningful spectating experiences, perhaps by confounding the expectations of arena designers and operators. As de Certeau notes, "room remains for microinventions, for the practice of reasoned differences, to resist with sweet obstinance the contagion of conformism."[66]

Former spectators remember spectating practices that were resistant in this way. Recall the junior players who hid in the Gardens' washrooms as a way to sneak into Maple Leafs games. Or the spectators who would litter the ice with their programmes in the event of unpopular referees' decisions. While patrons in the box and rail seats were on display – modelling behaviours that were either worthy of emulation or transgressive – programmes tossed to the ice (or onto other spectators below) often came from higher up in the stands. The distance from the ice surface of the second- and third-tier green and grey seats may have actually enabled resistance. Ticket holders in these seats operated largely in anonymity, able to interact with the spectacle in ways that, even if they were criticized as inappropriate or disreputable by the press, were somewhat removed from efforts at maintaining respectability, more able to self-define their spectating experience.

Such behaviours were not unique to Maple Leaf Gardens. Spectators at New York's Madison Square Garden would toss decks of cards onto the ice, the cards scattering when the pack hit the ice, making clean-up difficult and delaying the game. Meanwhile, spectators in Detroit "used to throw a lot of pennies," remembers Stuart, a former Maple Leaf player. This posed a danger because "a penny is warm, so it just goes down, melts in the ice," which meant that players and officials risked injury in case they skated over a hidden coin. (Stuart suffered a serious injury in a minor-league game when he tripped on a penny and slammed into the rink boards, no doubt sensitizing him to spectator behaviours of this sort.) Similarly, Maple Leafs star winger Charlie Conacher wrote in 1936 that in the past, spectators in Detroit "would take along everything, from cabbages to tomatoes still in the tins." As a consequence, Conacher noted, games at the Olympia "would last probably half an hour longer than anywhere else, due to the ice cleaners having to come out so often and clear away the missiles."[67]

Akin to Smythe's selling of transgression on the ice, although "hegemonic elements wanted to use" late nineteenth-century exhibitions "to impress the desirability of system and harmony, they also wanted to break down established habits, values, and expectations."[68] Their aim was to promote "new forms of behaviour" and create "new desires."[69] But as much as Toronto's late nineteenth-century Industrial Exhibition was about constructing meaning for people, Walden argues that the reception of meanings could not always be controlled and fairgoers made of the experience what they would. Often the entertainments surrounding the exhibition, rather than the industrial displays, were what people most wanted to consume. Exhibition grounds were used and experienced in a variety of ways, some conforming to and others transgressing the intentions of organizers and Victorian proscriptions on public behaviour. As a result, "the fairground was contested space."[70] The process of defining the spectating spaces of Maple Leaf Gardens was similarly open to contestation.

Foucault has observed that "a whole history remains to be written of spaces – which would at the same time be a history of powers."[71] What is central to such a history in the context of the hockey arena is how these "powers" were negotiated and distributed between the places of sport and the spectators who inhabited them. Consider these two configurations. John Bale notes that "in even the most sterile stadium the crowd acts as a form of 'noise,' creating a place out of nothing."[72] On the other hand, Mary Louise Adams asserts that the history of skating rinks "show[s] how spaces regulate identities and behaviour."[73] Both Bale and Adams write of spaces of sport and the people who inhabit them. The former points to the importance that spectators play in creating sport spaces out of sterile places, while the latter notes the role that spaces play in defining the identities (and limiting the behaviours) available to spectators. Ultimately a theorization of the historical sports spectator unites these two arguments and accommodates the dialectical relationship that Lefebvre asserts as central to the production of space.

The varied crowd welcomed into Maple Leaf Gardens in the 1930s may have been subject to enhanced regulation by strictures that paid special attention to what Foucault called "irregular bodies," those that did not conform to the norms and expectations of the respectable preferred spectator. But such bodies were not passive subjects to the power imposed on them by the architecture and operation of spectator facilities such as Maple Leaf Gardens. They were not "blank pages waiting to be inscribed with disciplinary power," but rather "bodies [that] come from somewhere, and they are produced out of conditions of their spatial origin."[74] Spectator facilities such as Maple Leaf Gardens may have altered the commercial and cultural codes of spectatorship, but the people who entered these buildings had their own histories and experiences of spectating within earlier facilities – such as Arena Gardens – that they brought with them into these new arenas.

One final (likely unintended) consequence of Maple Leaf Gardens' design, in conjunction with the nature of the game being played on the ice, was that there were occasions during games when spectators spent time in physical contact with one another. The pursuit of respectable spectators may not have anticipated this. Nevertheless, both Emily and Harry recall spectators in the grey seats rising to watch the play move down the ice and constantly leaning forward to get the best view of the ice. This rising and sitting, as well as passing by others on the way to one's seat and generally moving throughout the arena, meant that spectating bodies touched and interacted with other spectating bodies. The very physicality of this experience, evokes the "muscular bonding" that occurs between participants in mass physical activities. William McNeill contends that there is "a strange sense of personal enlargement" that comes from "participation in collective ritual."[75] Spectating was just such an embodied experience and, in these settings, cheering for the home team – being both corporally and emotionally involved in the game – spectators at Maple Leaf Gardens recall feelings of passion, partisanship, and community.

Conclusion

When Maple Leaf Gardens opened in 1931, it hosted indoor sports spectating on a scale previously unseen in the city. This book has focused primarily on the nature of that spectatorship, examining how Maple Leaf Gardens anticipated particular spectators and spectator behaviours, who the spectators were that attended hockey games at the new arena, and what the experience of spectating was for these people.

Implicit within these themes is an assumption about the nature of North American professional hockey in particular – and commercial sport more generally – in the 1920s and 1930s. Maple Leaf Gardens (and its counterparts operated by US-based NHL franchises) was an example of the changing nature of commercial sports facilities at the time. It offered Torontonians a perceptibly different commodified spectating experience from the arenas and ice rinks that had come before it. Toronto in 1931 had theatres, movie houses, and concert halls similar to the lights of Broadway and Carnegie Hall, and nearby theatres (Pantages) and movie houses (Loew's) meant that Maple Leaf Gardens was located in the vicinity of the city's other entertainment venues. In this era of increased consumption of entertainments, facilities were designed and operated to cater to consumers as spectators and, at the same time, to broaden the audience for commercial spectacle, both in terms of gender and economic accessibility.

Toronto is an important geographic location for enquiry into the emergence of commercial sport spectatorship culture in the 1920s and

1930s and not solely because of the presence of its modern new arena. In much the same way that Montreal's "position" in Canadian society in the late nineteenth century enabled its sport leaders to influence the national character of sport development, Toronto exerted economic and cultural influence over a wide hinterland.[76] It was a city steeped in English amateur sporting traditions, although professional sport in the mid-1920s still carried a certain amount of stigma.[77] Nevertheless, even as social and political leaders in 1920s Toronto worried as "American influences seeped in," a city whose populace was of largely British descent "was hardly any more cosmopolitan in a cultural than in an ethnic sense."[78]

To compete in the burgeoning entertainment economy of the late 1920s, entrepreneurs in cities throughout North America envisioned sport spaces that would exclude – or at least be seen attempting to exclude – disreputable elements such as gambling, and project an aura of middle-class respectability. In Toronto, Conn Smythe, the executives of the Maple Leafs, and their architects designed and operated Maple Leaf Gardens to anticipate and produce respectable spectators at a particular intersection of class and gender expectations. From the outset, this meant locating the new arena in the neighbourhood of another civic institution that was wooing the respectable middle-class consumer: Eaton's College Street department store. Smythe opted for the same architectural firm, Ross & Macdonald, that had designed Eaton's flagship store. Their architects created Toronto's largest indoor gathering space, one that supported the Maple Leafs' efforts to gentrify the practice of sport spectating without eliminating the possibility of distinctions within the arena. The nature of the seating, for example, was increasingly less comfortable as one travelled higher in the arena, and the building was designed to dissuade spectators from moving between the different tiers of seats. The arena was operated in such a way as to not challenge the class and gender identities of all who entered.

Although sport spectating, and hockey in particular, was a predominantly male pastime, Smythe sought to cloak it in stereotypical norms of feminine respectability. This entailed not only building a grander (and larger) arena than any previously erected in Toronto but also operating it in an appreciably different manner. Staff were attired in neat matching outfits, modelling, as did salespeople in department stores, the uniform of the respectable middle class. The staff roles were also gendered, with men in charge of ticket taking at the building's entrances and ushering in the uppermost tier of Maple Leaf Gardens, a predominantly male space where fears of unruly behaviour were greatest. Women, by contrast, operated the concession stands and worked as ushers in the more expensive box seats. They provided comfort and nourishment where male staff handled financial matters and any potentially physical tasks (such as disciplining disorderly patrons). Moreover, for spectators who entered Maple Leaf Gardens, Smythe's ardent support of Canada's position within the British Empire – though hardly unusual for the time – was on full display. From the portrait of the monarch hanging on the end wall of the arena to the military bands that paraded out onto the ice at every season-opening game, Maple Leaf Gardens could only be experienced as a space that was white, British, and Anglophone.

It was into this environment that Smythe hoped his preferred respectable middle-class spectator would enter, a spectator who was likely male and who, Smythe also hoped, would feel that Maple Leaf Gardens offered sufficient comfort to bring a female companion. But, in light of these expectations, who from among Toronto's more than six hundred thousand citizens opted to spend their evenings attending hockey games? Anecdotal evidence suggests that women were common attendees, often in the company of men. Although the crowd was still predominantly male, the gender disparity varied between sections within Maple Leaf Gardens, where men were far more common in the least expensive third tier (grey seats) and standing-room sections. Interviews with female spectators, however, reveal that women were far from absent in these spaces. Lillian proudly recalls the weekly Saturday-evening occasions she and five female friends spent in Maple Leaf Gardens' grey seats.

But perhaps the most revealing evidence of who populated Maple Leaf Gardens' seats comes from a ledger of Maple Leafs' ticket subscribers compiled by arena staff for the 1933–34 season, especially when cross-referenced with the 1934 *Might's City of Toronto Directory* and the 1931 *Seventh Census of Canada*. The ledger represented – if all subscribed tickets were used – more than 25 per cent of a capacity crowd on any given night at Maple Leaf Gardens in the 1930s and nearly 35 per cent of the average crowd for the 1933–34 season. Ticket subscribers were overwhelmingly male (88.1 per cent). These men earned higher incomes and were more commonly occupied in white-collar professions when compared to Toronto's contemporary wage-earning male population. While subscribers' estimated average annual income decreased as one moved away from the ice surface into the higher reaches of the arena, even those subscribers who worked in blue-collar industries were often employed in managerial positions. Similar patterns were evident among the ticket accounts associated with female consumers. These women earned on average substantially less than male subscribers but still had incomes more than one-third greater than Toronto's female wage-earners as a whole. The majority worked in service and clerical jobs, rather than in domestic service, factories, or the needle trades, and better paying positions, such as teaching, were common.

On the basis of this evidence, Maple Leaf Gardens attracted the crowd of middle-class men and women to whom Smythe aspired to cater. There is not enough evidence, especially from the pre-1931 period when the Maple Leafs played at Arena Gardens, to conclusively state that this represented a sea change, although Smythe's and Frank Selke's comments to this effect are persuasive. While Smythe was more interested in gentrifying the practice of watching hockey rather than the game itself, the presence of a middle-class audience, however, does not imply that its members spectated in "respectable" ways. The spectator experience cannot be easily distilled to a single experience – indeed it was a pastiche of many different experiences – but it was certainly less vanilla than is suggested by Selke's assertion that with the opening of Maple Leaf Gardens, "hockey crowds now had real class."[79] And while the crowds may have been "classy," the same could not be said of the men producing the on-ice spectacle.

Smythe's passion for the fortunes of his hockey club was so well regarded by the Toronto press – whose access to information was controlled by the hockey club's management – that he was rarely chastised and was often praised for incidents at Maple Leaf Gardens where he would curse at officials and occasionally charge out onto the ice after them if a controversial decision had gone against the Maple Leafs. While such behaviour appears paradoxical for the man attempting to create a respectable spectating environment within Maple Leaf Gardens, Smythe and his assistants went even further. The Maple Leafs used the media to stoke rivalries with other clubs and sell tickets to spectators who expected not only furious action but also the possibility of bloodshed. Toronto was not the only NHL team to employ this marketing tactic, but its use goes some way towards explaining why when press reports from Maple Leaf Gardens did highlight spectators, they focused so heavily on the arena patrons' presumed taste for physical play. Nevertheless, the reasons why spectators journeyed to Maple Leaf Gardens and what they took away from the experience were far more varied than this.

Certainly, many spectators took pleasure in the spectacle that unfolded on the ice surface before them, both in the speed of the game and its physicality. But it was not the spectacle alone that attracted the spectator. The opportunity to share the experience with others was also important. The fact that the average subscriber recorded in the 1933–34 Maple Leaf Gardens ledger purchased more than two tickets per account suggests that attending hockey games was a social experience. This held true regardless of social standing, although subscribers in Maple Leaf Gardens' expensive box seats – whose social networks extended beyond workplace and familial connections to include some of the more exclusive sport and social clubs in 1930s Toronto – were more likely to have purchased numerous tickets and host a group of spectators. In the less expensive seats, it was more common to find spectators with a connection to one another – for example, neighbours or co-workers – individually purchasing adjacent seats.

Former spectators recall the many ways in which hockey spectating was a social occasion: a parent taking a child to their first game; a heterosexual couple going on a date to the hockey game (and perhaps couples of all sexualities, although no interviewees spoke of this); as well as couples choosing to attend with other couples. Women were a significant minority within the Maple Leaf Gardens crowd, perhaps in response to Smythe's initiatives, although some former spectators such as Lillian dated their spectatorship *prior* to the opening of Maple Leaf Gardens. While many women entered the arena on the arms of the men escorting them to the game – who may also have paid for their tickets – there were also a number of instances where women went to hockey games in the company of other women. Spectating has been constructed as a masculine pastime, but in the new spaces of sport in the interwar years, women in Toronto used one of the city's most prominent public buildings as a site for their own socializing.

What is clear is that for ticket holders at Maple Leaf Gardens, their spectating meant something to them. This book foregrounds the experiences of these people, the consumers who patronized the new sport spaces of the interwar years, by combining contemporary press accounts and archival sources, including architectural drawings, with heretofore unexplored data in the Maple Leaf Gardens ticket ledger and the memories of former spectators. These experiences need to be understood within the evolving material conditions of commercial sport during the 1920s and 1930s. Little prior consideration has been given to the customers who contributed to the financial viability of the NHL as it expanded into the US in the interwar years and virtually no light has been shed on the spectator experience at the league's new facilities. Inserting spectators into the history of North American commercial sport generally and recognizing the active role that spectators had in shaping their experience of Maple Leaf Gardens specifically gives voice to the people whose engagement with these new arenas has been largely ignored by historical scholarship.

Notes

1. Historicizing the Hockey Spectator

1 Throughout this book, the sport of ice hockey will be referred to as "hockey," the name by which it is most commonly known in North America.

2 "Paid Attendance, Pro Hockey Games," F223-3-1-60: NHL – Summary of Box Office Receipts, Conn Smythe Fonds, Archives of Ontario.

3 Tommy Munns, "Free-For-All Produces 6 Penalties as Leafs Win," *Globe and Mail* (Toronto), March 1, 1937, 20.

4 "Places Blame on Conacher," *Globe and Mail* (Toronto), March 2, 1937, 16.

5 Charles Wilkins, "Maple Leaf Gardens (and How It Got That Way)," in *Maple Leaf Gardens: Memories & Dreams, 1931–1999*, ed. Dan Diamond (Toronto: Maple Leaf Sports and Entertainment, 1999), 46.

6 Frank J. Selke with H. Gordon Green, *Behind the Cheering* (Toronto: McClelland and Stewart, 1962), 94.

7 The most influential text is Tony Mason's *Association Football and English Society, 1863–1915* (Brighton, UK: Harvester, 1980), which is considered below. Much of the soccer scholarship cited here builds upon Mason's important contributions.

8 Jeffrey Hill, *Sport, Leisure and Culture in Twentieth-Century Britain* (Houndmills, Basingstoke, Hampshire, UK: Palgrave, 2002), 30. See also Allen Guttmann, *Sports Spectators* (New York: Columbia University Press, 1986), 109.

9 John K. Walton, "Football, Fainting and Fatalities, 1923–1946," *History Today* 53, no. 1 (January 2003): 11.

10 See Philip White and Brian Wilson, "Distinctions in the Stands: An Investigation of Bourdieu's 'Habitus,' Socioeconomic Status and Sport Spectatorship in Canada," *International Review for the Sociology of Sport* 34, no. 3 (1999): 245–64; Ivan Waddington, Dominic Malcolm, and Roman Horak,

"The Social Composition of Football Crowds in Western Europe: A Comparative Study," *International Review for the Sociology of Sport* 33, no. 2 (1998): 155–69.

11 Guttmann, *Sports Spectators*, 121.

12 Mason, *Association Football*, 150.

13 Ibid.

14 Martin Johnes, *Soccer and Society: South Wales, 1900–1939* (Cardiff: University of Wales Press, 2002), 119.

15 Guttmann, *Sports Spectators*, 71, 116.

16 Lewis A. Erenberg, *Steppin' Out: New York Nightlife and the Transformation of American Culture, 1890–1930* (Chicago: University of Chicago Press, 1984), xiv–xv.

17 Mark Jancovich, Lucy Faire, and Sarah Stubbings, *The Place of the Audience: Cultural Geographies of Film Consumption* (London: British Film Institute, 2003), 42.

18 *New York Chronicle*, August 22, 1867, quoted in Melvin Adelman, *A Sporting Time: New York City and the Rise of Modern Athletics, 1820–70* (Urbana: University of Illinois Press, 1986), 158.

19 Colin D. Howell, *Northern Sandlots: A Social History of Maritime Baseball* (Toronto: University of Toronto Press, 1995), 75.

20 Ibid. Guttmann, *Sports Spectators*, 114–15, makes a similar argument about baseball in the US in the second half of the nineteenth century, as does R.J. Anderson, "'On the Edge of the Baseball Map' with the 1908 Vancouver Beavers," *Canadian Historical Review* 77, no. 4 (1996): 538–74, about Vancouver, BC, during the 1908 baseball season.

21 Johnes, *Soccer and Society*, 119. As Fiona Skillen has noted, the history of women's participation in football in Britain at this time also needs to be recuperated. Fiona Skillen, "Women, Identity, and Sports Participation in Interwar Britain," in *Consuming Modernity: Gendered Behaviour and Consumerism Before the Baby Boom*, ed. Cheryl Krasnick Warsh and Dan Malleck (Vancouver: UBC Press, 2013).

22 Peter Levine, *Ellis Island to Ebbets Field: Sport and the American Jewish Experience* (New York: Oxford University Press, 1992), 17.

23 Steven A. Riess, *Touching Base: Professional Baseball and American Culture in the Progressive Era*, 2nd ed. (Urbana: University of Illinois Press, 1999), 47, 48.

24 Hill, *Sport, Leisure and Culture*, 29; Jack Williams, *Cricket and England: A Cultural and Social History of the Inter-war Years* (London: Frank Cass, 1999), 45.

25 Guttmann, *Sports Spectators*, 121.

26 Dave Russell, *Football and the English: A Social History of Association Football in England, 1863–1995* (Preston: Carnegie Publishing, 1997), 56.

27 Mason, *Association Football*, 153.

28 Riess, *Touching Base*, 28, 33.

29 Mason, *Association Football*, 151.
30 Ibid., 155.
31 Dean A. Sullivan, "Faces in the Crowd: A Statistical Portrait of Baseball Spectators in Cincinnati, 1886–1888," *Journal of Sport History* 17, no. 3 (1990): 365.
32 Nicholas Fishwick, *English Football and Society, 1910–1950* (Manchester: Manchester University Press, 1989), 58; Johnes, *Soccer and Society*, 115.
33 Riess, *Touching Base*, 29.
34 Ibid., 39. Richard Cashman makes a similar argument about decreasing entry fees for cricket in Australia and a broadening consumer base for entertainment in the 1920s: Richard Cashman, *'Ave a Go, Yer Mug! Australian Cricket Crowds from Larrikin to Ocker* (Sydney: Collins, 1984), 70ff.
35 Benjamin G. Rader, *American Sports: From the Age of Folk Games to the Age of the Spectators* (Englewood Cliffs, NJ: Prentice-Hall, 1983), 196; Bruce Kidd, in *The Struggle for Canadian Sport* (Toronto: University of Toronto Press, 1996), 210, makes the same argument about rule changes in ice hockey.
36 Fishwick, *English Football and Society*, 58.
37 Bruce Kuklick, *To Every Thing a Season: Shibe Park and Urban Philadelphia, 1909–1976* (Princeton, NJ: Princeton University Press, 1991), 56.
38 Fishwick, *English Football and Society*, 65–6.
39 Ibid., 59.
40 Johnes, *Soccer and Society*, 123.
41 Ibid., 133–4.
42 Ibid., 124.
43 Ibid., 126.
44 Ibid., 114.
45 See Gunther Paul Barth, *City People: The Rise of Modern City Culture in Nineteenth-Century America* (New York: Oxford University Press, 1980); Gregory Bush, "'Genial Evasion' in the Big Time: Changing Norms of Respectability within an Expansive Urban Culture," *Journal of Urban History* 19, no. 3 (1993): 121–38; Lizabeth Cohen, "The Mass in Mass Consumption," *Reviews in American History* 18, no. 4 (1990): 548–55; Mark Dyreson, "The Emergence of Consumer Culture and the Transformation of Physical Culture: American Sport in the 1920s," *Journal of Sport History* 16, no. 3 (1989): 261–81; Stephen Hardy, "The City and the Rise of American Sport: 1820–1920," *Exercise and Sports Sciences Reviews* 9, no. 1 (1981): 183–219; Stephen Hardy, "Sport in Urbanizing America: A Historical Review," *Journal of Urban History* 23, no. 6 (1997): 675–708; David Nasaw, *Going Out: The Rise and Fall of Public Amusements* (Cambridge, MA: Harvard University Press, 1993); William R. Taylor, "The Launching of a Commercial Culture: New York City, 1860–1930" in *Power, Culture, and Place: Essays on New York City*, ed. John Hull Mollenkopf (New York: Russell Sage Foundation, 1988).

46 Fishwick, *English Football and Society*, 55.

47 Johnes, *Soccer and Society*, 117.

48 Fishwick, *English Football and Society*, 51.

49 Hill, *Sport, Leisure and Culture*, 29.

50 For a discussion of the NHL's expansion to the US and the economic implications of this, see Stephen Hardy and Andrew C. Holman, *Hockey: A Global History* (Urbana: University of Illinois Press, 2018), 219–22, and Kidd, *The Struggle for Canadian Sport*, chapter 5. See also J. Andrew Ross, *Joining the Clubs: The Business of the National Hockey League to 1945* (Syracuse: Syracuse University Press, 2015); John Chi-Kit Wong, *Lords of the Rinks: The Emergence of the National Hockey League, 1875–1936* (Toronto: University of Toronto Press, 2005).

51 Kidd, *The Struggle for Canadian Sport*, 199; Richard S. Gruneau and David Whitson, *Hockey Night in Canada: Sport, Identities, and Cultural Politics* (Toronto: Garamond, 1993), 102, make a similar argument.

52 "Unmusical Montreal," *Musical Canada* 2, no. 4 (July 1907): 163, quoted in Maria Tippett, *Making Culture: English-Canadian Institutions and the Arts before the Massey Commission* (Toronto: University of Toronto Press, 1990), 10; also quoted in Gruneau and Whitson, *Hockey Night in Canada*, 84.

53 D'Arcy Jenish, *The Stanley Cup: A Hundred Years of Hockey at Its Best* (Toronto: McClelland and Stewart, 1992), 118.

54 Gruneau and Whitson, *Hockey Night in Canada*, 102.

55 Major Frederic McLaughlin to Frank Calder, April 22, 1927, quoted in John Wong, "The Development of Professional Hockey and the Making of the National Hockey League" (PhD diss., University of Maryland, 2001), 265.

56 Kidd, *The Struggle for Canadian Sport*, 211–12.

57 Gruneau and Whitson, *Hockey Night in Canada*, 102.

58 The financial impact of the building of Maple Leaf Gardens is considered in Russell Field, "Passive Participation: The Selling of Spectacle and the Construction of Maple Leaf Gardens, 1931," *Sport History Review* 33, no. 1 (May 2002): 35–50.

59 Brian McFarlane, *Proud Past, Bright Future: One Hundred Years of Canadian Women's Hockey* (Toronto: Stoddart, 1994), 6.

60 Quoted in Michael McKinley, *Putting a Roof on Winter: Hockey's Rise from Sport to Spectacle* (Vancouver: Greystone, 2000), 10.

61 Kidd, *The Struggle for Canadian Sport*, 199ff.

62 See Gruneau and Whitson, *Hockey Night in Canada*; Colin Howell, *Blood, Sweat, and Cheers: Sport and the Making of Modern Canada* (Toronto: University of Toronto Press, 2001), chapter 4: Cheers; John Herd Thompson and Allen Seager, *Canada, 1922–1939: Decades of Discord* (Toronto: McClelland and Stewart, 1985), 158–92; Tippett, *Making Culture*.

63 Gruneau and Whitson, *Hockey Night in Canada*, 101.

64 Kidd, *The Struggle for Canadian Sport*, 300n7. While the number of popular hockey histories is extensive, the list provided by Kidd, which includes works by Fischler and McFarlane, is an excellent starting point. More recent popular histories of hockey include McKinley, *Putting a Roof on Winter*, while Jenish, *The Stanley Cup*, is a popular history of the NHL.

65 See Gruneau and Whitson, *Hockey Night in Canada*; Hardy and Holman, *Hockey: A Global History*; Kidd, *The Struggle for Canadian Sport*, chapter 5; Ross, *Joining the Clubs*; Howard Shubert, *Architecture on Ice: A History of the Hockey Arena* (Montreal and Kingston: McGill-Queen's University Press: 2016); and Wong, *Lords of the Rinks*. Other significant contributions include Andrew Carl Holman, ed., *Canada's Game: Hockey and Identity* (Montreal: McGill-Queen's University Press, 2009); Colin D. Howell, ed., *Putting It on Ice*, vol. 1: *Hockey and Cultural Identities* (Halifax: Gorsebrook Research Institute, 2002); Colin D. Howell, ed., *Putting It on Ice*, vol. 2: *Internationalizing "Canada's Game"* (Halifax: Gorsebrook Research Institute, 2002); Colin D. Howell, ed., *Putting It on Ice*, vol. 3: *Women's Hockey – Gender Issues On and Off the Ice* (Halifax: Gorsebrook Research Institute, 2005); John Chi-Kit Wong, ed., *Coast to Coast: Hockey in Canada to the Second World War* (Toronto: University of Toronto Press, 2009).

66 For sociological explorations and critiques of the notion of hockey's cultural significance in Canada, see, for example, Courtney Szto, *Changing on the Fly: Hockey Through the Voices of South Asian Canadians* (Vancouver: University of British Columbia Press, 2020); Richard Gruneau and David Whitson, eds., *Artificial Ice: Hockey, Culture, and Commerce* (Toronto: University of Toronto Press, 2019).

67 Kidd, *The Struggle for Canadian Sport*, 192.

68 Wong, "The Development of Professional Hockey," 266.

69 Howard Shubert, "The Changing Experience of Hockey Spectatorship: Architecture, Design, Technology, and Economics" in *Putting It on Ice*, 1: 60.

70 Andrew Craig Morrison, *Opera House, Nickel Show, and Palace: An Illustrated Inventory of Theater Buildings in the Detroit Area* (Dearborn, MI: Greenfield Village & Henry Ford Museum, 1974), 1.

71 Harold Kalman, *A History of Canadian Architecture* (Toronto: Oxford University Press, 1994), 742–4.

72 Constance Olsheski, *Pantages Theatre: Rebirth of a Landmark* (Toronto: Key Porter, 1989), 34.

73 Selke with Green, *Behind the Cheering*, 59.

74 Frank "King" Clancy, 1967, audio recording 275747, Brian McFarlane Collection, R9327-0-5-E, Library and Archives Canada, Ottawa, Ontario.

75 Foster Hewitt, *Foster Hewitt: His Own Story* (Toronto: Ryerson Press, 1967), 47.

76 Selke with Green, *Behind the Cheering*, 60.

77 *The Rocket*, directed by Charles Binamé (Montreal: Cinémaginere, 2005).

78 Shubert, "The Changing Experience," 60.

79 Stephen Hardy, "Long before Orr," in *The Rock, the Curse, and the Hub: A Random History of Boston Sports*, ed. Randy Roberts (Cambridge, MA: Harvard University Press, 2005), 269.

80 *Boston Arena Programme*, December 22, 1925, 8, File 18A: NHL programs, Thomas Patrick Gorman Fonds, MG30-C129, Library and Archives Canada, Ottawa, Ontario.

81 On the masculine nature of smoking in public, see Jarrett Rudy, *The Freedom to Smoke: Tobacco Consumption and Identity* (Montreal: McGill-Queen's University Press, 2005).

82 Hardy, "Long before Orr," 266.

83 The Madison Square Garden "franchise" plan ended with Rickard's death in Miami in 1929.

84 "Arrest Connie Smythe on Assault Charge," *Daily Star* (Toronto), December 13, 1933, 2.

85 "Fans Make Early Start Showering Torn Paper on Boston Gardens Ice," *Globe and Mail* (Toronto), March 30, 1938, 18.

86 See, for example, "Syracuse Wins from London," *Globe* (Toronto), March 4, 1936, 7: "Fans rushed to the ice, and police were called to restore order"; or "Oshawa Upsets Brantford, 6–5," *Globe* (Toronto), March 19, 1940, 14: "fights broke out among the fans, police had to be called to quell riots in two different sections of the rink and at least one Brantford spectator needed a doctor's attention."

87 "Quick Action," *Globe* (Toronto), December 14, 1933, 8.

88 See William J. Smyth, *Toronto, the Belfast of Canada: The Orange Order and the Shaping of Municipal Culture* (Toronto: University of Toronto Press, 2015).

89 James T. Lemon, *Toronto since 1918: An Illustrated History* (Toronto: James Lorimer, 1985), 50.

90 Quoted in Lemon, *Toronto since 1918*, 50.

91 Thompson and Seager, *Canada, 1922–1939*, 98.

92 Lemon, *Toronto since 1918*, 45.

93 Ibid., 76.

94 Thompson and Seager, *Canada, 1922–1939*, 77.

95 Lemon, *Toronto since 1918*, 41.

96 Quoted in Thompson and Seager, *Canada, 1922–1939*, 138.

97 Thompson and Seager, *Canada, 1922–1939*, 151.

98 Lemon, *Toronto since 1918*, 26; Randall White, *Too Good to Be True: Toronto in the 1920s* (Toronto: Dundurn, 1993), 69.

99 Thompson and Seager, *Canada, 1922–1939*, 175.

100 Lemon, *Toronto since 1918*, 33; see also White, *Too Good to Be True*, 72–5.

101 Susan E. Houston, "A Little Steam, a Little Sizzle and a Little Sleaze: English Language Tabloids in the Interwar Period," *Papers of the Bibliographical Society of Canada* 40, no. 1 (2002): 38.

102 Editorial, *Hush* (Toronto), February 8, 1936, 3.

103 Lemon, *Toronto since 1918*, 26.

104 Quoted in White, *Too Good to Be True*, 133.

105 See William Kilbourn, *Intimate Grandeur: One Hundred Years at Massey Hall* (Toronto: Stoddart, 1993).

106 Olsheski, *Pantages Theatre*, 42. The Pantages was renamed the Imperial Theatre in 1930 when Nathanson sold his holdings to Famous Players. See "Ed Mirvish Theatre," Cinema Treasures, http://cinematreasures.org/theaters/871.

107 For architectural and historical details on Massey Hall, Loew's Yonge Street and Winter Garden theatres, and Toronto's "theatre block," see Paul Dilse, *Toronto's Theatre Block: An Architectural History* (Toronto: Toronto Region Architectural Conservancy, 1989).

108 Conn Smythe with Scott Young, *If You Can't Beat 'Em in the Alley* (Toronto: McClelland and Stewart, 1981), 102–3.

109 Wilkins, "Maple Leaf Gardens," 46.

110 Bruce Kidd, "Solman, Lawrence," *Dictionary of Canadian Biography*, vol. 16: *1931–1940* (University of Toronto/Université Laval: 2021), http://www.biographi.ca/en/bio/solman_lawrence_16E.html; Hilary Russell, *Double Take:* The Story of the Elgin and Winter Garden Theatres (Toronto: Dundurn, 1989), 27.

111 Russell, *Double Take*, 27.

112 See Jason Wilson, Kevin Shea, and Graham MacLachlan, *J.P. Bickell: The Life, the Leafs, and the Legacy* (Toronto: Dundurn, 2017).

113 Kidd, *The Struggle for Canadian Sport*, 205.

114 Kelly McParland, *The Lives of Conn Smythe: From the Battlefield to Maple Leaf Gardens; A Hockey Icon's Story* (Toronto: Fenn/McClelland and Stewart, 2012), 156.

115 Ibid., 79.

116 Henry Roxborough, "The Heart of the City," *Maple Leaf Gardens Official Programme,* January 1950, 56, Hockey Hall of Fame, Resource Centre, Toronto, Ontario; "Public Skating Expected Next Saturday Night," *Daily Star* (Toronto), November 26, 1912, 11.

117 "Public Skating."

118 Field, "Passive Participation," 38n16 details the many seating capacity estimates for Arena Gardens, ranging from seven thousand to nine thousand.

119 Tom Gaston with Kevin Shea, *A Fan for All Seasons* (Toronto: Fenn, 2001), 13.

120 "Historic Sites of Manitoba: Winnipeg Amphitheatre," Manitoba Historical Society, updated June 4, 2022, http://www.mhs.mb.ca/docs/sites/winnipegamphitheatre.shtml.

121 Gaston with Shea, *A Fan for All Seasons*, 13.
122 Roxborough, "The Heart of the City," 56.
123 Gaston with Shea, *A Fan for All Seasons*, 13.
124 Quoted in Roy MacGregor, "The First Fifty Years," in *The Leafs: The First Fifty Years*, ed. Stan Obodiac (Toronto: McClelland and Stewart, 1976), 27.
125 Nutsy Fagan [Ted Reeve], "Why We Need a New Arena," *Arena Gardens Programme*, 1930–31 season (game-specific insert missing), 17, Box 234159, File 23, Larry Becker Fonds, City of Toronto Archives, Toronto, Ontario.
126 Clancy, audio recording.
127 "Superior Experience Beat Toronto in First Pro. Game," *Daily Star* (Toronto), December 26, 1912, 13.
128 Clancy, audio recording.
129 Unsigned letter addressed to 105 Mary Street West, Whitby, Ontario, undated, found in Toronto Toros hockey team program, February 27, 1976, Box 234159, File 17, Larry Becker Fonds, City of Toronto Archives, Toronto, Ontario.
130 "All Sports," *Hush* (Toronto), April 2, 1931, 8.
131 F 223-3-1-60: NHL – Summary of Box Office Receipts, Conn Smythe Fonds, Archives of Ontario, Toronto, Ontario.
132 Gaston with Shea, *A Fan for All Seasons*, 13.
133 Smythe with Young, 102.
134 Russell Field, "Profits, Playoffs, and the Building of Maple Leafs Gardens," in *Putting It On Ice*, 1: 49–50.
135 Kidd, *The Struggle for Canadian Sport*, 213; Field, "Profits, Playoffs," 55, table 3.
136 Moaner McGruffey [Ted Reeve], "Why We Need a New Arena," *Arena Gardens Programme*, 1930–31 season (game-specific insert missing), 56, Box 234159, File 23, Larry Becker Fonds, City of Toronto Archives, Toronto, Ontario.
137 McParland, *The Lives of Conn Smythe*, 112.
138 Alice Snippersnapper [Ted Reeve], "Why We Need a New Arena," *Arena Gardens Programme*, 1930–31 season (game-specific insert missing), 56, Box 234159, File 23, Larry Becker Fonds, City of Toronto Archives, Toronto, Ontario.
139 Fagan [Reeve], "Why We Need a New Arena," 56.
140 Kidd, *The Struggle for Canadian Sport*, 198.
141 See Field, "Passive Participation." See also Ross, *Joining the Clubs*.
142 Tony Bennett, *The Birth of the Museum: History, Theory, Politics* (London: Routledge, 1995).

2. Constructing the Preferred Spectator

1 Conn Smythe, quoted in John Barber, "Ghosts of the Gardens Tell Tales of Glory and Disgrace," *Globe and Mail* (Toronto), February 13, 1999, A12.

2 *Maple Leaf Gardens Official Programme*, November 12, 1931, 28, Resource Centre, Hockey Hall of Fame, Toronto, Ontario.

3 Conn Smythe with Scott Young, *If You Can't Beat 'Em in the Alley* (Toronto: McClelland and Stewart, 1981), 102–3.

4 Maple Leaf Gardens prospectus, 1931, F 223-3-1-53, Conn Smythe Papers, Archives of Ontario, Toronto, Ontario.

5 Smythe with Young, *If You Can't Beat 'Em in the Alley*, 103.

6 For a discussion of separate spheres and its strengths and limitations as an explanatory device, see Linda K. Kerber, "Separate Spheres, Female Worlds, Woman's Place: The Rhetoric of Women's History," *The Journal of American History* 75, no. 1 (1988): 9–39.

7 Cynthia Wright, "'The Most Prominent Rendezvous of the Feminine Toronto': Eaton's College Street and the Organization of Shopping in Toronto, 1920–1950," (PhD diss., University of Toronto, 1992), 147.

8 Ibid., 130.

9 Ibid., 123. Wright cites William Dendy, *Lost Toronto* (Toronto: Oxford University Press, 1978), 157.

10 Dendy, *Lost Toronto*, 201.

11 Frank J. Selke with H. Gordon Green, *Behind the Cheering* (Toronto: McClelland and Stewart, 1962), 89.

12 Memorandum, James Elliott, January 3, 1931, Maple Leaf Gardens: General Matters, File M-103, General Files of James Elliott, F229–82, T. Eaton Company Fonds, Archives of Ontario, Toronto, Ontario.

13 Charles Wilkins, "Maple Leaf Gardens (and How It Got That Way)," in *Maple Leaf Gardens: Memories & Dreams, 1931–1999*, ed. Dan Diamond (Toronto: Maple Leaf Sports and Entertainment, 1999), 47.

14 J.A. Gibson to James Elliott, April 29, 1930, Maple Leaf Gardens: General Matters, File M-103, General Files of James Elliott, F229–82, T. Eaton Company Fonds, Archives of Ontario, Toronto, Ontario.

15 Gibson's letter identifies E.W. Bickle as the president of the hockey club. There is room for confusion here. Bickle was certainly an executive with both the hockey club and the arena, but J.P. Bickell, a Toronto mining executive, was president of Maple Leaf Gardens (the arena corporation). At this point in the franchise's history, Conn Smythe was the manager of the hockey club. But while Bickle and Bickell had high profile positions, for all intents and purposes, Smythe was running both the business and hockey affairs of the team, including planning the new arena.

16 J.A. Gibson to T. Eaton Company Limited, December 30, 1930, Maple
    Leaf Gardens: General Matters, File M-103, General Files of James Elliott,
    F229–82, T. Eaton Company Fonds, Archives of Ontario, Toronto, On-
    tario. McParland contends that Bickle's statement is "a suggestion he can
    only have made without Smythe's knowledge." Kelly McParland, *The Lives
    of Conn Smythe: From the Battlefield to Maple Leaf Gardens; A Hockey Icon's Story*
    (Toronto: Fenn/McClelland and Stewart, 2012), 118.

17 Quoted in Selke with Green, 89.

18 Dendy, *Lost Toronto*, 201.

19 Ross & Macdonald to J.A. Gibson, January 26, 1931, Maple Leaf Gardens:
    General Matters, File M-103, General Files of James Elliott, F229–82,
    T. Eaton Company Fonds, Archives of Ontario, Toronto, Ontario.

20 Note for files, James Elliott, November 20, 1930; J.A. Gibson to T. Eaton
    Company Limited, December 30, 1930, Maple Leaf Gardens: General
    Matters, File M-103, General Files of James Elliott, F229–82, T. Eaton Com-
    pany Fonds, Archives of Ontario, Toronto, Ontario.

21 "Toronto's Red Light Babies: The Big Vice Clean-Up Has Started," *Hush*
    (Toronto), June 18, 1931, 21.

22 "Is It Really True That – ," *Hush* (Toronto), February 9, 1935, 1; "Things
    We Would Like to Know," *Hush* (Toronto), March 9, 1935, 1.

23 James Elliott to C.N. Mills, January 27, 1931, Maple Leaf Gardens: General
    Matters, File M-103, General Files of James Elliott, F229–82, T. Eaton Com-
    pany Fonds, Archives of Ontario, Toronto, Ontario.

24 A.E. Stuart to James Elliott, February 10, 1931, Maple Leaf Gardens: Gen-
    eral Matters, File M-103, General Files of James Elliott, F229–82, T. Eaton
    Company Fonds, Archives of Ontario, Toronto, Ontario.

25 James T. Lemon, *Toronto since 1918: An Illustrated History* (Toronto: James
    Lorimer, 1985), 43, 45. See also John Herd Thompson and Allen Seager,
    Canada, 1922–1939: Decades of Discord (Toronto: McClelland and Stewart,
    1985), 85.

26 Wright, "'The Most Prominent Rendezvous,'" 134; Smythe with Young, *If
    You Can't Beat 'Em in the Alley*, 103.

27 James Elliott to C.N. Mills, January 27, 1931, Maple Leaf Gardens: General
    Matters, File M-103, General Files of James Elliott, F229–82, T. Eaton Com-
    pany Fonds, Archives of Ontario, Toronto, Ontario.

28 J.E. Dodds to James Elliott, January 26, 1931, Maple Leaf Gardens: Gen-
    eral Matters, File M-103, General Files of James Elliott, F229–82, T. Eaton
    Company Fonds, Archives of Ontario, Toronto, Ontario.

29 J.A. Gibson to James Elliott, March 10, 1931; Note for files, James Elliott,
    January 27, 1931, Maple Leaf Gardens: General Matters, File M-103, Gen-
    eral Files of James Elliott, F229–282, T. Eaton Company Fonds, Archives of
    Ontario, Toronto, Ontario.

30 Cynthia Wright, "'Feminine Trifles of Vast Importance': Writing Gender into the History of Consumption" in *Gender Conflicts: New Essays in Women's History*, ed. Franca Iacovetta and Mariana Valverde (Toronto: University of Toronto Press, 1992), 230.

31 Wright, "'The Most Prominent Rendezvous,'" 121.

32 Memorandum, James Elliott, May 3, 1930, Maple Leaf Gardens: General Matters, File M-103, General Files of James Elliott, F229–82, T. Eaton Company Fonds, Archives of Ontario, Toronto, Ontario.

33 Geo. A. Ross to Harry McGee, May 21, 1931, Maple Leaf Gardens: General Matters, File M-103, General Files of James Elliott, F229–82, T. Eaton Company Fonds, Archives of Ontario, Toronto, Ontario. The sale price of $375,000 was subsequently reduced to $350,000 and also granted Eaton's "the right to approve the exterior of the building" (McParland, *The Lives of Conn Smythe*, 119).

34 J. Elliott to J.A. Livingstone, February 16, 1931; Geo. A. Ross to Harry McGee, May 21, 1931, Maple Leaf Gardens: General Matters, File M-103, General Files of James Elliott, F229–82, T. Eaton Company Fonds, Archives of Ontario, Toronto, Ontario.

35 "Cross Section," February 20, 1931, Folder 13-164-02M, Maple Leaf Gardens file, Ross & Macdonald Collection, Canadian Centre for Architecture, Montreal, Quebec.

36 Stan Obodiac, *Maple Leaf Gardens: Fifty Years of History* (Toronto: Van Nostrand Reinhold, 1981), 14. The event depicted by this photograph likely took place in 1936, since McBride died during his second term as mayor in 1936, after only four months in office. His first term as mayor occurred before the opening of Maple Leaf Gardens.

37 Wright, "'The Most Prominent Rendezvous,'" 135.

38 Sherry McKay, "Designing Discipline: The Architecture of a Gymnasium," in *Disciplining Bodies in the Gymnasium: Memory, Monument, Modernism*, ed. Patricia Vertinsky and Sherry McKay (London and New York: Routledge, 2004), 133.

39 Patricia Vertinsky, "Designing the Million Dollar Gym: Modernism and Masculinity," in *Disciplining Bodies in the Gymnasium*, 47.

40 Leslie Maitland, Jacqueline Hucker, and Shannon Ricketts, *A Guide to Canadian Architectural Styles* (Peterborough, ON: Broadview, 1992), 132.

41 Patricia McHugh, *Toronto Architecture: A City Guide* (Toronto: Mercury, 1985), 174.

42 Tim Morawetz, "Gardens a Masterful Combination of Art Deco and Streamlined Moderne Styling," Friends of Maple Leaf Gardens, https://web.archive.org/web/20060620095827/ http://www.friendsofmapleleafgardens.ca:80/history.cfm.

43 John Bentley Mays, *Emerald City: Toronto Visited* (Toronto: Viking, 1994), 276. Mays quotes from an uncited report by Anne M. Fort-Menares. Interestingly, Maple Leaf Gardens does not merit mention in some of the seminal texts of Canadian architectural history, for example, Alan Gowans, *Building Canada: An Architectural History of Canadian Life* (Toronto: Oxford University Press, 1966) and Harold Kalman, *A History of Canadian Architecture* (Toronto: Oxford University Press, 1994).

44 "First Floor Plan," Maple Leaf Gardens – Arena, RG 7–137, rolls, L133–1140, Factory Inspection Branch blueprints and drawings, Archives of Ontario, Toronto, Ontario.

45 Sinaiticus, "Maple Leaf Gardens, Toronto," *Construction*, 24, no. 12 (December 1931), 370.

46 Andrew Podnieks, *The Blue and White Book, 1997* (Toronto: ECW, 1996), 7.

47 Wilkins, "Maple Leaf Gardens," 53.

48 Sinaiticus, "Maple Leaf Gardens," 370.

49 "Interior Study," August 18, 1931, Folder 13-164-01, Maple Leaf Gardens file, Ross & Macdonald Collection, Canadian Centre for Architecture, Montreal, Quebec.

50 "Details of Boxing Ring," October 21, 1931, Folder 13-164-08; "Boxing Ring Elec. Fixture," undated, Folder 13-164-09, Maple Leaf Gardens file, Ross & Macdonald Collection, Canadian Centre for Architecture, Montreal, Quebec.

51 Lou Marsh, "Lamping the Arena Opening with Frau – and Others," *Daily Star* (Toronto), November 13, 1931, 10.

52 Rinkside rail seats were the only spaces that could accommodate, for example, patrons in wheelchairs.

53 James Elliott to Harry McGee, February 26, 1931, Maple Leaf Gardens: General Matters, File M-103, General Files of James Elliott, F229–82, T. Eaton Company Fonds, Archives of Ontario, Toronto, Ontario.

54 "First Floor Plan," Maple Leaf Gardens – Arena, RG 7–137, rolls, L133–1140, Factory Inspection Branch blueprints and drawings, Archives of Ontario, Toronto, Ontario.

55 Phyllis M. Griffiths, "The Girl and the Game," *Telegram* (Toronto), November 13, 1931, 27.

56 Jarrett Rudy, *The Freedom to Smoke: Tobacco Consumption and Identity* (Montreal: McGill-Queen's University Press, 2005), 20, 164.

57 Donald F. Davis and Barbara Lorenzkowski, "A Platform for Gender Tensions: Women Working and Riding on Canadian Urban Public Transit in the 1940s," *Canadian Historical Review* 79, no. 3 (1998): 443.

58 Rudy, *The Freedom to Smoke*, 6.

59 Ibid., 39.

60 Maple Leaf Gardens file and *Maple Leaf Gardens Official Programme*, January 23, 1934, Resource Centre, Hockey Hall of Fame, Toronto, Ontario.
61 Sinaiticus, "Maple Leaf Gardens," 370; emphasis added.
62 "Diagrams Showing Types of Seats," July 6, 1931, Folder 13-164-03, Maple Leaf Gardens file, Ross & Macdonald Collection, Canadian Centre for Architecture, Montreal, Quebec.
63 "Plan of Box Seating," July 20, 1931, Folder 13-164-03; "Seating Plan," undated, Folder 13-164-05, Maple Leaf Gardens file, Ross & Macdonald Collection, Canadian Centre for Architecture, Montreal, Quebec.
64 J.P. Fitzgerald, "Maple Leaf Gardens Formally Opened," *Telegram* (Toronto), November 13, 1931, 26.
65 Selke with Green, *Behind the Cheering*, 94.
66 Tommy Munns, "Scanning the Sport Field," *Globe* (Toronto), March 27, 1936, 6.
67 Edwin Allan, "Sporting Gossip," *Mail and Empire* (Toronto), December 13, 1933, 13.
68 "The President's Message to Maple Leaf Fans," *Maple Leaf Gardens Official Programme*, January 23, 1934, 2, Resource Centre, Hockey Hall of Fame, Toronto, Ontario.
69 "Toronto Maple Leaf Ticket Prices," Maple Leaf Sports and Entertainment corporate files; Sinaiticus, "Maple Leaf Gardens," 372.
70 W.A. Hewitt, "Sporting Views and Reviews," *Daily Star* (Toronto), November 12, 1931, 16.
71 Selke with Green, *Behind the Cheering*, 94.
72 For commentary on Smythe's role in enforcing a dress code, see Tom Gaston with Kevin Shea, *A Fan for All Seasons* (Toronto: Fenn, 2001), 71.
73 Paul O'Leary, "Networking Respectability: Class, Gender and Ethnicity among the Irish in South Wales, 1845–1914," *Immigrants & Minorities* 23, no. 2–3 (July–November 2005): 265–6.
74 Gareth Stedman Jones, "Working-Class Culture and Working-Class Politics in London, 1870–1900; Notes on the Remaking of a Working Class," *Journal of Social History* 7, no. 4 (Summer 1974): 475.
75 Kate Boyer, "Place and the Politics of Virtue: Clerical Work, Corporate Anxiety, and Changing Meanings of Public Womanhood in Early Twentieth-Century Montreal," *Gender, Place & Culture* 5, no. 3 (1998): 266.
76 Sammy Taft was the operator of a well-known Toronto haberdasher. During the 1930s, his business offered a hat to any player who scored three goals in a single game at Maple Leaf Gardens, a promotion that is credited with originating the term "hat trick." See Jamie Bradburn, "Toronto Invents: The Hat Trick," Torontoist, April 3, 2013, https://torontoist.com/2013/04/toronto-invents-the-hat-trick/.

77 Neil Campbell, "The Gardens: It's Still Hockey's Home," *Globe and Mail* (Toronto), October 10, 1981, S4. Campbell interviews Charlie Good, who had been an usher since 1931, and John Moor, who had once played coronet in the Toronto Irish Regiment band at the Gardens before becoming staff at Maple Leaf Gardens and moving up to supervisor of ticket takers.

78 Quoted in George Gross, "The Hallowed Halls," *Sun* (Toronto), November 12, 1980, 91.

79 Bruce Kidd, *The Struggle for Canadian Sport* (Toronto: University of Toronto Press, 1996), 199.

80 Lou Marsh, "With Pick and Shovel," *Daily Star* (Toronto), November 12, 1931, 16.

81 "Weekly Whoopee by Rounder," *Hush* (Toronto), November 12, 1931, 14.

82 "Weekly Whoopee by Rounder," *Hush* (Toronto), December 10, 1932, 10. The $3.00 seats were the most expensive tickets at Maple Leaf Gardens.

83 "Weekly Whoopee," *Hush* (Toronto), December 26, 1933, 2. "S.R.O." is short for standing room only.

84 "Weekly Whoopee by Rounder," *Hush* (Toronto), November 26, 1932, 2.

85 For a discussion of racialized space, see Sherene Razack, "When Place Becomes Race," in *Race, Space, and the Law: Unmapping a White Settler Society*, ed. Sherene Razack (Toronto: Between the Lines, 2002).

86 Lemon, *Toronto since 1918*, 196–7, tables 7–9.

87 See, for example, Douglas Hunter, *War Games: Conn Smythe and Hockey's Fighting Men* (Toronto: Penguin, 1997).

88 Cyril H. Levitt and William Shaffir, *The Riot at Christie Pits* (Toronto: Lester & Orpen Dennys, 1987).

89 "Is It True," *Hush* (Toronto), November 26, 1931, 16.

90 Quoted in "Smythe Defends Shore," *Mail and Empire* (Toronto), December 14, 1933, 15.

91 C.W. MacQueen, "Maple Leaf Players Return Home and Give Their Version of Battle," *Mail and Empire* (Toronto), December 17, 1931, 14.

92 Susan Porter Benson, "Palace of Consumption and Machine for Selling: The American Department Store, 1880–1940," *Radical History Review* 21 (Fall 1979): 207.

93 Ibid.

94 See Veronica Strong-Boag, *The New Day Recalled: Lives of Girls and Women in English Canada, 1919–1939* (Toronto: Penguin, 1988).

95 Alexandrine Gibb, "No Man's Land of Sport," *Daily Star* (Toronto), November 12, 1931, 17.

96 See Alice Kessler-Harris, "Gender Ideology in Historical Reconstruction: A Case Study from the 1930s," *Gender & History* 1, no. 1 (1989): 31–49; Margaret Hobbs, "Rethinking Antifeminism in the 1930s: Gender Crisis or Workplace Justice? A Response to Alice Kessler-Harris," *Gender & History* 5,

no. 1 (1993): 4–15; Alice Kessler-Harris, "Reply to Hobbs," *Gender & History* 5, no. 1 (1993): 16–19.

97 Hobbs, "Rethinking Antifeminism," 6.

98 Ibid., 11.

99 "Is It True," *Hush* (Toronto), March 31, 1932, 16; "Things We Would Like to Know," *Hush* (Toronto), November 25, 1933, 1.

100 "Places Blame on Conacher," *Globe and Mail* (Toronto), March 2, 1937, 16.

101 Sandra Weathers Smith, "Spectators in Public: Theatre Audiences in New York City, 1882–1929," (PhD diss., University of California, Berkeley, 2001), 207.

102 Smythe with Young, *If You Can't Beat 'Em in the Alley*, 115–16.

103 Frank Selke to Conn Smythe, January 14, 1944, F223-3-1-102: Hockey – Miscellaneous, 1925–1947, Conn Smythe Fonds, Archives of Ontario, Toronto, Ontario.

104 "Weekly Whoopee by Rounder," *Hush* (Toronto), April 22, 1933, 10.

105 Robert Bothwell, Ian M. Drummond, and John English, *Canada, 1900–1945* (Toronto: University of Toronto Press, 1987), 285–6.

106 Foster Hewitt, *Foster Hewitt: His Own Story* (Toronto: Ryerson Press, 1967), 56. The 1941 *Eighth Census of Canada* listed the Canadian population as 11,506,655.

107 "Weekly Whoopee by Rounder," *Hush* (Toronto), November 26, 1932, 2.

108 Hewitt, *Foster Hewitt: His Own Story*, 39.

109 Marsh, "Lamping the Arena Opening."

110 "Recalling Toronto the Good," *Toronto Star*, March 9, 2003, F7.

111 Gaston with Shea, *A Fan for All Seasons*, 54.

112 Jack Dennett on Foster Hewitt's broadcast of the first game at Maple Leaf Gardens, "Great Moments in Hockey," Hockey Night in Canada, produced by Canadian Sports Network Ltd., audio recording, LP.

113 Bobbie Rosenfeld, "Feminine Sports Reel," *Globe and Mail* (Toronto), February 27, 1939, 18.

114 Hewitt, *Foster Hewitt: His Own Story*, 43.

115 Barry Broadfoot, *Ten Lost Years, 1929–1939: Memories of Canadians Who Survived the Depression* (Toronto: Doubleday Canada, 1973), 250.

116 Quoted in Charles Wilkins, "Maple Leaf Gardens: What Fate Awaits This Icon of Canadian Culture?" *Canadian Geographic* 114 (January/February 1994): 33.

117 Gibb, "No Man's Land of Sport"; Hewitt, "Sporting Views and Reviews."

118 Sinaiticus, "Maple Leaf Gardens," 369.

119 James Elliott to Harry McGee, November 2, 1931, Maple Leaf Gardens: General Matters, File M-103, General Files of James Elliott, F229–82, T. Eaton Company Fonds, Archives of Ontario, Toronto, Ontario.

120 Marsh, "Lamping the Arena Opening."

121 Hewitt, "Sporting Views and Reviews."

122 L.S.B. Shapiro, "Canadiens Show Improvement to Tie Toronto, 1–1," Montreal *Gazette*, November 16, 1931, 20.

123 Sinaiticus, "Maple Leaf Gardens," 372.

124 Ibid., 370.

125 Marsh, "Lamping the Arena Opening." The term "gallery gods" was a moniker used to describe spectators in the seats furthest from the ice, stage, etc., in performance venues (i.e., those people sitting in the gallery).

126 Ted Reeve, "Sporting Extras," *Telegram* (Toronto), November 13, 1931, 27.

127 Marsh, "Lamping the Arena Opening."

128 Quoted in Gross, "The Hallowed Halls."

129 Gaston with Shea, *A Fan for All Seasons*, 50.

130 Ibid. Vic R., who was "sitting in the west blues" for the first game at Maple Leaf Gardens, also recalls dressing in a jacket and tie.

131 "Thousands Throng Gardens as Leafs Open New Home," *Telegram* (Toronto), November 13, 1931, 26; Gaston with Shea, *A Fan for All Seasons*, 51.

132 Reeve, "Sporting Extras."

133 Marsh, "Lamping the Arena Opening."

134 C.W MacQueen, "Chicago Black Hawks Beat Leafs in Opening Game at New Gardens," *Mail and Empire* (Toronto), November 13, 1931, 16.

135 "Thousands Throng Gardens"; Gaston with Shea, *A Fan for All Seasons*, 51, also mentions this particular spectator.

136 "Thousands Throng Gardens"; J.P. Fitzgerald, "Maple Leaf Gardens Formally Opened," *Telegram* (Toronto), November 13, 1931, 26.

137 Edwin Allan, "Sporting Gossip," *Mail and Empire* (Toronto), November 14, 1931, 19.

138 "That Question of Manners at the Arena Opening," *Mail and Empire* (Toronto), November 13, 1931, 6.

139 J.P. Fitzgerald, "Toronto Citizens Must Measure Up to Hockey," *Telegram* (Toronto), November 12, 1931, 43.

140 Gibb, "No Man's Land of Sport."

141 Fitzgerald, "Toronto Citizens."

142 Marsh, "Lamping the Arena Opening"; Frank "King" Clancy, 1967, audio recording 275747, Brian McFarlane Collection, R9327-0-5-E, Library and Archives Canada, Ottawa, Ontario.

143 "Weekly Whoopee by Rounder," *Hush* (Toronto), June 11, 1931, 10.

144 *Labour Leader*, November 27, 1931, 1.

3. Filling the Stands

1 Russell Field, "Passive Participation: The Selling of Spectacle and the Construction of Maple Leaf Gardens, 1931," *Sport History Review*, 33, no. 1 (May 2002): 35–50.

2 Rogan Taylor, "Walking Alone Together: Football Supporters and Their Relationship with the Game," in *British Football and Social Change: Getting into Europe,* ed. John Williams and Stephen Wagg (Leicester: Leicester University Press, 1991), 111.

3 James T. Lemon, *Toronto since 1918: An Illustrated History* (Toronto: James Lorimer, 1985), 68, 64.

4 The discrepancy between the number of subscribers and subscribed seats listed in Table 3.1 and the figures derived from the 1933–34 ledger, which are listed in Table 3.2 and discussed below, are due to recording methods. Table 3.1 represents a snapshot in time, taken on 22 December 1933, while the ledger was amended and updated through to the end of the 1933–34 NHL season.

5 Conn Smythe with Scott Young, *If You Can't Beat 'Em in the Alley* (Toronto: McClelland and Stewart, 1981), 109; Kelly McParland, *The Lives of Conn Smythe: From the Battlefield to Maple Leaf Gardens; A Hockey Icon's Story* (Toronto: Fenn/McClelland and Stewart, 2012), 142.

6 "Maple Leaf Home Games Season 1933–34," F 223-3-1-60: NHL – Summary of Box Office Receipts, Conn Smythe Fonds, Archives of Ontario, Toronto, Ontario.

7 For the purposes of this study, income and employment data were taken from vol. 5, "Wage Earners," of the 1931 *Seventh Census of Canada.*

8 Ingrid Botting, "Understanding Domestic Service through Oral History and the Census: The Case of Grand Falls, Newfoundland," *Resources for Feminist Research* 28, no. 1–2 (2000): 103. See also Bruce Curtis, *The Politics of Population: State Formation, Statistics, and the Census of Canada, 1840–1875* (Toronto: University of Toronto Press, 2001).

9 Botting, "Understanding Domestic Service," 109.

10 Harold Carter and C. Roy Lewis, *An Urban Geography of England and Wales in the Nineteenth Century* (London: Edward Arnold, 1990), 17.

11 Gareth Shaw, *British Directories as Sources in Historical Geography,* Historical Geography Research Series, no. 8 (Norwich: Geo Abstracts,1982), 34; see also Gareth Shaw and Tim Coles, "Directories as Elements of Town Life: The Case of National Socialist Germany," *The Geographical Journal* 161, no. 3 (November 1995): 296–306.

12 The description of Maple Leaf Gardens' seating plan is based upon "Seating Plan," presentation drawings, October 6, 1931, folder 13-164-04, Maple Leaf Gardens file, Ross & Macdonald Collection, Canadian Centre for Architecture, Montreal, Quebec. The total number of seats in each section are listed in "Summary of Seats for Hockey," Maple Leaf Gardens Seating Plans, F 223-3-1, box k663, Conn Smythe Fonds, Archives of Ontario, Toronto, Ontario.

13 "Seating Plan," drawing No. 3.04 C, revision B, July 6, 1931, folder 13-164-05, Maple Leaf Gardens file, Ross & Macdonald Collection, Canadian Centre for Architecture, Montreal, Quebec.

14 For a discussion of spectator cultures at New York's Madison Square Garden, see Russell Field, "A Night at the Garden(s): A History of Professional Hockey Spectatorship in the 1920s and 1930s" (PhD diss., University of Toronto, 2008).

15 "A.E. Marie Parkes," University of Toronto Sports Hall of Fame, https://varsityblues.ca/honors/hall-of-fame/a-e-marie-parkes/9.

16 Andrew Podnieks, *The Blue and White Book, 1997* (Toronto: ECW, 1996), 5.

17 Advertisement, "Charlie Querrie's Palace Theatre (Danfort[h] at Pape) Plays Only Big League Pictures," *Arena Gardens Official Programme*, March 7, 1931, 14, Resource Centre, Hockey Hall of Fame, Toronto, Ontario.

18 "Toronto Wrestling History: An Annotated Scrapbook," Gary Will's Toronto Wrestling History: An Annotated Scrapbook, https://web.archive.org/web/20160507231756/ http://www.garywill.com/toronto/index.htm.

19 Bruce Kidd, "'Making the Pros Pay' for Amateur Sports: The Ontario Athletic Commission 1920–1947," *Ontario History* 87, no. 2 (1995): 105–28. The OAC was one of the beneficiaries of a provincial amusement tax levied against entertainments such as those hosted at Maple Leaf Gardens.

20 Andy Lytle, *Daily Star* (Toronto), October 17, 1949, quoted in McParland, *The Lives of Conn Smythe*, 151.

21 A. Victoria Bloomfield and Richard Harris, "The Journey to Work: A Historical Methodology," *Historical Methods* 30, no. 2 (Spring 1997): 100; emphasis added.

22 When totalled, the figures for individual categories of occupation listed in Tables 3.5, 3.6, and 3.8 do not reflect the published totals. This is accounted for, in part, by a small number of people listed as being employed in occupations of fewer than ten persons. Despite this, there are still minor errors in the figures in the published census data. The calculations in this chapter and reflected in Tables 3.5, 3.6, and 3.8 are based upon the published figures in the *Seventh Census of Canada* (1931).

23 Robert Bothwell, Ian M. Drummond, and John English, *Canada, 1900–1945* (Toronto: University of Toronto Press, 1987), 258.

24 Lemon, *Toronto since 1918*, 60.

25 Ibid., 59.

26 This portion of the analysis excludes the small number of account holders both male and female (153) who were listed in the *Might's City of Toronto Directory* with occupational details but no place of employment. Some worked out of their home or were self-employed, including a wide variety of professions from milliners and grocers to physicians and dentists.

27 Bloomfield and Harris, "The Journey to Work," 101.

28 "Free Tickets for Hockey Matches," *Flash*, October 14, 1935, 3, F229-141-0-171: Employee Magazines, T. Eaton Company Records, Archives of Ontario, Toronto, Ontario.

29 Jesse Edgar Middleton, *Toronto's 100 Years* (Toronto: City of Toronto Centennial Committee, 1934), 161.

30 *Maple Leaf Gardens Official Programme*, January 23, 1934, 34, Resource Centre, Hockey Hall of Fame, Toronto, Ontario.

31 "Turning on Toronto: Hiding in Plain Sight," City of Toronto, https://www.toronto.ca/explore-enjoy/history-art-culture/online-exhibits/web-exhibits/web-exhibits-local-government/turning-on-toronto-a-history-of-toronto-hydro/turning-on-toronto-hiding-in-plain-sight/.

32 Maple Leaf Gardens prospectus, 1931, F 223-3-1-53, Conn Smythe Papers, Archives of Ontario, Toronto, Ontario.

33 The registrar was the company responsible for keeping a record of the holders of Maple Leaf Gardens' public securities. Maple Leaf Gardens' board members also included directors at Canada Life Assurance, National Life Assurance, North American Life Assurance, and, not surprisingly, Sun Life Assurance Corp., which held the largest mortgage on the arena.

34 Tom Gaston with Kevin Shea, *A Fan for All Seasons* (Toronto: Fenn, 2001), 52–3.

35 Local histories of Toronto's Jewish community make no mention of the elder Levinsky. City directories of the early twentieth century have been critiqued for omitting immigrants, yet Bloomfield and Harris ("The Journey to Work," 99) argue that in Toronto the "listings of Jews and Italians … were extensive."

36 These figures are for "partial" account holders, who represented the vast majority of subscribers.

37 William J. Covington, ed., *The Torontonian Society Blue Book and Club Membership Register: The Social Register, 1934* (Toronto: Torontonian Society, 1934).

38 Suzanne Morton, *Ideal Surroundings: Domestic Life in a Working-Class Suburb in the 1920s* (Toronto: University of Toronto Press, 1995), 120.

39 When considering subscribers apart from the social networks of their relations, there are five such clubs.

40 Donald Kerr, "The Emergence of the Industrial Heartland c. 1750–1950," in *Heartland and Hinterland: A Geography of Canada*, ed. L.D. McCann (Toronto: Prentice-Hall, 1982), 94–5, cited in Gunter Gad and Deryck Holdsworth, "Building for City, Region, and Nation: Office Development in Toronto 1834–1984," in *Forging a Consensus: Historical Essays on Toronto*, ed. Victor L. Russell (Toronto: University of Toronto Press, 1984), 301.

41 *Maple Leaf Gardens Official Programme*, January 23, 1934, 72.

42 Frank J. Selke with H. Gordon Green, *Behind the Cheering* (Toronto: McClelland and Stewart, 1962), 88. Selke notes that Rogers was president of Canada Building Materials, while Smythe with Young (*If You Can't Beat 'Em in the Alley*, 105) labels Rogers as president of Elias Rogers Co. Ltd. and St. Mary's Cement Co. Ltd. Selke also states that Larkin Maloney, whom

Smythe calls "[m]y oldtime pal from the racetracks" (Smythe with Young, *If You Can't Beat 'Em in the Alley*, 103), convinced Rogers to invest in Maple Leaf Gardens, and who, in turn, encouraged J.P. Bickell to increase his $25,000 in the team by investing a further $10,000 in the new arena. Smythe's memoirs, however, recall the same event in reverse: Bickell talking Rogers into investing in the arena.

43 *Maple Leaf Gardens Official Programme,* January 23, 1934, 39.

44 The president of O'Keefe's Beverages Ltd., W.B. Cleland, appeared in the 1933–34 ledger as the purchaser of four box seats, however "Not taking" was handwritten next to this particular entry. The Maple Leaf Gardens 1933–34 *Programme* included a full-page advertisement for O'Keefe's Stone Ginger Beer. *Maple Leaf Gardens Official Programme,* January 23, 1934, 29, Resource Centre, Hockey Hall of Fame, Toronto, Ontario.

45 W.A. Hewitt, "Sporting Views and Reviews," *Daily Star* (Toronto), November 12, 1931, 16.

46 Gruneau and Whitson, *Hockey Night in Canada,* 101. The auto manufacturer's hockey broadcasts had become such a ubiquitous part of the Toronto airwaves in the 1930s that the local tabloid, *Hush,* asked "why General Motors should be allowed to tie up three stations with Foster Hewitt's bleatings is beyond comprehension" ("Weekly Whoopee by Rounder," *Hush* (Toronto), December 31, 1932, 4).

47 Barry Broadfoot, *Ten Lost Years, 1929–1939: Memories of Canadians Who Survived the Depression* (Toronto: Doubleday Canada, 1973), 250.

48 The 1931 census lists Toronto's population as 631,207: 305,427 men (48.39 per cent) and 325,780 women (51.61 per cent).

49 Bloomfield and Harris, "The Journey to Work." They note that "directories provided poor coverage of married women and hence of those lines of work, such as nursing, where married women were widely employed" (107).

50 Veronica Strong-Boag, *The New Day Recalled: Lives of Girls and Women in English Canada, 1919–1939* (Toronto: Penguin, 1988), 51.

51 Strong-Boag, *The New Day Recalled,* 51ff; Graham S. Lowe, "Women, Work, and the Office: The Feminization of Clerical Occupations in Canada, 1901–1931," in *Rethinking Canada: The Promise of Women's History,* ed. Veronica Strong-Boag and Anita Clair Fellman, 3rd ed. (Toronto: Oxford University Press, 1997), 257, table 2.

52 Gad and Holdsworth, "Building for City, Region, and Nation," 304.

53 Bloomfield and Harris, "The Journey to Work," 107.

54 See Joan Sangster, *Earning Respect: The Lives of Working Women in Small-Town Ontario, 1920–1960* (Toronto: University of Toronto Press, 1995), 94–5, for the argument about "self-supporting single women."

4. Community in the Stands

1 Linda Shopes, "Making Sense of Oral History," *History Matters: The U.S. Survey Course on the Web*, February 2002, http://historymatters.gmu.edu /mse/oral/oral.pdf, 2, 3; Nancy Cook, "The Thin within the Thick: Social History, Postmodern Ethnography, and Textual Practice," *Histoire sociale/ Social History* 32, no. 63 (1999): 90.

2 Shopes, "Making Sense of Oral History," 6.

3 Alessandro Portelli, *The Death of Luigi Trastulli, and Other Stories: Form and Meaning in Oral History* (Albany: State University of New York Press, 1991), 26.

4 Paul Quarrington, "Introduction," in *Maple Leaf Gardens: Memories & Dreams, 1931–1999*, ed. Dan Diamond (Toronto: Maple Leaf Sports and Entertainment, 1999), 6.

5 Conn Smythe with Scott Young, *If You Can't Beat 'Em in the Alley* (Toronto: McClelland and Stewart, 1981), 104.

6 Roger E. Riendeau, "Servicing the Modern City, 1900–30," in *Forging a Consensus: Historical Essays on Toronto*, ed. Victor L. Russell (Toronto: University of Toronto Press, 1984), 166.

7 James T. Lemon, *Toronto since 1918: An Illustrated History* (Toronto: James Lorimer, 1985), 77.

8 Riendeau, "Servicing the Modern City," 77.

9 "A Big Job Well Done," *Globe* (Toronto), November 14, 1931, 4.

10 Ibid.

11 Tom Gaston with Kevin Shea, *A Fan for All Seasons* (Toronto: Fenn, 2001), 50.

12 "Recalling Toronto the Good," *Toronto Star*, March 9, 2003, F7.

13 "Dowling's Grill," located east of the arena's main entrance, is visible in exterior photos of Maple Leaf Gardens from the 1930s. Maple Leaf Gardens file, Resource Centre, Hockey Hall of Fame, Toronto, Ontario.

14 No doubt former spectators were also confronted with smells as well, however few of them dwelled upon this during interviews.

15 Bobby Hewitson, "Inside the Blue Line," *Telegram* (Toronto), March 24, 1937, 45.

16 Edwin Allan, "Sporting Gossip," *Mail and Empire* (Toronto), November 13, 1931, 17.

17 Bobby Hewitson, "Inside the Blue Line," *Telegram* (Toronto), January 18, 1937, 22.

18 Gaston with Shea, *A Fan for All Seasons*, 50.

19 "Seating Plan," drawing No. 3.04 C, revision B, July 6, 1931, folder 13-164-05, Maple Leaf Gardens file, Ross & Macdonald Collection, Canadian Centre for Architecture, Montreal, Quebec.

20 L.S.B. Shapiro, "Canadiens Show Improvement to Tie Toronto, 1–1," Montreal *Gazette*, November 16, 1931, 20.

21 Bruce Hunter, email message to Paul Beirne, Maple Leaf Sports and Entertainment, July 5, 2005.

22 "Recalling Toronto the Good."

23 Allan, "Sporting Gossip."

24 Alexandrine Gibb, "No Man's Land of Sport," *Daily Star* (Toronto), November 12, 1931, 17.

25 Gaston with Shea, *A Fan for All Seasons*, 78. Spectator memories may be somewhat unreliable on the nature of organ music at Maple Leaf Gardens. In 1956, Smythe acquired the Wurlitzer organ from the soon-to-be demolished Shea's Hippodrome. Whether this replaced an existing organ at the arena is unclear. Jim Amodeo, "The Sound of Music," *Hockey Then & Now* (blog), https://hockeythenandnow.blogspot.com/2011/01/sound-of-music.html; Lloyd E. Klos, "A man … a Castle … and a Wurlitzer," TTOS: The Toronto Theatre Organ Society, http://www.theatreorgans.com/toronto/history.html, reprinted from *Theater Organ* 16, no. 1 (February 1976): 5–11.

26 Bobbie Rosenfeld, "Feminine Sports Reel," *Globe and Mail* (Toronto), February 27, 1939, 18.

27 William Kilbourn, *The Toronto Book: An Anthology of Writings Past and Present* (Toronto: Macmillan of Canada, 1976), 238.

28 Craig Heron, "The Boys and Their Booze: Masculinities and Public Drinking in Working-Class Hamilton, 1890–1946," *Canadian Historical Review* 86, no. 3 (September 2005): 411–52. Prohibition in Ontario lasted from 1926 to 1934. As Heron notes, the ban on the public sale of alcohol only made its consumption "more awkward and clandestine" (434). After 1934, alcohol could be consumed in licensed drinking places that were, at least in working-class Hamilton, "relatively unattractive" (445).

29 Quoted in Neil Campbell, "The Gardens: It's Still Hockey's Home," *Globe and Mail* (Toronto), October 10, 1981, S4.

30 M.J. Rodden, "On the Highways of Sport," *Globe* (Toronto), March 4, 1932, 12. It is unclear whether Montreal's fans were "grouped together" in Maple Leaf Gardens by the arena's ticket staff or by choice.

31 Gaston with Shea, *A Fan for All Seasons*, 52.

32 Kevin Shea, "Stanley Cup Journal," Hockey Hall of Fame, https://web.archive.org/web/20101203180944/http://www.hhof.com/html/exSCJ05_12.shtml.

33 Tommy Munns, "Scanning the Sport Field," *Globe* (Toronto), March 27, 1936, 6.

34 J.P. Bickell, "President's Address to Sports Followers of the Queen City," *Maple Leaf Gardens Official Programme*, November 12, 1931, 28, Resource Centre, Hockey Hall of Fame, Toronto, Ontario.

35 Quoted in Phyllis M. Griffiths, "The Girl and the Game," *Telegram* (Toronto), February 27, 1939, 21.

36 Bert Perry, "Bruins Beat Leafs in Lively Fracas," *Globe* (Toronto), March 11, 1935, 6.

37 Andy Lytle, "Big Boston Bears Show Leafs the Way to Go Home," *Daily Star* (Toronto), March 11, 1935, 10.

38 "Chicago Hawks Spoil Gardens Opening by Beating Leafs," *Telegram* (Toronto), November 13, 1931, 26.

39 Griffiths, "The Girl and the Game," 27.

40 Foster Hewitt, *Foster Hewitt: His Own Story* (Toronto: Ryerson Press, 1967), 44.

41 Andy Lytle, "Leafs Obliged to Knock Karakas Out to Get Win," *Daily Star* (Toronto), January 18, 1937, 10.

42 Don Cowie, "Leafs Trim Hawks in Stormy Battle," *Globe and Mail* (Toronto), January 18, 1937, 19.

43 W.T. Munns, "On the Highways of Sport," *Globe* (Toronto), February 8, 1935, 6.

44 Bill Chadwick, "Whistling the Playoffs," in *The Official National Hockey League Stanley Cup Centennial Book*, ed. Dan Diamond (Toronto: McClelland and Stewart, 1992), 117–18.

45 M.J. Rodden, "On the Highways of Sport," *Globe* (Toronto), November 26, 1934, 12.

46 "Bruins' Last Period Rally Upsets Leafs," *Telegram* (Toronto), March 11, 1935, 22.

47 "Maple Leaf Home Games [by season]," F 223-3-1-60: NHL – Summary of Box Office Receipts, Conn Smythe Fonds, Archives of Ontario, Toronto, Ontario.

48 Frank Selke to Conn Smythe, January 14, 1944, F223-3-1-102: Hockey – Miscellaneous, 1925–47, Conn Smythe Fonds, Archives of Ontario, Toronto, Ontario.

49 Edwin Allan, "Sporting Gossip," *Mail and Empire* (Toronto), December 24, 1932, 13.

50 "Maple Leaf Home Games [by season]," F 223-3-1-60: NHL – Summary of Box Office Receipts, Conn Smythe Fonds, Archives of Ontario, Toronto, Ontario. Attendance records of earlier Maple Leafs seasons make mention of Young Canada Night, but do not include specific figures for the numbers of children admitted.

51 Frank Selke to Conn Smythe, 30th Battery, Canadian Army Overseas, January 11, 1944, F223-3-1-102: Hockey – Miscellaneous, 1925–47, Conn Smythe Fonds, Archives of Ontario, Toronto, Ontario.

52 Ava Baron, "On Looking at Men: Masculinity and the Making of a Gendered Working-Class History," in *Feminists Revision History*, ed. Ann-Louise Shapiro (New Brunswick, NJ: Rutgers University Press, 1994), 148.

53 Ibid., 150.

54 Michael S. Kimmel, *Manhood in America: A Cultural History*, 2nd ed. (New York: Oxford University Press, 2006), 5.

55 Ibid.

56 Suzanne Morton, *Ideal Surroundings: Domestic Life in a Working-Class Suburb in the 1920s* (Toronto: University of Toronto Press, 1995), 109. Morton cites Andrew Tolson, *The Limits of Masculinity* (London: Tavistock, 1977), 12–13.

57 Joy Parr, *The Gender of Breadwinners: Women, Men, and Change in Two Industrial Towns* (Toronto: University of Toronto Press, 1990), 186.

58 Morton, *Ideal Surroundings*, 121.

59 Craig Heron, "The Boys and Their Booze," 419.

60 Ibid., 449.

61 Judith Fingard, "Masculinity, Fraternity, and Respectability in Halifax at the Turn of the Twentieth Century," in *Gender and History in Canada*, ed. Joy Parr and Mark Rosenfeld (Toronto: Copp Clark, 1996), 211; Lynne Sorrel Marks, *Revivals and Roller Rinks: Religion, Leisure, and Identity in Late-Nineteenth-Century Small-Town Ontario* (Toronto: University of Toronto Press, 1996), 110.

62 Morton, *Ideal Surroundings*, 125.

63 See, for example, Nancy B. Bouchier, *For the Love of the Game: Amateur Sport in Small-Town Ontario, 1838–1895* (Montreal and Kingston: McGill-Queen's University Press, 2003).

64 Quoted in Kimmel, *Manhood in America*, 113; Ernest Thompson Seton, "The Boy Scouts in America," *Outlook* 95 (1910): 630, quoted in David I. Macleod, *Building Character in the American Boy: The Boy Scouts, the YMCA, and Their Forerunners, 1870–1920* (Madison: University of Wisconsin Press, 1983), 49.

65 Morton, *Ideal Surroundings*, 125.

66 Kimmel, *Manhood in America*, 116.

67 Morton, *Ideal Surroundings*, 119.

68 Ibid., 125.

69 Fingard, "Masculinity, Fraternity, and Respectability," 211.

70 Dorothy McAnally, personal communication to author, July 29, 2005.

71 Bruce Hunter, personal communication to author, July 30, 2005.

72 Heron, "The Boys and Their Booze," 449.

73 Ibid., 450.

74 For Canadian scholarship on this issue in English Canada, see Veronica Strong-Boag, *The New Day Recalled: Lives of Girls and Women in English Canada, 1919–1939* (Toronto: Penguin, 1988). For francophone Canada, see Denyse Baillargeon, *Making Do: Women, Family and Home in Montreal during the Great Depression*, trans. Yvonne Klein (Waterloo, ON: Wilfrid

Laurier University Press, 1999). More focused Canadian studies include Morton, *Ideal Surroundings*; Parr, *The Gender of Breadwinners*; Ruth A. Frager, *Sweatshop Strife: Class, Ethnicity, and Gender in the Jewish Labour Movement of Toronto, 1900–1939* (Toronto: University of Toronto Press, 1993); and Carolyn Strange, *Toronto's Girl Problem: The Perils and Pleasures of the City, 1880–1930* (Toronto: University of Toronto Press, 1995).

75 For American scholarship, focusing on the pre–First World War period and working-class women, see Kathy Lee Peiss, *Cheap Amusements: Working Women and Leisure in Turn-of-the-Century New York* (Philadelphia: Temple University Press, 1986). The literature on Canadian women and sport from this period is dominated understandably by the opportunities and challenges women faced as participants and organizers, rather than as spectators. See, for example, M. Ann Hall, *The Girl and The Game: A History of Women's Sport in Canada*, 2nd ed. (Peterborough, ON: Broadview, 2016); Carly Adams, "'I Just Felt Like I Belonged to Them': Women's Industrial Softball, London, Ontario 1923–35," *Journal of Sport History* 38, no. 1 (2011): 75–94.

76 Katrina Srigley, *Breadwinning Daughters: Young Working Women in a Depression-Era City, 1929–1939* (Toronto: University of Toronto Press, 2010). See chapter 5.

77 Joan Sangster, *Earning Respect: The Lives of Working Women in Small-Town Ontario, 1920–1960* (Toronto: University of Toronto Press, 1995), 85–8.

78 Franca Iacovetta and Mariana Valverde, "Introduction," in *Gender Conflicts: New Essays in Women's History*, ed. Franca Iacovetta and Mariana Valverde (Toronto: University of Toronto Press, 1992), xvi.

79 In what follows, I do not want to discount or disrespect men's accounts; rather I want to understand their characterization of female fans as socially constructed memories.

80 Andy Lytle, "Once Overs," *Daily Star* (Toronto), March 29, 1935, 16.

81 Hewitt, *Foster Hewitt: His Own Story*, 41.

82 Gibb, "No Man's Land of Sport"; Griffiths, "The Girl and the Game."

83 See Strong-Boag, *The New Day Recalled*.

84 Griffiths, "The Girl and the Game." "Big Boy Blues" is a reference to the Maple Leafs' team colours.

85 Cynthia Wright, "'Feminine Trifles of Vast Importance': Writing Gender into the History of Consumption," in *Gender Conflicts: New Essays in Women's History*, ed. Franca Iacovetta and Mariana Valverde (Toronto: University of Toronto Press, 1992), 250–1.

86 Hockey: Activities at Maple Leaf Gardens, film recording 284846, Brian McFarlane Collection, Library and Archives Canada, Ottawa, Ontario.

87 "The Fan's Corner," *Globe and Mail* (Toronto), January 19, 1937, 21.

88 Gaston with Shea, *A Fan for All Seasons*, 78.

5. The State of Smythe's Respectability Project

1 For a discussion of the "memories" constructed around the closing of Maple Leaf Gardens, see Russell Field, "Manufacturing Memories and Directing Dreams: Commemoration, Community, and the Closing of Maple Leaf Gardens," *International Journal of Canadian Studies* 35 (2007): 61–93.

2 Stephen Brunt, "Building on Maple Leaf Memories," *Globe and Mail* (Toronto), February 13, 1999, A32.

3 John Barber, "Ghosts of the Gardens Tell Tales of Glory and Disgrace," *Globe and Mail* (Toronto), February 13, 1999, A12.

4 W.A. Hewitt, "Sporting Views and Reviews," *Daily Star* (Toronto), November 13, 1931, 10; see also Bruce Kidd, "Toronto's SkyDome: The World's Greatest Entertainment Centre," in *The Stadium and the City*, ed. John Bale and Olof Moen (Keele, UK: Keele University Press, 1995).

5 Bert Perry, "Chihawks Victorious as Great New Arena Gets Official Start," *Globe* (Toronto), November 13, 1931, 1.

6 M.J. Rodden, "On the Highways of Sport," *Globe* (Toronto), November 13, 1931, 8.

7 J.P. Fitzgerald, "Toronto Citizens Must Measure Up to Hockey," *Telegram* (Toronto), November 12, 1931, 43.

8 Colin Howell, *Blood, Sweat, and Cheers: Sport and the Making of Modern Canada* (Toronto: University of Toronto Press, 2001), 7.

9 J.P. Fitzgerald, "Public Has No Right to Enter Sport Fights," *Telegram* (Toronto), December 17, 1931, 45.

10 Henri Lefebvre, *The Production of Space* (Oxford: Blackwell, 1991).

11 On six-day bicycle racing, see Ari de Wilde, "Six-Day Racing Entrepreneurs and the Emergence of the Twentieth Century Arena Sportscape, 1891–1912," *Journal of Historical Research in Marketing* 4, no. 4 (2012): 532–3.

12 E.A. Heaman, *The Inglorious Arts of Peace: Exhibitions in Canadian Society during the Nineteenth Century* (Toronto: University of Toronto Press, 1999), 28.

13 Keith Walden, *Becoming Modern in Toronto: The Industrial Exhibition and the Shaping of a Late Victorian Culture* (Toronto: University of Toronto Press, 1997), 119.

14 Michel Foucault, *Discipline and Punish: The Birth of the Prison* (New York: Vintage, 1995), 201.

15 Ibid.

16 Ibid., 202.

17 Tony Bennett, *The Birth of the Museum: History, Theory, Politics* (London: Routledge, 1995), 68.

18 Ibid., 69.

19 Ibid., 55.

20 Patricia Vertinsky, "'Power Geometries': Disciplining the Gendered Body in the Spaces of the War Memorial Gymnasium" in *Disciplining Bodies in*

the Gymnasium: Memory, Monument, Modernism, ed. Patricia Vertinsky and Sherry McKay (London and New York: Routledge, 2004), 50.

21 Heaman, *The Inglorious Arts of Peace,* 135; Bennett, *The Birth of the Museum,* 47.

22 Cynthia Wright, "'The Most Prominent Rendezvous of the Feminine Toronto': Eaton's College Street and the Organization of Shopping in Toronto, 1920–1950" (PhD diss., University of Toronto, 1992), 131.

23 Sandra Weathers Smith, "Spectators in Public: Theatre Audiences in New York City, 1882–1929" (PhD diss., University of California, Berkeley, 2001), 17.

24 Wright, "'The Most Prominent Rendezvous,'" 203, 205.

25 Ibid., 205.

26 Weathers Smith, "Spectators in Public," 26.

27 Heaman, *The Inglorious Arts of Peace,* 119.

28 Bennett, *The Birth of the Museum,* 31.

29 Ibid., 32.

30 Heaman, *The Inglorious Arts of Peace,* 263.

31 Bennett, *The Birth of the Museum,* 33.

32 Donald F. Davis and Barbara Lorenzkowski, "A Platform for Gender Tensions: Women Working and Riding on Canadian Urban Public Transit in the 1940s," *Canadian Historical Review* 79, no. 3 (1998): 435, 443.

33 Ibid., 431.

34 Henning Eichberg, "Stadium, Pyramid, Labyrinth: Eye and Body on the Move," in *The Stadium and the City,* ed. John Bale and Olof Moen (Keele, UK: Keele University Press, 1995), 336–7.

35 Neil Campbell, "The Gardens: It's Still Hockey's Home," *Globe and Mail* (Toronto), October 10, 1981, S4.

36 Cornell Sandvoss, *Fans: The Mirror of Consumption* (Oxford: Polity, 2005), 34.

37 Richard Giulianotti, *Sport: A Critical Sociology* (Cambridge: Polity, 2005), 156–7.

38 Pierre Bourdieu, *Distinction: A Social Critique of the Judgement of Taste* (Cambridge, MA: Harvard University Press, 1984), 291.

39 See Pierre Bourdieu, "Sport and Social Class," *Social Science Information* 17, no. 6 (1978): 819–40.

40 Cornell Sandvoss, *A Game of Two Halves: Football, Television and Globalization* (London: Routledge, 2003), 22.

41 See, for example, Philip White and Brian Wilson, "Distinction in the Stands: An Investigation of Bourdieu's 'Habitus,' Socioeconomic Status and Sport Spectatorship in Canada," *International Review for the Sociology of Sport* 34, no. 3 (1999): 245–64.

42 Richard Giulianotti argues that there is a need for increased flexibility in applying Bourdieu. Giulianotti, *Sport: A Critical Sociology,* 169.

43   Foster Hewitt, *Down the Ice: Hockey Contacts and Reflections* (Toronto: S.J.R. Saunders, 1934), 108.

44   Andy Lytle, "Once Overs," *Daily Star* (Toronto), February 8, 1935, 12.

45   "Fighting Hockey Players," editorial, *Globe* (Toronto), December 14, 1933, 4.

46   Tommy Munns, "Free-For-All Produces 6 Penalties as Leafs Win," *Globe and Mail* (Toronto), March 1, 1937, 20.

47   Hewitt, *Down the Ice*, 109.

48   Don Cowie, "Leafs Trim Hawks in Stormy Battle," *Globe and Mail* (Toronto), January 18, 1937, 19.

49   Bobby Hewitson, "Inside the Blue Line," *Telegram* (Toronto), January 18, 1937, 22.

50   Andy Lytle, "Big Boston Bears Show Leafs the Way to Go Home," *Daily Star* (Toronto), March 11, 1935, 10.

51   Hewitson, "Inside the Blue Line"; Andy Lytle, "Leafs Obliged to Knock Karakas Out to Get Win," *Daily Star* (Toronto), January 18, 1937, 10.

52   J.P. Fitzgerald, "Hockey Gains Nothing from Rough Appeal," *Telegram* (Toronto), December 14, 1933, 26.

53   Frank Selke to Conn Smythe, January 14, 1944, F223-3-1-102: Hockey – Miscellaneous, 1925–47, Conn Smythe Fonds, Archives of Ontario, Toronto, Ontario. Smythe was overseas serving in the military in 1944 and Selke was left running the club.

54   Conn Smythe with Scott Young, *If You Can't Beat 'Em in the Alley* (Toronto: McClelland and Stewart, 1981), 79. Smythe outlines, from his perspective, the origins of his rivalry with Ross.

55   C.W. MacQueen, "Leafs' Loose Defensive Play Helps Bruins to 7–4 Victory," *Mail and Empire* (Toronto), March 11, 1935, 12; "Weekly Whoopee by Rounder," *Hush* (Toronto), March 31, 1932, 8.

56   J.P. Fitzgerald, "Hockey Gains Nothing."

57   Ted Reeve, "Sporting Extras," *Telegram* (Toronto), March 1, 1937, 23.

58   Frank Selke to Conn Smythe, January 14, 1944, F223-3-1-102: Hockey – Miscellaneous, 1925–47, Conn Smythe Fonds, Archives of Ontario, Toronto, Ontario.

59   Wright, "'The Most Prominent Rendezvous,'" 140. See also Susan Porter Benson, "Palace of Consumption and Machine for Selling: The American Department Store, 1880–1940," *Radical History Review* 21 (Fall 1979): 207.

60   J.P. Bickell, "President's Address to Sports Followers of the Queen City," *Maple Leaf Gardens Official Programme*, November 12, 1931, 28, Resource Centre, Hockey Hall of Fame, Toronto, Ontario.

61   Frank Selke to Conn Smythe, January 14, 1944, F223-3-1-102: Hockey – Miscellaneous, 1925–47, Conn Smythe Fonds, Archives of Ontario, Toronto, Ontario.

62   Lefebvre, *The Production of Space*, 129.

63 Quoted in "Arrest Connie Smythe on Assault Charge," *Daily Star* (Toronto), December 13, 1933, 2.
64 Lynne Marks, *Revivals and Roller Rinks: Religion, Leisure, and Identity in Late-Nineteenth-Century Small-Town Ontario* (Toronto: University of Toronto Press, 1996), 116.
65 Michel de Certeau, *The Practice of Everyday Life* (Berkeley: University of California Press, 1984), 37.
66 Michel de Certeau, Luce Giard, and Pierre Mayol, *The Practice of Everyday Life.* Volume 2: *Living and Cooking* (Minneapolis: University of Minnesota Press, 1998), 188.
67 Charles Conacher, "Conacher's Comment," *Globe and Mail* (Toronto), December 4, 1936, 23.
68 Walden, *Becoming Modern in Toronto*, 334–5.
69 Ibid., 335.
70 Ibid.
71 Michel Foucault, "The Eye of Power," quoted in Margaret E. Farrar, "Health and Beauty in the Body Politic: Subjectivity and Urban Space," *Polity* 33, no. 1 (Fall 2000): 1.
72 John Bale, "Virtual Fandoms: Futurescapes of Football," in *Fanatics! Power, Identity and Fandom in Football*, ed. Adam Brown (London and New York: Routledge, 1998), 271.
73 Mary Louise Adams, "Freezing Social Relations: Ice, Rinks, and the Development of Figure Skating," in *Sites of Sport: Space, Place, Experience*, ed. Patricia Vertinsky and John Bale (London and New York: Routledge, 2004), 58. See also Mary Louise Adams, *Artistic Impressions: Figure Skating, Masculinity, and the Limits of Sport* (Toronto: University of Toronto Press, 2011).
74 Foucault, quoted in Farrar, "Health and Beauty," 21.
75 William H. McNeill, *Keeping Together in Time: Dance and Drill in Human History* (Cambridge, MA: Harvard University Press, 1995), 2.
76 Alan Metcalfe, "Organized Sport and Social Stratification in Montreal, 1840–1901," in *Canadian Sport: Sociological Perspectives*, ed. Richard Gruneau and John Albinson (Don Mills, ON: Addison-Wesley, 1976).
77 See for example, Bruce Kidd, *The Struggle for Canadian Sport* (Toronto: University of Toronto Press, 1996), 185. Kidd recounts the 1920 story of the "University of Toronto star Bill Box [who] turned down an NHL contract because his parents objected to his playing with the pros."
78 James T. Lemon, *Toronto since 1918: An Illustrated History* (Toronto: James Lorimer, 1985), 19, 57.
79 Frank J. Selke with H. Gordon Green, *Behind the Cheering* (Toronto: McClelland and Stewart, 1962), 94.

Index